D1590948

SUGAWARA AND THE SECRETS OF CALLIGRAPHY

Translations from the Oriental Classics

Sugawara and the Secrets of Calligraphy

EDITED AND TRANSLATED
by *Stanleigh H. Jones, Jr.*

COLUMBIA UNIVERSITY PRESS   *New York 1985*

Columbia University Press
New York   Guildford, Surrey

Printed in the United States of America

Library of Congress Cataloging in Publication Data

Sugawara denju tenarai kagami.   English.
  Sugawara and the secrets of calligraphy.

  Translation of: Sugawara denju tenarai kagami.
  Play written by Izumo Takeda and others.   Cf.
Engeki gedai yōran.
  Includes bibliography.
  I. Jones, Stanleigh H. II. Takeda, Izumo, 1691–1756.
III. Title.
PL795.S84E5 1985   895.6'23   84-15550
ISBN 0-231-05974-4
ISBN 0-231-05975-2 (pbk.)

Clothbound editions of Columbia University Press Books are
Smyth-sewn and printed on permanent and durable acid-free
paper.

Dedicated with affection
to
Henrietta and Stanleigh Sr.

Translations from the Oriental Classics

Contents

Acknowledgments

Many people have helped in various ways to bring this translation into being. It is impossible to thank them all by name or to dwell at commensurate length on my gratitude to them. Yet, I cannot let pass the opportunity to acknowledge several kindnesses for which I have a particular feeling. To begin at the beginning, my thanks to Mabel Suzuki, who first introduced me both to the puppet theater and to many other appealing aspects of Japanese culture. To Donald Keene I owe a great deal, not only for what he has taught me but for much inspiration. Robert Borgen read the manuscript and provided valuable comments which can only have improved it. Nakamura Tetsurō and Ozawa Seiichi have both been warm friends and endless sources of information and insight regarding Japanese theater in general as well as this play in particular. Thanks are due also to Fujito Yoshiko, who rescued me from mental mayhem on several occasions by clarifying puzzling passages. Yoshinaga Takao has been the very personification of cordiality and encouragement as well as being a veritable gold mine of information on the puppet theater.

One would have to look long and far to discover any more gracious hospitality than I found among the members of the Bunraku Kyōkai in Osaka, both the performers who carry on the long tradition and those in the administrative office who support them. To them all I owe a very deep debt of gratitude. They went out of their way on numerous occasions to help me better understand and appreciate this finest flower of Edo culture. I am especially grateful to Ikoma Takami, who has made so many things possible for me at the Asahiza Theater in Osaka and who has regularly supplied virtually any materials possible which I have sought in my studies. Among the performers themselves, who took time from terribly busy schedules to offer assistance, I should like to thank Yoshida Kotama, Yoshida Minoshi, Yoshida Minosuke, Yoshida Tamamatsu, Kiritake Kamematsu, Kiritake Kanjūrō, Kiritake Monju, and Toyomatsu Seijūrō.

Lori Harnack, Jacqi Jernigan and, Judy Warhol have performed typing wonders that have much eased the whole process of preparing the manuscript. The Faculty Research Committee of the Claremont Graduate School and in particular the National Endowment for the Humanities provided funds which enabled me to travel to and live in Japan, and for this indispensable assistance words alone seem a small measure of gratitude. With these thanks, it should go without saying that all of the above are fully absolved of any errors or infelicities that may still remain despite careful searches; if my foot is in my mouth at any point, I put it there myself.

And finally, but by no means in least standing, for their patience with the fits and starts that have marked the lengthy gestation of this book, and for timely proddings that helped move it all ahead, warm thanks to my family.

SUGAWARA AND THE SECRETS OF CALLIGRAPHY

Introduction

When *Sugawara and the Secrets of Calligraphy (Sugawara denju tenarai kagami)* was first performed at the Takemoto Theater (Takemotoza) in Osaka on the twenty-first day of the eighth month 1746,[1] both the play and its performers were the objects of immediate critical acclaim. A contemporary critique, for example, after quoting snatches of the final lines of the play's most famous scene, "The Village School" ("Terakoya"), went on to note that "so many in the audience of the Takemoto Theater were in tears, word has it that the price of tissue paper has gone way up."[2] The play continued its run for over six months, with a star-studded list of performers that included such outstanding narrators as Takemoto Masadayū, Takemoto Konodayū, Takemoto Yuridayū and others. Leading the doll handlers was Yoshida Bunzaburō, the most famous manipulator in the history of the puppet theater and the man credited with a host of important innovations in the dolls themselves. Bunzaburō was the principal handler of the puppets for the characters Sugawara, Shiradayū, and Matsuōmaru's wife, Chiyo.[3] The Edo puppet theater, known as the Toyotake Hizen-no-jō-za, quickly sent one of its puppeteers and a narrator down to Osaka to study the performance firsthand. Several narrators and doll handlers from the

[1] A more precise translation of the title would be *A Mirror of the Transmission and Learning of Sugawara's Calligraphic Secrets.*

[2] Quoted in Tsurumi Makoto, *Takeda Izumo Shū*, p. 32.

[3] For a list of all of the performers, see *ibid.*, pp. 30–31.

Takemoto-za were then brought to Edo to assist in mounting the play there, where it began a successful showing from the second month of 1747. The enterprising Edo showmen are said to have helped assure a full house for the play by passing out free tickets to calligraphy teachers of the city.[4]

Quick to spot a winner, kabuki also jumped on the bandwagon, and slightly over a month after the play's premiere at the Takemoto-za it was appearing at the Asao Gengorō Theater in Kyoto. By the fifth month of 1747 *Sugawara and the Secrets of Calligraphy* had been adapted to kabuki in Edo, appearing simultaneously at the Ichimura-za and the Nakamura-za, the latter theater's production winning the greatest praise because of Yoshizawa Ayame's interpretation of Tonami and Ichikawa Ebizō's portrayal of the role of Genzō.[5] Three months later the play reached the kabuki stage in Osaka, at Ichikawa Ryūzō's Naka no Shibai. While the Kyoto and Osaka productions were faithful renderings of the original play, the performances in Edo embellished the work with the characteristic extravagance and bravura of Edo's kabuki acting style, a feature that was to influence subsequent puppet performances of the play.

The central character in *Sugawara and the Secrets of Calligraphy* is Sugawara no Michizane, born in 845, a man who through his Chinese learning rose to become a distinguished scholar and teacher, famed as a writer of Chinese verse and prose, and eventually in 899 the holder of the second highest post in the government, Minister of the Right. Michizane's rise in official position brought with it an ever-increasing apprehension and jealousy on the part of the Fujiwara family, which was developing what was to become a tradition of political power based

[4]*Ibid.*, p. 34.
[5]*Ibid.*

on strategic marriages between their own members and those of the imperial family. Through such maneuvers they eventually gained both the highest offices in government and close kinship ties to the emperor himself.

As time went on, this latter connection usually meant that young Fujiwara grandchildren ascended the throne at tender ages, thus enabling Fujiwara patriarchs to assume the influential role of regent. The fortunes of the family were progressing well until the accession in 887 of Emperor Uda, an ambitious young man who sought to diminish Fujiwara influence in government. A lover of scholarship, literature, and Chinese poetry, Uda was attracted to the gifted Michizane, and it was through the emperor's patronage that Michizane's star rose in the firmament of court and government.

Emperor Uda abdicated in 897 and two years later, the same year that Michizane became Minister of the Right, he entered holy orders. His son, Emperor Daigo, succeeded him, and not long thereafter came Michizane's downfall. Michizane's ascendancy had been marked at one point by his daughter Nobuko becoming one of Uda's consorts. Though she was not the mother of the imperial prince Tokiyo, the latter did marry one of Michizane's daughters (name unknown). These factors gave Michizane the kind of access to the emperor that the Fujiwara were trying to contrive for themselves. Thus, while many of the details in *Sugawara and the Secrets of Calligraphy* are fictional, the overall story is based on historical fact.

Rising in the bureaucracy along with Michizane was Fujiwara no Tokihira. The rivalry between the two men grew as they rose in position and influence, and early in 900 Tokihira moved to rid himself and the Fujiwara of the outsider Michizane. Many documents pertaining to the coup no longer exist, and we cannot be precisely sure of the accusations brought against Michi-

zane. It appears most likely, however, that he was charged with
lese majesty in a plot (hatched with retired Emperor Uda's con-
sent) to depose Emperor Daigo and replace him with Prince Tokiyo. There is no reason to believe that Michizane was in fact
guilty of such machinations, but the allegation was made to stick
and Michizane was dispatched into exile in Kyushu, at the old
government headquarters in Dazaifu some five hundred miles west
of the Capital. This took place in the first month of 901. Michizane died in his lonely place of banishment in the second month
of 903. He was fifty-eight at the time.

If matters had ended at this point, Michizane would probably
have remained an obscure figure noted laconically in the
chronicles as a prominent victim of the ruthless Fujiwara grasp
for power. But Michizane lived out his career in a highly super-
stitious age, and subsequent events were to catapult him to a far
more illustrious place in Japanese history and popular culture than
most of the Fujiwara themselves were ever able to achieve. In
909, six years after Michizane had gone to his grave, his enemy
Tokihira died suddenly at the early age of thirty-eight and at the
height of his career. Over the next several years there followed
an extraordinary series of deaths within the imperial house and
among leading members of the Fujiwara family. It was finally
determined that these misfortunes were caused by the angry spirit
of Michizane, who was wreaking vengeance upon those who had
wronged him. In 923, in an effort to placate the vindictive ghost,
the court posthumously restored to Michizane his offices and ti-
tles and elevated him in court rank. The spirit still seemed un-
appeased, however, for the Capital continued to be visited by such
calamities as fearful storms of thunder and lightning, earth-
quakes, plagues, and other natural disasters. Finally in 947, at
the urgings of an oracle, a shrine was erected in Michizane's honor

at Kitano in the northern part of the Capital. It was called the Kitano Tenmangū, The Kitano Heaven-Filling Shrine, and it remains there today. Forty years later, in 987, Michizane became the first subject in Japanese history to be canonized as a god and by imperial decree was named Tenjin, or Heavenly Deity.[6]

Though Michizane was in life a gentle and studious man, the credulous superstition of his day gave him an initial posthumous image of vengeful wrath as the dreaded god of thunder. Eventually, as time passed, his achievements as a poet and scholar were given emphasis so that, as the deity Tenjin, he became the divine patron of literature and learning. And, though no examples of his brushwork survive as evidence, he also came to be regarded as the god of that art of arts in Japan—calligraphy. With the exception of the shrines of Hachiman, the god of war, and the Inari shrines that commemorate the goddess of rice, there are today more Shinto shrines in Japan dedicated to Tenjin and his spiritual nurturing of scholarship and calligraphy than to any other deity.[7]

The vitality of the cult of learning that surrounds Michizane's memory today may be measured by the thousands of students who annually throng the Tenjin shrines all over the country to offer prayers that they will pass the rigorous entrance examinations for admission into Japan's colleges and universities. Few Americans are likely to be aware of it, but Michizane has even

[6]The general outline of the foregoing account of Michizane is drawn from Ivan Morris, *The Nobility of Failure,* pp. 41–66; and Burton Watson, "Michizane and the Plums," pp. 217–220. For corrections of details in Morris's account, I am indebted to Robert Borgen, who has written a very full biography, "Sugawara no Michizane."

[7]Morris, p. 61.

gained a certain immortality in the United States, where his name appears along the frieze of the Boston Public Library.[8]

In the play *Sugawara and the Secrets of Calligraphy*, Shihei (the Sino-Japanese reading for the name Tokihira) is an unredeemable blackguard, the unvarnished villain whom the audience is quite happy to see receive his just deserts in the end. Yet the historical Tokihira, though rather Machiavellian in his approach to politics, appears to have been essentially a hard-working and conscientious aristocrat administrator who probably deserves a better press. The legends and romance that had grown up around Michizane, however, cast a long shadow, and the eighteenth-century Japanese popular mind was predisposed to the evil image of Tokihira, made all the more sinister when placed against the purity and sincerity ascribed to Michizane. Whatever merits Tokihira may in fact have possessed as a man and a government official, it was Michizane, after all, who became a god.

Some of the legends about Michizane bear directly on the play. We know, for instance, from Michizane's own writings that he had a strong and particular fondness for the plum tree *(ume)*, and the plum has thus come to have a close association with him. Michizane often wrote about the plum. One of his most famous poems, and one that figures in the play, is his farewell to the beloved plum tree in his garden, written shortly before going into exile.

> When blows the eastern wind,
> Send to me your fragrance,

[8] The background of this is somewhat obscure, but I understand that the library was built during the time that Okakura Tenshin, famous for his *Book of Tea*, was curator of the Asiatic collection of the Boston Museum of Fine Arts, and it may well have been Okakura's influence that led to the inclusion in the frieze of Michizane's name.

O flower of the plum.
Though absent from your master,
Forget not the season of spring.

Michizane is also said to have had a special attachment for two other trees: a cherry *(sakura)* and a pine *(matsu)*. When he left for exile, so the legend goes, the cherry tree withered and died because of loneliness; the plum tree, upon hearing Michizane's poem "When blows the eastern wind," uprooted itself and flew to be with him in exile. Another of Michizane's poems, which is central to the theme of the play but whose authenticity is questioned, has Michizane noting the death of his cherry tree, acknowledging the arrival of the plum, and then chiding the pine for its lack of feeling.

The plum has flown to my side,
The cherry has withered away.
Why in this indifferent world
Yet stands so heartless the pine.

From this poem came the names of the three brothers in *Sugawara and the Secrets of Calligraphy.*

To a remarkable degree this last poem and the tradition surrounding the three favored trees accounted for important plot elements in the play and a good deal of nuance associated with the trees. Though ostensibly about incidents in the last years of Michizane's life and its thunderous aftermath, *Sugawara and the Secrets of Calligraphy* is in fact concerned more with the adventures of the namesakes of Michizane's beloved trees, the three brothers Umeōmaru, Sakuramaru, and Matsuōmaru. In the poem, for instance, the cherry withers and dies—the cherry has long been for the Japanese a metaphor for the brevity of human existence. Sakuramaru, named for the cherry, is thus the triplet who dies and, like the tree in the poem, he does so after his master has gone into exile. Sakuramaru displays an almost feminine quality. His character is soft and gentle, reminiscent of the fragile cherry blossoms so quickly scattered by the wind; yet he possesses an inner strength that his outward appearance belies. Sakuramaru's wife Yae, whose name means "the double cherry blossom," is the best drawn of the wives of the brothers, and she shares both the gentle aspects of her husband's personality as well as the intrinsic fortitude of his character: in one scene Sakuramaru shows his mettle as a valiant adversary; later Yae singlehandedly drives off a band of marauders. And, of the wives, Yae is the one who dies.

Like his namesake the plum tree in the poem, it is Umeōmaru who follows his lord to his place of banishment. Since the delicate white flowers of the plum bloom from knotted branches in the cold of winter, the tree symbolizes inner fortitude and determination, and such is the doughty character of Umeōmaru. His wife's name is Haru, meaning "spring," the season under the old lunar calendar when the plum blooms.

As the poem questions the sentiments of the pine tree, so does the audience as it watches Matsuōmaru's antagonism toward his brothers and his father. In answer to the question of loyalty, however, the playwright allows him finally to redeem himself, though at the terrible cost of the sacrifice of his son. The name of his wife, Chiyo, means "a thousand generations," a reminder that the evergreen pine is the emblem of longevity. From the beginning of act 3, each brother wears a costume decorated with his namesake among the trees, each wife's clothing also similarly marked by the same pattern as that of her husband.

From the early 1720s the practice of some form of multiple authorship of plays had grown up in the world of the puppet theater, so much so that by the time of *Sugawara and the Secrets of Calligraphy* the practice had become virtually the rule. It had apparently developed out of conferences between the theater manager, the chief playwright, and other experienced members of the dramatic staff at the time a new play was being prepared. As plays became increasingly long and complex in their plots and subplots, combining the talents of several playwrights was seen as desirable. Moreover, given the tight schedules for productions, especially as the competition between the Takemoto-za and the rival Toyotake-za intensified, it was also probably simply deemed more efficient for a team to write a play than to leave the task to one man alone. This approach to playwriting could, of course, lead to a certain unevenness of literary and dramatic quality, especially over the course of a long and involved play which might require ten hours or more for a full performance. In the hands of a smoothly working team of talented playwrights, on the other hand, great things could be accomplished. Nowhere is this more clearly shown than in the years 1746, 1747, and 1748 when the same playwriting team of the Takemoto-za produced the three greatest masterpieces of the Japanese puppet theater: *Sugawara and the Secrets of Calligraphy* (1746), *Yoshitsune and the Thousand Cherry Trees* (1747, *Yoshitsune senbon zakura*) and *A Treasury of Loyal Retainers* (1748, *Kanadehon chūshingura*).[9]

Four names appear as the playwrights of *Sugawara and the Secrets of Calligraphy*. At the beginning of the printed version of the play, beneath the title, is the phrase "written by Takeda Izumo." At the end of the text, beneath the premiere date, are listed (in this order) Namiki Senryū, Miyoshi Shōraku, and Takeda Koizumo. The inference would be that the principal author

[9]For a full translation of the last of these, see Donald Keene, *Chūshingura: The Treasury of Loyal Retainers*.

was Izumo, the other three being subordinate writers. This has been the accepted notion of the play's authorship until relatively recent years.

The name Takeda Izumo appears on a large number of plays spanning the years 1723 to 1756, but this name in fact refers to two men: Izumo I and his son Koizumo ("Little Izumo"). Koizumo is listed among the playwrights of twenty-six plays produced between 1739 and 1746. The last work bearing the Koizumo name was the 1746 play *Sugawara and the Secrets of Calligraphy*. By that year, Izumo the father was already advanced in years; he died in the sixth month of 1747, less than a year after the play had its premiere.[10] Upon his death, his son Koizumo inherited from his father both the directorship of the Takemoto Theater and the name Izumo (making him Izumo II, though he never signed himself thus). Though the elder Izumo may have had some role in determining the overall structure of the Sugawara play, it is likely that his was largely a formal relationship, most, if not all, of the creative process being conducted by the other three playwrights.[11]

As a young man Namiki Senryū (1695?–1751?), a native of Osaka, became a disciple of the well-known playwright of the Toyotake-za, Nishizawa Ippū (1665–1731). His first public appearance as a playwright came when he was one of the subordinate collaborators with Ippū on a play first performed in 1726. The play was a great hit, running for some eleven months, thus establishing Senryū's career as a dramatist. The following year Ippū retired and Senryū became the chief playwright, the *tate-*

[10] Yokoyama Tadashi, *Jōruri Shū*, p. 38.

[11] For a very interesting discussion of the general subject of collaborative authorship in the puppet theater and the case of *Sugawara and the Secrets of Calligraphy* in particular, see Eduard Klopfenstein, "*Gassaku*—Co-authorship in Classical *Jōruri* of the 18th Century." On the differentiation between the two Izumos, see Yūda Yoshio, "Takeda Izumo no Shūmei to Sakuhin."

sakusha, of the Toyotake Theater. As with virtually all of the playwrights of the eighteenth century, Senryū's career has for later researchers a number of gaps. He appears to have been doing extremely well at the Toyotake-za when in 1742, for reasons unknown, he resigned his position as head playwright, wrote a few works with some other dramatists, and for a couple of years dropped out of sight. Then unexpectedly in 1745 we find him having joined the Toyotake's rival playhouse, the Takemoto-za. During the time he had served as chief playwright at the Toyotake-za he had used the name Namiki Sōsuke; upon joining the Takemoto-za he changed his name to Senryū.

It was fortunate for the history of the puppet theater that Senryū spent the six years from 1745 to 1750 at the Toyotake-za, for in that period he was an important collaborator in the writing of the three masterworks already mentioned as well as another favorite, *The Mirror of the Osaka Summer Festival (Natsu matsuri Naniwa kagami*, 1745), which also is still frequently performed. Senryū appears to have worked congenially with his fellow playwrights at the Takemoto Theater, but in 1751 he again switched theaters, returning to the Toyotake-za. He died in the sixth month of the same year while working on another major drama, *The Battle of Ichinotani (Ichinotani futaba gunki).* This play too appears often on both the puppet and kabuki stages, and though Senryū (he was back to the name Sōsuke at the time) did not live to finish the work or to see its premiere in the twelfth month of 1751, he is generally believed to have been the creator of the play's best scene from the end of the third act, "Kumagai's Camp" ("Kumagai jinya").[12]

We have even less information about Miyoshi Shōraku (1696?–1771?). Coming originally from the island of Shikoku, he is said

[12]Tsurumi, pp. 25–28.

variously to have been a Buddhist priest of the Shingon sect, a physician, and the proprietor of a tea house. He was well along in years, around forty-one, when his name first appeared among the writers of a play that went on the boards of the Takemoto-za in 1736. For all his years as a writer at the Takemoto-za (he was around seventy-six when he died), Shōraku never rose to the position of chief playwright. Perhaps he lacked the dash and brilliance of the other, often younger, writers who surrounded him. Yet he collaborated on more than fifty plays, including more than a dozen that have become standard classics of both the puppet and kabuki stages.[13] Apparently a writer of more subdued qualities than his contemporaries, until his life can be delineated in more detail (if that will ever be possible) he must probably be counted as one of the more important puppet dramatists of the eighteenth century.[14]

Accounts vary regarding the inspiration for writing *Sugawara and the Secrets of Calligraphy*. A string of unprofitable productions at the Takemoto Theater, according to one story, prompted the playwrights to offer prayers at the Tenjin Shrine in Osaka, and from this came the idea of a play about Tenjin/Sugawara himself.[15] The more commonly recounted tale, however, runs as follows. *An Ancient Tale of Kusunoki Masashige (Kusunoki mukashi banashi)* had opened the 1746 season in the first month and had enjoyed a successful run. To celebrate the triumph, a

[13] *Ibid.*, pp. 22–25. Also, Waseda Daigaku Engeki Hakubutsukan, *Engeki Hyakka Daijiten*, 5:336.

[14] For other brief accounts of the three playwrights, plus a different appraisal of Shōraku, see the following works by Donald Keene: *Chūshingura*, pp. 8–10, and *World Within Walls, Japanese Literature of the Pre-Modern Era, 1600–1867*, pp. 282–285.

[15] Yokoyama, p. 32.

theater party was held, at which time Miyoshi Shōraku proposed that the next play be one dealing with the life of Sugawara no Michizane, the second, third, and fourth acts each to portray a tragic separation between parent and child. The idea won immediate approval and there began the business of allocating the acts to the several playwrights. As a result, Shōraku was assigned the end of act 2, in which Sugawara bids a sorrowful farewell to his daughter Kariya; Senryū got act 3, at the end of which Sakuramaru commits suicide and is thus parted from this father Shiradayū; the ending of act 4, the scene in which Matsuōmaru sacrifices his own child to protect Sugawara's son, went to Izumo II (then signing himself Koizumo).[16]

About a month before the play received its first performance an unusual event in Osaka provided another element that lent the play a contemporary note. On the twenty-eighth day of the seventh month, triplets were born to a family living in the Tenma ward of the city. The incident was considered so remarkable that it was soon the subject of widespread gossip, and city officials bestowed a sum of money upon the parents. From this came the idea of triplet brothers in the play.[17] The playwrights were also said to have been inspired by the names of bridges they passed beneath while cruising Osaka's Chijimi River: Umeda Bridge, Sakura Bridge, and Midoribashi, or Green Bridge, hence a connotation of the evergreen pine.[18]

It is difficult to ascertain the truth of such stories; the play is ingenious in many of its details, and the playwrights may well have been equally ingenious in their conception of the work. As for the assignments of parts of the play among the playwrights,

[16] Fujino Yoshio, *Sugawara Denju Tenarai Kagami Hyōkai*, pp. 8–9; Tsurumi, p. 34.

[17] Tsurumi, p. 35.

[18] Bunraku program for April 1976, p. 15.

while it is probably equally impossible to determine accurately who wrote which part, there is at the same time no reason to disbelieve the traditional attributions.

We do, however, have a fair idea of the sorts of sources used by the playwrights in plotting various incidents and characters in the play. The earliest known source is the late fifteenth-century Nō play *Raiden (Thunder and Lightning)*, attributed to the playwright Miyamasu. In *Raiden* the spirit of Michizane visits his former teacher, the priest Hosshōbō on Mount Hiei, thanking him for kindnesses during his life. Michizane then tells Hosshōbō that he has become the god of thunder and that he plans to go to the imperial palace and take revenge on his enemies there. He warns Hosshōbō not to accept any summons to go to the palace, but the priest answers that if he receives as many as three calls he will be obliged to attend. Michizane then picks up a pomegranate on a Buddhist altar, bites into it and spits out the seeds at a temple door, causing it to burst into flames. Hosshōbō quells the fire with his holy powers. The scene shifts to the palace, where Michizane's thundering ghost is wreaking havoc. Hosshōbō arrives and gradually weakens the ghost with his exorcising spells as he pursues the spirit from one chamber of the palace to another. Finally, with the issuance of an imperial decree that Michizane is to be worshiped as the Heavenly God (Tenjin) of Tenma, the god of thunder flies off into the sky.[19] Several passages in the last act of *Sugawara and the Secrets of Calligraphy* have clearly been lifted from *Raiden*, as has been the character Hosshōbō and his attempt to exorcise the spirits of Yae and Sakuramaru.

---

[19] See Tsukamoto Tetsuzo, ed., *Yōkyoku Shū*, 2:494–499.

Raiden, however, provided only a minor contribution to the work. The playwrights also went to a body of puppet plays written over the preceding four decades, several of which had been written by Namiki Senryū during the time he was chief playwright at the Toyotake-za and signing himself Namiki Sōsuke.[20] Their most important single source was the play *Tenjin-ki (A Chronicle of Tenjin)*, written by the most important playwright in the history of the puppet theater, Chikamatsu Monzaemon (1653–1725), and first performed in the second month of 1713 at the same Takemoto Theater. One finds the names of some characters, certain situations, and some of the language of that work incorporated into *Sugawara and the Secrets of Calligraphy*.[21] While the borrowings from *Tenjin-ki* are pervasive, they are always in the form of smaller details within the overall play.

As with most plays of this period, one may find parallels with earlier puppet dramas for elements scattered throughout the work. Such indebtedness, however, should not be overemphasized, for the broader conception of the play, its strong emotional appeal and high drama, and the great scenes that have become standard repertoire in the puppet and kabuki theaters are due mainly to the genius of its creators. Small wonder that of the several plays that have taken as their subject the life and legends of Sugawara no Michizane only *Sugawara and the Secrets of Calligraphy* has remained a viable and perennially popular drama on Japan's traditional popular stage.

Chikamatsu Monzaemon, so the story goes, stopped writing for kabuki in part because he disliked the liberties taken with his

---

[20] For details, see Tsurumi, pp. 36–38, and Sonoda Tamio, *Jōruri Sakusha no Kenkyū*, pp. 286–292.

[21] Fujino, pp. 12–17, notes several of the specific parallels.

texts by the actors performing them. And kabuki writers borrowing plays from the puppet repertoire have ever been wont to make changes where they felt such alterations were, for kabuki, warranted. They were quite right to do so, of course, for the kabuki stage has many potentials not open to the puppet theater. There is the electricity that a great actor can generate; the kabuki stage itself is far larger than that of the puppets and is fitted with numerous theatrical devices that are generally less effective (and therefore usually eschewed) in the doll theater; and one cannot overlook the fact that in any number of instances kabuki playwrights or technicians have come up with original dramatic touches, great and small, that have often enriched dramas originally created for the puppets. Moreover, such kabuki innovations have often found their way back to become standard practices in the puppet theater.

Kabuki, to begin with, simply never or rarely performs certain parts of plays borrowed from the puppet theater, primarily because such scenes do not provide an actor with sufficient opportunity to display his skills. For this reason, the following scenes are routinely cut from kabuki productions of *Sugawara and the Secrets of Calligraphy:* "The Imperial Palace" (act 1), "The Journey" and "Yasui Beach" scenes (act 2), the first part of "Sata Village" (act 3), "North Saga Village" (act 4), and all of act 5. Indeed, except in those comparatively rare instances of a complete production of the play, the puppet theater itself tends to edit the work in much the same manner.

The narrative tradition that informs the puppet stage remains to a degree in kabuki, but it is important that actors be fairly continuously involved in the action on stage. Long descriptive passages delivered by the narrator in puppet plays often become lines spoken by actors, and the lines will sometimes be broken up so that each performer participates. One example of this occurs at the end of act 3 where two long narrative passages following Sakuramaru's suicide are distributed among the four performers remaining on stage—Shiradayū, Yae, Umeōmaru, and Haru. And elsewhere in the kabuki version occurs a similar manipulation of lines in order to enhance the vitality of the actors.[22]

Kabuki adaptations also characteristically seek to develop the personalities of characters in ways that puppet works do not. From the opening scene of act 3, "Tearing the Carriage Apart," Matsuōmaru is presented as a miscreant who has traded his proper loyalty to his benefactor Lord Sugawara for allegiance to Shihei, the archvillain whose fortunes are at that point in the ascendant. His evil nature and his conflict with his brothers is further developed in the "Sata Village" scene where he also alienates himself from his father, Shiradayū. Kabuki adaptors, apparently mindful of Michizane's poetic characterization of Matsuōmaru's namesake the pine tree ("Why in this indifferent world/Yet stands so heartless the pine"), decided to blacken Matsuōmaru's personality even further. In the puppet play, he asks his father to disown him because he is now loyal solely to Shihei. After a tongue-lashing by Shiradayū, his only line is "Come on, wife." Kabuki gives the scene a bitter edge as Chiyo confronts her husband Matsuōmaru.

CHIYO: How can you say such a thing to father! Please, father, don't forget your grandchild.

SHIRADAYŪ: I love no grandchild! Now go! Still haven't gone? Perhaps you want back the cap you gave me? Here, quickly, take it and go!

(He throws the cap at her.)

---

[22] For some further discussion of kabuki treatment of its adaptations from the puppet theatre, see Stanleigh H. Jones, Jr., "Miracle at Yaguchi Ferry."

CHIYO: You even return my gift to you?

MATSUŌMARU: Since he's returned it, pick it up. If he won't wear it, I will.

SHIRADAYŪ: Why, you wretch! I'll beat you!

(He brandishes a broom at Matsuō.)

MATSUŌMARU: You'd better not! Tomorrow I'll shave off my fore-locks and become a samurai in Shihei's service. I'll be known as Matsuō, Lord of Harima. You'll not be forgiven any dis-respect then! Come on, wife.[23]

In a similar fashion kabuki highlights with an added touch of harsh bravado the strident villainy of Shihei's minion Genba in "The Village School" (act 4). At the end of the head inspection scene, the puppet Genba simply marches off the stage, satisfied that he possesses for his master the head of Michizane's son Kan Shūsai. The kabuki Genba, however, cannot leave without pausing outside Genzō's gate to deliver a final sneer.

GENBA: Lately, Genzō, you've paid a lot of lip service to loyalty, loyalty. But when you find yourself put to the fire, you'd even cut off your own master's head. When you come down to it, life is pretty dear, isn't it. Ha ha ha ha ha.[24]

Elsewhere in the kabuki version there is a different kind of ex-pansion of the original puppet play. For instance, in the first half of the "Mount Tenpai" scene (act 4), Shihei's henchman Heima makes his entrance locked in combat with Umeōmaru. His mis-sion becomes known in his monologue after he has been sub-dued. This is a somewhat static moment on stage, and the creed of kabuki that an actor must *act*, not merely talk, is served by an

[23] Fujino, p. 145. For a similar but variant text, see Toita Yasuji et al., eds., *Meisaku Kabuki Zenshū*, 2:202.

[24] *Ibid.*, p. 224.

entirely new scene depicting Heima and his own followers de-
barking from a boat, Heima briefing his men on the assassina-
tion plot against Michizane.[25]

As the "Mount Tenpai" scene progresses, the point is reached
where Michizane becomes the god of thunder, and here kabuki
creates a spectacle worthy of the size and technical refinement
of its stage. A cluster of crags, Michizane on top, rises amid clouds
of mist on the main stage lift. Thunder rolls and lightning flashes
in the background as, in some productions, real water falls as
rain, and a pine tree atop the crags is torn apart by a hidden
device. Attackers seek to climb the slope in pursuit of Michizane, engaging in spirited fight scenes and being flung from the
mountain (dummies, of course). Michizane ties to a plum branch
a paper bearing his vow to the gods and Buddhas that he will
protect the emperor, and a white cloud descends and carries the
vow off to the heavens. Boatmen, who are Heima's henchmen,
arrive at the foot of the mountain where Umeōmaru confronts
them and cuts them down. The curtain closes amid the roar of
thunder, the glare of lightning, and torrential rain, or sound effects suggesting a downpour.[26]

Kabuki is much more ready to introduce comedy into its plays
than is the puppet theater. Accordingly, in certain kabuki scenes
of *Sugawara and the Secrets of Calligraphy* there are elements of
ribaldry not found in puppet productions, many of them serving
as a kind of comic relief juxtaposed against scenes of pathos and
tragedy in somewhat the same way that Shakespeare used them.
The best single example is the kabuki treatment of the class dunce,
Noodlehead, in the most popular part of the play, "The Village
School." Though in current puppet productions some of his an-

[25] *Ibid.*, pp. 206–207.

[26] *Ibid.*, pp. 212–213; Fujino, p. 190.

tics derive from kabuki-inspired innovations, it is basically as the clumsy bumpkin of fifteen in a class of children half his age that we find him funny. In kabuki he is still an awkward lout, but he is also an impertinent pilferer who shows a certain sharpness of wit. As punishment for having started a brawl with the other children, Tonami makes him stand on one of the school desks, a cup of water in one hand and a lighted stick in the other. He starts bawling shortly after Chiyo arrives, thus prompting her to intercede for him. Chiyo has him blow his nose in some tissue paper, whereupon he jumps down from the desk and deftly steals a cake from the box Chiyo has brought and puts it in his sleeve. Sansuke, Chiyo's servant, sees him.

SANSUKE: Hey, hey, what're you going to do with that cake?

NOODLEHEAD: Oh, I'm not going to do anything. The teacher's away right now, so I'm going to look after these cakes till he gets back.

SUNSUKE: Rubbish! I just saw you stick your hand in that box and put a cake into your sleeve.

NOODLEHEAD: I don't remember doing that.

SANSUKE: What do you mean you don't remember. Then turn out your sleeve.

NOODLEHEAD: Well . . . uh . . .

SANSUKE: Well?

NOODLEHEAD: Well . . .

BOTH: Well! Well! Well!

SANSUKE: Quickly now, give me that cake!

NOODLEHEAD: What a lousy piece of luck, I had it all figured out how to get one, and that darned Sansuke spotted me. Lousy luck. *(Poses awkwardly.)*

SANSUKE: You good for nothing, I ought to take it back right now.

But to celebrate Kotarō's first day of school, I'll forget about it this time.[27]

The exchange continues briefly before Tonami and Chiyo resume their conversation. As Chiyo takes her leave, she goes out the gate, pauses, then returns, saying she has left her fan, though obviously it is still in her hand. This is but a ruse to allow her one last look at her son. Tonami points out the fan in Chiyo's hand, and the two women laugh embarrassedly as Chiyo finally departs, hiding her tearful face with the opened fan. After she has disappeared down the *hanamichi*, Noodlehead comes out and wakes the dozing Sansuke, teasing the sleepy servant by pointing first in one direction then another as the way that Chiyo has gone. The two of them then replay in hilarious parody the touching farewell that has just taken place between Chiyo (in this case Sansuke) and Tonami (Noodlehead taking her part). The effect is an absurd piece of farce hard on the heels of an affecting scene of a mother knowingly looking upon her only child for the last time.

Sugawara and the Secrets of Calligraphy is unique among plays of the puppet theater for its wholesale adoption of kabuki performance practice in one scene, "Tearing the Carriage Apart" (act 3), or "Kurumabiki" as it is called in Japanese. As originally conceived, it was a relatively minor scene whose main dramatic purpose was to highlight Matsuōmaru's alignment with the play's principal villain, Shihei, and to establish his estrangement from his brothers and later his father. This would make all the more startling in the later "Village School" scene the revelation that, despite the depravity he had earlier shown, he had remained at heart faithful to Michizane, willing even to sacrifice the life of

[27] Fujino, pp. 195–196.

his own child in that service. Kabuki took "Kurumabiki" and created what is today one of the finest examples of that quintessential feature of kabuki, *aragoto*. Often translated "rough business" or the "rough-house" style of acting, *aragoto* is marked by characters who are drawn larger than life and who engage in exaggerated movements accompanied by much theatrical posing, extravagant histrionics and declamation, and the use of costumes and props designed to hyperbolize the actor and his total performance. Kabuki's *aragoto* treatment of "Kurumabiki" became so popular that the puppet theater adopted the performance style virtually intact, even writing in the minor role of Sugiōmaru, a kabuki embellishment not present in the puppet original. I know of no other scene in a puppet play which shows such a thoroughgoing genuflection to the techniques of its major dramatic rival, kabuki.

Chikamatsu Monzaemon, already noted as the almost universally acknowledged titan of the Japanese puppet theater, was a dramatist of genius and a highly gifted writer, who was also largely responsible for raising that theater from the sphere of rudimentary entertainment to the level of serious and literate drama. Without his ingenuity and inspiration, the puppet theater would surely not have developed and matured as it did. In the nineteenth century, when the Japanese felt the need to find in their own cultural tradition counterparts to the newly discovered arts of the West, he was given the title "The Shakespeare of Japan," and studies of the puppet theater, both in Japan and in the West, have since then centered on Chikamatsu and his works. Yet, it is a fact that the majority of plays that have from their premieres remained continuously in the doll repertoire have come from the brushes of later playwrights. With very few exceptions, Chikamatsu's works have either not been performed after their initial appearances or they have had to be rewritten in order to appeal to changes in dramatic tastes and to suit a variety of altered conditions in the puppet theater.[28] This adulation of an admittedly great dramatist and pioneer has thus produced a rather lopsided view of the Japanese puppet theater and has tended to accord an unjustifiably second-rate status to the writers and plays of later years.

The playwriting team of Takeda Izumo (II), Namiki Senryū, and Miyoshi Shōraku represents the pinnacle of the post-Chikamatsu period of the puppet theater's development. Between 1745 and 1749 they wrote a total of nine plays, no fewer than six of which continue in regular performance to the present. That, as we have seen, three of these plays should have become the accepted masterworks not only in their original home of the puppet theater but also in kabuki is a tribute to the theatrical genius of this exceptional trio.

I was in Japan for some six months in 1972 on a grant from the National Endowment for the Humanities, under which I had hoped to pursue a study of the life and works of the playwright Chikamatsu Hanji (1725–1783). The project turned out to be rather frustrating, partly because only a few of Hanji's plays were performed during the time I was in Japan, but more so because it became clear that precious little material existed which would support a study of the man's life. In a somewhat different way, however, I did have a remarkable stroke of good fortune: in May 1972, at the National Theater in Tokyo, *Sugawara and the Secrets of Calligraphy* was mounted by the Bunraku Kyōkai (Bunraku Association) in the most complete performance of the play in some 140 years. Quite apart from the fact that it was a thor-

[28]For a description of some of these changes, see Keene, *World Within Walls*, pp. 268–269, 276ff, and Donald Keene, *Major Plays of Chikamatsu*, pp. 7–8.

oughly absorbing and moving drama, this production afforded virtually all of the opportunities I had hoped for in the case of Chikamatsu Hanji's plays. It was possible to view the play repeatedly—I spent some six or seven full days at the theater from about eleven in the morning till nearly ten at night, literally eating on the run. Consequently, I could make notes on stage movement, sound effects, sets, costumes and props, none of which gain mention in the text of a puppet play. I was graciously given permission to photograph the production extensively in dress rehearsal and in public performance; and I was able to obtain audio tapes of the complete play, a feature that I believe has been of enormous help in my attempt to convey in English a sense of the drama taking place on stage. Narrators, for instance, often enliven a play in performance in ways which a text alone gives hardly any hint.

Because part of the narrator's role is descriptive, stage action will be clear in many instances from his lines. When this is the case in the present translation, I have added no stage directions. On the other hand, where action goes unmentioned in the narrator's *recitativo*, but where an awareness of movement would enhance a perception of the work as a vehicle for the theater, I have drawn from my notes and photographs to indicate what is happening on stage. It should be understood, however, that the absence of specific notes hardly means that the scene is static, for the puppet stage is very much alive, with subtle as well as broad activity in progress most of the time. To include all of this would unduly inhibit a smooth reading of the play. Such notes as appear, therefore, represent what I have felt important in attempting to provide in print some experience of the vitality of the stage itself.

There are several terms used throughout the stage notes which perhaps call for explanation. *SR* and *SL* mean, respectively, the

Stage Right and *Stage Left* of conventional theatrical usage, referring to a side of the stage from the performer's point of view. *Shōji* are sliding doors or partitions made of wooden latticework covered on one side by translucent paper.

This translation is based primarily on the text annotated by Yokoyama Tadashi on pages 486–630 of *Jōruri Shū* (see bibliography). Generally excellent annotations plus a translation into modern colloquial Japanese have made this the most useful single source. I have also been helped by the annotations in Fujino Yoshio, *Sugawara Denju Tenarai Kagami Hyōkai*, and in Yūda Yoshio's treatment of parts of the play, pages 42–141, in *Bunraku Jōruri Shū*.

Music in the puppet theater cannot go unmentioned. It is a continuous and highly important part of the performance, setting the pace for both the narration and the puppets' movements and responsible for creating various atmospherics for successive scenes. Though other instruments find occasional use, the workhorse of musical accompaniment is the three-stringed samisen. Known as the futozao samisen, it is a larger and heavier instrument with richer base resonances than the more commonly encountered nagauta instrument that figures prominently in kabuki performances. The puppet theater without its samisen would be like an opera without an orchestra, but the whole question of music in the puppet theater is quite complex. I simply have not the musical background to deal with it in any adequate way; accordingly, there is scant mention of it in this translation. Few things would give me more pleasure than for someone qualified to treat the subject to write about it in some detail, thus adding another dimension to a Western appreciation of this unique drama form.

A final note about the illustrations accompanying this translation. The Bunraku Kyōkai was wonderfully generous in allow-

ing me to take extensive photographs of the play in dress rehearsal, when it was possible to move close to the stage and capture
on film moments that would have eluded me from the glassed
director's booth at the back of the theater. During formal performances at least two of the puppet manipulators are always hooded;
the principal operator, however, is not always dressed in the same
manner. In dress rehearsals, on the other hand, all of the puppet
handlers, while wearing their black smocks, forego the hood. Some
of the photographs that appear here will show all of the manipulators without hoods, an indication that the photograph was taken
during dress rehearsal. If they appear hooded, the picture was
taken during a regular performance.

*Sugawara
and the Secrets
of Calligraphy*

Dramatis Personae

As might be expected of a complex play requiring virtually a whole day to stage, *Sugawara and the Secrets of Calligraphy* boasts a sizable cast: nearly forty characters of greater or lesser importance, not counting such supernumeraries as gatemen, guards, boatmen, maids, peasants, school children, and the like. The following is a dramatis personae, arranged in alphabetical order according to the name each goes by in the play. Some have fuller names, used mainly when they are introduced in the narrator's recitativo, and these are noted in parentheses. In the case of the triplet brothers, two are known by shortened versions of their names. Sakuramaru is always referred to by his full name; Umeōmaru and Matsuōmaru are often called, respectively, Umeō and Matsuō, a practice found in the original text and followed here.

CHIKARA (Arashima Chikara), retainer of Shihei
CHIYO, wife of Matsuōmaru
GENBA (Shundō Genba), retainer of Shihei
GENZŌ (Takebe Genzō), former calligraphy disciple of
     Sugawara; now a teacher in a remote village.
HARU, wife of Umeōmaru
HEIMA (Washizuka Heima), retainer of Shihei
HOSHIZAKA (Hoshizaka Gengo), retainer of Shihei
HOSSHŌBŌ, Buddhist priest
HYŌE (Haji no Hyōe), father of Sukune Tarō

JŪSAKU, neighbor of Shiradayū

KAKUJU, Sugawara's aunt; mother of Tatsuta and Kariya

KAN SHŪSAI, Sugawara's young son

KARIYA, Sugawara's adopted daughter (her real parent is Kakuju)

KATSUNO, maid in Sugawara's household

KIYOTSURA (Miyoshi no Kiyotsura), retainer of Shihei

KOTARŌ, Matsuōmaru's son

LADY SUGAWARA, wife of Sugawara no Michizane

MAREYO, court official and Sugawara's calligraphy disciple

MATSUŌMARU, groom in Shihei's service; triplet brother of Umeōmaru and Sakuramaru

NAISHI (Iyo no Naishi), lady in waiting at the imperial court

NOODLEHEAD, student in Genzō's village school

SAKURAMARU, groom in Prince Tokiyo's service; triplet brother of Umeōmaru and Matsuōmaru

SANSUKE, Chiyo's servant

SHIHEI (Fujiwara no Shihei), Minister of the Left

SHIRADAYŪ, retainer of Sugawara no Michizane; father of the triplets

SUGIŌMARU, retainer of Shihei

SUGAWARA (Sugawara no Michizane), Minister of the Right

TAKUNAI, servant in Kakuju's house

TARŌ (Sukune Tarō), husband of Tatsuta

TATSUTA, daughter of Kakuju and older sister of Kariya

TENRANKEI, Chinese priest

TERUKUNI (Hangandai Terukuni), official in the court of the Retired Emperor; Sugawara's escort

TOKIYO (Prince Tokiyo), younger brother of the Emperor

TONAMI, Genzō's wife

TSUBONE, maid in the Sugawara household

UMEŌMARU, groom in Sugawara's service; triplet brother of Sakuramaru and Matsuōmaru

YAE, wife of Sakuramaru

Prologue

NARRATOR: The stately pines that stand
Verdant, ageless on Mount Hakoya,
Were transformed, they say,
Into slender, graceful girls.[1]
And the famed plum trees of Mount Rafu,
Pink as precious coral,
Became transfigured in a dream
To beauties rare,
To beauties, gracious, lovely.[2]
These are tales of transformations
Wrought by deep meditation.
Can one truly say that these
Have been the souls of trees?
Yet not alone in distant China,
But here too in Japan
Are persons named for trees—
Matsu, for the pine,

---

[1] Mount Hakoya (Mount Ku I in Chinese) is a legendary home of immortals. The place is mentioned in *Chuang Tzu*: see Fung Yu-lan's selected translations in *Chuang Tzu* (Shanghai: Commercial Press, 1933), pp. 36–37. It is not clear from where came the story of the pines of this mountain becoming beautiful girls.

[2] From a story of a man who went to Mt. Rafu (Lo-fu in Chinese) and there dreamed he met a beautiful woman who was the spirit of the plum. Recounted by the T'ang writer Liu Tsung-yuan (ca. 773–819) in his *Lung Ch'eng Lu*. See Fujino, *Sugawara Denju Tenarai Kagami Hyōkai*, p. 32, n. 2.

Ume, for the plum,
Sakura, for the flowering cherry.
And so even unto blossoms
We impart compassion.
The great heavenly god[3]
Of the Tenman Shrine—
The Heaven-Filling Shrine—
Composed a poem to his beloved plum,
And this is handed down
Most gratefully
To us of later ages.[4]

[3] I.e., Sugawara no Michizane.

[4] The poem by Sugawara, composed while he was in exile in Kyushu, is quoted in act 4, scene 1.

Act I

Scene 1. The Imperial Palace

(The rear half of the stage is a raised platform with a black lacquered railing running across its front edge and a three-tiered black lacquered stairway in the middle. Behind this are seated Sugawara (SR) and Shihei (SL). Between them is a portion of stage hidden by blinds that roll upward. Both Sugawara and Shihei are dressed in flowing black robes with red linings visible at the neck and sleeve openings. Each wears a tall black cap of state.)

NARRATOR: When this god was yet
>A great minister of state,
>Sugawara no Michizane he was called.
>Master of literature,
>Wise in secrets deep
>Of the calligraphic art,
>Such was his scholarship
>And the virtue of his wisdom
>That he was commended to the post
>Of Minister of the Right,
>And was so appointed.
>Known respectfully as Kan Shōjō,[1]

---

[1] The first character of the name Sugawara is read alone as *Kan* and here stands for Lord Sugawara. Shōjō, a term of Chinese origin denoting the highest ranking governing official, is used in Japanese as an alternate term for "great minister" *(daijin)*. Michizane is referred to throughout most of the play by the name Kan Shōjō, but for the sake of clarity and consistency I have for the most part called him Lord Sugawara.

His prestige equals that
Of Fujiwara no Shihei,
Despotic Minister of the Left.
Auspicious this age of Engi when he serves[2]
As the Emperor's protector.
Of late, however, a cold has sent
His Majesty to his sickbed.
The youthful Prince Tokiyo,
Yet lacking in imperial preferment,[3]
Has proceeded to the palace
To inquire after His Majesty's health.
His escort: Hangandai Terukuni,
Officer in the secretariat
Of the Retired Sovereign Uda.
While at the staircase base
Waits Terukuni in attendance,
Prince Tokiyo assumes his seat.

(Terukuni and Prince Tokiyo enter from SR.)

TOKIYO: When I called this morning at the Retired Sovereign's
palace, he expressed concern that the Emperor's illness was
showing no signs of improvement. He asked me to hurry to
the palace for an audience with His Majesty, and to report
back upon his condition. Hangandai Terukuni was dispatched to accompany me. How is His Majesty feeling?

NARRATOR: Grasping his ceremonial baton,
    Sugawara replies with solemn dignity.

SUGAWARA: There appears to be little change. For a further report, however, rather than hear it from me, you had best
inquire directly of His Majesty.

[2] The Engi era spanned the years 901 to 923.

[3] That is, an imperial prince not yet assigned one of the four grades within the
ranks of such princes.

TOKIYO: Perhaps I should.

NARRATOR: Offering to Shihei his compliments,
        Prince Tokiyo departs
        For the chambers of the Emperor.

(Tokiyo exits at SL.)

        At this point Shundō Genba,[4]
        A lesser officer in the Chancellery,
        Enters at the garden's edge and bows.

(Genba enters from SR carrying a wooden tray bearing woven goods of red brocade. He places it just above the stairway, withdraws to SR.)

GENBA: A Chinese priest named Tenrankei has arrived from Pohai bearing a request.[5] The Emperor of China, having heard of our Emperor's imperial virtue and wishing somehow that he might be able to see his face, has ordered this priest to come to our country and paint a likeness of the Emperor. The Chinese Emperor's hope is that by viewing this portrait it will be as though he were confronting our Emperor personally, and so he has sent these numerous gifts.

NARRATOR: As Lord Sugawara listens,

        The presents are brought forth.

SUGAWARA: It is a most remarkable request that this priest brings. It is widely known that our present Emperor is a sage ruler, and it is a distinct honor for Japan that the Chinese Emperor wishes to see our Emperor. Unfortunately, however,

---

[4] Genba is actually the name of a Heian period governmental office whose duties resembled those of a secretary dealing with foreign affairs, overseeing the reception of foreign missions as well as handling the affairs of Buddhist institutions. Shundō Genba's name is given as Tomokage. Since throughout the play he is regularly referred to as Genba and not by his name, the same practice has been followed in the translation.

[5] Envoys from Pohai, in eastern Manchuria, appeared with some regularity at the Japanese court from the eighth to the tenth centuries.

you must tell him the truth of the matter that His Majesty is ill. We should probably send back to China both these gifts and this priest. Perhaps Lord Shihei has some views on this.

NARRATOR: At the words, abruptly
Shihei turns his head,
His tall court hat aquiver.

SHIHEI: I disagree, Michizane. Though we have been told that the Emperor is ill, I doubt that such is the case. Our Emperor is a wise ruler, but he would seem most unlike an emperor if he were described as a cripple, blind of an eye, or hare-lipped, or deformed. Hence, for us to say that he is sick would be taken as a makeshift excuse, to Japan's shame. Rather than have this priest report us as people who are troublesome to deal with, we should get a substitute and pretend that he is the Emperor. Then the Chinese priest will see him, and the matter will be concluded without complication. Now, instead of discussing who will undertake the impersonation, I, Shihei, will act in his stead. I shall put on the imperial robes, become the Emperor, and have audience with this priest.

NARRATOR: With an air of finality
He asserts himself, and yet
The hint therein of traitorous design
Is fearsome indeed.
Terukuni brings himself up sharply
At the foot of the stairs.

TERUKUNI: Your command is a most novel one, but I doubt that the Chinese priest Tenrankei will paint a picture of Lord Shihei. The Japanese Emperor with eyes that tilt upward? With a broad lower jaw? With high cheekbones? Our Chinese priest is hardly likely to accept that sort of a face!

Should Lord Shihei take the place of Emperor Buretsu, the only evil ruler of Japan from Emperor Jimmu to our time, then he would be most suitable. But to take the place of our present Emperor would be as grotesque as calling a deer a horse. Ha ha ha ha ha! The idea is absurd.

NARRATOR: He laughs derisively,

But Shihei rebukes him.

SHIHEI: Your remarks are uncalled for. Withdraw, Terukuni. You there, Genba. Conduct Tenrankei into the palace. I, Shihei, will make preparations to be the Emperor.

NARRATOR: He stands, but Lord Sugawara stops him.

SUGAWARA: Shihei's suggestion is most appropriate that for the sake of our country a substitution be made. However, if this priest is capable of reading a person's character by observing his face, then should he look carefully at the face of a minister he would know that such a person was not of imperial blood but merely a subordinate. What would we do then?

NARRATOR: For reply to such reasoning

Shihei is at a loss.

Miyoshi no Kiyotsura steps forth.

(Till now Kiyotsura has been seated at SL.)

KIYOTSURA: I cannot go along with what Lord Sugawara suggests. To say that that priest can read a person's character is simply too great a flight of imagination. You are being overly cautious. Isn't that right, Mareyo?

SUGAWARA: What you say may be true, yet it often happens that mistakes still occur even when one has exercised great caution. This audience is with an important visitor from China, and so we cannot reach a decision thoughtlessly.

NARRATOR: Briefly he is deep in thought.

SUGAWARA: In any case, an inferior cannot take the place of the Emperor. Fortunately for us, however, we can pay rever-

ence as Emperor, for just this day, to the young Prince Tokiyo, who is of imperial lineage. And even if his portrait is
carried back to China, it will be one about which we need
feel no shame. What do you think of this arrangement?

NARRATOR: On so logical an argument
       Shihei's scheme founders.
       Exchanging glances,
       Shihei and Kiyotsura
       Are left with mouths agape.
       Now from a room screened off by bamboo blinds
       Emerges Iyo no Naishi,
       Waiting lady to the court.

(Naishi enters from SL):

NAISHI: Your discussion has been reported fully to the Emperor,
and he has issued an imperial command that Prince Tokiyo
be his substitute. The Prince is at this moment changing
into the imperial robes. I was instructed to inform you of
this.

NARRATOR: Naishi returns to the inner room.
       Shihei's face quickly turns to angry scorn,
       While Terukuni feels both relief and joy.
       The eastern palace gate opens,
       And, Genba as his guide,
       In comes the Chinese priest Tenrankei,
       His foreign robes, so different from those of Japan,
       Spreading over the garden as he bows.

(Tenrankei enters from downstage right.)

SHIHEI: Hmm—So you are the priest Tenrankei from China. You
are fortunate that your request to paint a portrait of the imperial countenance has been granted. Be thankful.

NARRATOR: A sign from Shihei,
       And a herald's voice is heard
       Announcing the Emperor,

As a bamboo curtain rises higher, higher.
Within sits youthful Prince Tokiyo,
The golden coronet of state
Set straight upon his head,
Elegant in the royal robes.
In recognition of his true regal lineage,
The Chinese priest and all officials
Acknowledge the royal presence
And bow low in reverence.
At length, Tenrankei lifts his head
And gazes intently on the jewel-like personage.

TENRANKEI: Ah, a splendid and sage ruler. How fully he lives up to the expectations of my Emperor Hsi Tsung.[6] He is as beautiful as the thirty-two manifestations of the Buddha, so handsome I cannot find words to describe him. Unworthy though I am, I shall now trace his features with my brush.

NARRATOR: He brings out silken canvas
And box containing inkstone.
Then, with a brush of cypress wood,
Fluently he starts to paint.
Observing the shape of the eyebrows, the set of the brow,
He continues his work,
Now painting, now gazing on his subject.
How the flat baton of state is held,
The fall of the robes—nothing is amiss,
As he paints away with wondrous speed.
So rare his display of artist's skill,
One might take him as a scion

[6] Also known as Li Yen (862–888), the eighteenth emperor of the T'ang Dynasty, who reigned from 873 to 888. Most of his reign was plagued with rebel unrest as the T'ang was in a steep decline. See Herbert A. Giles, A Chinese Biographical Dictionary p. 473. Yokoyama, Jōruri Shū, p. 490, identifies him in error as Hui Tsung, 8th emperor of the Northern Sung Dynasty; this would place him in the twelfth century.

Of that famous painter Yen Hui.
Discreetly, Terukuni gathers up
The gifts the priest has brought.

SUGAWARA *(to the priest):* You will surely be rewarded for your
efforts. You may now return to your lodgings.

NARRATOR: At Michizane's command,
Genba allows the priest to pay his respects.
With Genba as escort, the two withdraw.
Pausing only till the priest has gone,
Shihei dashes to the royal dais,
Grabs Prince Tokiyo's shoulder, drags him down,
And flings aside the imperial robe and coronet.

SHIHEI: Now that the Chinese priest has left, you may wear this
regalia not a moment longer. For such as you, with neither
court office nor court rank—not even the lowest ninth rank—
to be wearing these robes and this coronet is to sully them.
They shall not be left in the palace. I will take charge of
them. As to the events of the day, the Minister of the Right
may report them to the Emperor. I shall withdraw and return home.

NARRATOR: He is about to make off with the royal raiment
When Sugawara stands and takes them from him.

SUGAWARA: How thoughtless, Shihei! Without a word from the
Emperor you seize the imperial robes and coronet to take
them to your residence. Would you have this misunder-
stood and become marked as a traitor?

NARRATOR: For Michizane, merely a casual remark
Meant only for Shihei's own good;
But for Shihei, who knows his own intentions,
The words are like a nail thrust in the breast.
Unable to reply, he turns away.
Prince Tokiyo addresses Sugawara.

TOKIYO: His Majesty had a second command. Nothing is sure, he said, whether one is old or young. In a world where one never knows when he may die, to leave behind an illustrous name may be a personal gratification, but to leave behind one's skills is a gratification for generations yet unborn. Your older child, to whom you might pass on the calligraphic skill you have mastered with your brush, is a girl, and for that there is no help. And, because he is still but a youth you probably should not pass it on to your son Kan Shūsai. Since you, Michizane, have many disciples, it is the Emperor's wish that you choose one of these who is truly competent and transmit to him the inner secrets of the calligraphic art so that it may be a treasure for many ages to come.

NARRATOR: As he speaks, Mareyo runs up to the Prince.

(Mareyo approaches from SL.)

MAREYO *(speaks very rapidly)*: Among Lord Sugawara's pupils possessing both court rank and skill, none of them is a better calligrapher than I, Mareyo. I request that you take advantage of this and decree that Lord Sugawara transmit the secrets to me right now.

NARRATOR: Before he can finish, Sugawara smiles.

SUGAWARA: Within the palace you are my senior; however, in matters of calligraphy you are my disciple. Therefore, when it comes to the way of the brush, do not make selfish requests that disregard the opinions of your teacher.

NARRATOR: The reprimand is sharp.

Sugawara straightens his robes

And responds to the Prince.

SUGAWARA: I am grateful for His Majesty's kindness. My calligraphic studies are important, for they serve to hand down our written language from the age of the gods. I will, therefore, enter into a fast of seven days and make prayers and offerings to the deities of our land and to the Buddhas, using the ceremonies of both China and Japan. There are many tens of thousands of written characters, but my teachings omit not one. Children everywhere who practice the way of the brush are all my disciples, though they may not know it. Starting this day I will seclude myself in my house and select a worthy disciple to whom I may entrust the secrets of the brush.

NARRATOR: And constant to his words,

> The way of the brush that lives for us today
> Is that authentic way taught by Michizane.
> An imperial age of genuine greatness it was,
> That era of the Engi years in which
> Michizane's very name itself
> Stood for the true and faithful way.

(Curtain)

Scene 2. The Bank of the Kamo River

(The backdrop depicts a scene of rice fields and a few farm houses in the foreground, with mountains in the distance against a pale blue sky. Pines appear in the near foreground to the right and left. At center stage stands a black and gold lacquered carriage drawn by a black ox draped in a red cloth. Before the carriage, lying on a low grassy mound, heads supported on their arms, are Matsuōmaru on the right and Umeōmaru on the left. Both are dressed identically, and Sakuramaru, when he enters, will be dressed the same.)

NARRATOR: Drawn off beneath a pine tree,
      Palace carriages rest their wheels,
      And two grooms doze lazily,
      Heads cradled on their arms.
      Two carriages stand side by side,
      One from Fujiwara,
      The other of Sugawara.
      Lord Sugawara's deputy is Mareyo;
      Miyoshi no Kiyotsura serves
      As the emissary of Lord Shihei.
      Prayers are being offered at the Kamo Shrine
      For the Emperor's health.
      While priestesses conduct the rituals
      Of purification within the holy precincts,
      Here on the Kamo riverbank,

What dreams are joined with dreams?
At the sound of the wind in the pines,
Umeōmaru, groom of Lord Sugawara,
Opens his eyes.

UMEŌMARU: Eh, Matsuōmaru, your master, Lord Shihei, may be an irritable sort, but by natural gifts he is a distinguished man. His deputy, Lord Kiyotsura, on the other hand, is a short-tempered blow-hard. You really have to stay awake in case some servant comes looking for you and sends you off about some business.

MATSUŌMARU: You're one to talk, Umeō. Your master's deputy, Mareyo, is the real son-of-a-bitch. Everyone to his own tastes, but I'd certainly like to know why Lord Sugawara takes as a disciple or dispatches as his deputy such a wretch as that.

UMEŌMARU: Oh, his outlook is not so narrow as yours. I know quite well how generous he is. Sakuramaru, who takes care of Prince Tokiyo's carriage, and then you and I, the three of us, are triplets, and that's pretty rare in this world. Our faces and our hearts may differ, but all three of us wear the same garb, all because Lord Sugawara interceded when he heard our father lamenting the difficulty of caring for the children of so remarkable a birth. The birth of triplets is a good omen of peace for all the country, Lord Sugawara said. If they are made pages at court, they will become protectors of the Emperor. Raise them, he told our father, and I will have them appointed as carriage attendants. Why, we are even given our own stipends. Our father Shirokurō now lives in comfort on the land granted to him in the village of Sata, where he looks after Lord Sugawara's beloved trees—the cherry, the plum, and the pine. Lord Sugawara even named us after these three trees; guessing me to be the eldest, he called me Umeōmaru and took me into his own service.

You, Matsuōmaru and Sakuramaru, became grooms at the palace. We are indebted to Lord Sugawara, who became our godfather. We may serve different houses, but we should never think slightingly of Lord Sugawara.

MATSUŌMARU: Ah, you're certainly a long-winded one! Say, Prince Tokiyo must have arrived. It looks like Sakuramaru has come to give his ox a rest.

UMEŌMARU: You have some business to discuss with him?

MATSUŌMARU: Yes, father in Sata Village sent a message for all three of us and our wives to come next month and celebrate his seventieth birthday. I must let Sakuramaru know.

UKEŌMARU: Oh, messengers came to each of us. He already knows about it. You know, when I think about it, I can see that our father is really very fortunate. Just as the proverb says, "neither lender nor borrower, and blessed with three children."

NARRATOR: Seed of the same womb,
Born at the same time,
In the same year,
Which is the elder brother?
Which the younger? One cannot tell.
To Umeō, the plum, and Matsuō, the pine,
Comes Sakuramaru, namesake of the cherry—
A trio of grooms.
His carriage parked nearby
In the shadow of a tree,
Sakuramaru calls from above the riverbank.

SAKURAMARU: Well, well. You two are certainly taking it easy. The ceremonies are already half finished. You'd better go before you're sent for.

NARRATOR: He speaks with a serious look.

UMEŌMARU: When the ceremonies are over, Prince Tokiyo will

probably be the first to leave. So why have you come over
here?

SAKURAMARU: Oh, the Prince is resting at the priest's quarters, so
I don't know when he'll be leaving. The deputies you brought
here are all excited, saying they have business back at the
palace. You're sure to be scolded if you're late.

MATSUŌMARU: Of course, the Prince, who has no office, is different from the busy Kiyotsura, who has caught the fancy
of Lord Shihei. I don't know when he'll leave, so I'm going.

NARRATOR: He is about to take hold of the carriage.

UMEŌMARU: Wait a moment, Matsuō. If Kiyotsura is departing,
his honor Mareyo will also be leaving. If they aren't ready
to depart yet and we pull these two carriages into that crowd,
then people may get hurt or the carriages damaged, and any
blunders will surely be blamed on us. Let's go quickly and
have a look. We can come back later to pick up the carriages. Our rest will have to wait. Let's go.

NARRATOR: The pair set off together
        Running toward the shrine.
        Sakuramaru watches their departure.

SAKURAMARU: Ha ha ha ha ha. They swallowed it all.

NARRATOR: Chuckling to himself,
        He claps his hands as a signal.
        Beckoned by love,
        Traversing grasses moist with dew,
        Forward comes the gentle Lady Kariya,
        Daughter of Lord Sugawara.
        In the tender bloom of maidenhood,
        A picture of loveliness,
        Her hands hold arching about her face
        A mantle of translucent lace,
        Thin and diaphanous.

In charm and bearing
A fitting member is she of her father's house.
Behind her follows the beautiful Yae,
Beloved wife of Sakuramaru.
These two have arranged this tryst
Between the lady and him who has won her heart,
Prince Tokiyo.

YAE: Ah, my husband. Is everything arranged?

SAKURAMARU: Of course, of course. Today this riverbank is just for parking carriages. It's blocked off to people, and I thought that no one would be passing by, not even a mouse around. But when I accompanied the Prince here, to my disappointment I ran into Umeōmaru and Matsuōmaru. They were all goggle-eyed at seeing me here, but I told them the biggest fib of my life, and sent them scattering. Now, now, my lady, you needn't be so shy. Come along over here, over here. Let me lift this blind and you will see before you a veritable Buddha.

NARRATOR: The carriage blind is raised,
And from within appears
The bashful face of the Prince.
At this meeting, more shy is he
Than Lady Kariya, as she smiles sweetly
And buries her face in her sleeve.

SAKURAMARU: Ah, they're not commoners like us. It's hard to get them to take advantage of the situation. Oh Yae, if only I could make it completely dark!

YAE: What are you talking about. That's easy, even in broad daylight. They can't be seen inside this fine carriage.

SAKURAMARU: Yae, you're a smart one! Now, I'll leave you all alone for a bit.

NARRATOR: He goes off into the shadows.

YAE: Excellent, good idea. Men are a nuisance at times like this. Now, my lady, if you have anything to say, you can feel quite at ease.

NARRATOR: She pushes Lady Kariya forward.

KARIYA (*speaking to the prince*): I am both thankful and happy for your replies to all of the notes I have sent you, and for your own note saying we would have an opportunity to meet. I have been waiting anxiously for this meeting today, and I have come as you bade me.

NARRATOR: She hides her face in her sleeve.

And Prince Tokiyo too, but seventeen
And this his young first love,
Can find no words to woo her.

TOKIYO: Sakuramaru has been most helpful. Each time I read your notes, my longing to meet you grew and grew. I am glad you have come. But . . . ah . . . don't you find the spring breeze chilling?

NARRATOR: The Prince's words call forth
The lady's tender feelings;
But, for her, more penetrating
Than the breezes of the spring
Are the zephyrs of love.
From behind the carriage
Sakuramaru pokes out his head.

SAKURAMARU: Good heavens, wife, put yourself in their place and think of something! I'm so impatient, I'm having palpitations! Can't you hurry up and help them get on with it?

YAE: You're exactly right. Oh, as the Prince says, the spring breeze *is* chilling. Excuse me, but why don't you get out of the wind for a bit inside the carriage. Here, let me help you.

NARRATOR: She picks the lady up
And pushes her inside.

KARIYA: Oh! What are you doing? This isn't right!

NARRATOR: But even as she speaks,
Into the carriage she goes.

SAKURAMARU: Now, down with the blind!

NARRATOR: From within can be heard the Prince,
"How happy I am!"
And also Lady Kariya:
"Entering the sacred carriage like this
Will surely summon the wrath of the gods.
Well, let it come!"
Hearing this tender exchange,
Sakuramaru and Yae quickly withdraw.

SAKURAMARU: Wife, I can't stand it! With things like this going on right next to us, the wildest feeling has come over me.

NARRATOR: He is fairly squirming.

YAE: Hush, you'll be heard. The two of them are in such good spirits, so happy, aren't they.

SAKURAMARU: They're in rather overly good spirits if you ask me, and it's giving me a hard time. But that's another matter. I really must hand it to you for arranging this meeting. How on earth were you able to get in to see Lady Kariya?

YAE: Just as you told me to do, I disguised myself as one of the ladies of the court and got all the way into the priests' quarters. When I approached Lady Kariya I said, "I am Sakuramaru's wife, Yae." She seemed to have been waiting anxiously for me, for she said, "Ah, you've come. Quickly, shall we go?" She had her maids wait there, and then she came out secretly by a back way.

SAKURAMARU: Ah, that's just as it was supposed to be. I made the arrangements the other day. As luck would have it, Lord Sugawara had closeted himself to prepare for transmitting his secrets of calligraphy. So I had Lady Kariya ask her

mother for permission to visit a shrine. To keep her attendants quiet, I bribed them heavily, as though I were sprin-
kling water about. Speaking of water reminds me, we're going
to need some water before long, you know.

YAE: What are you talking about? You mean for those two in-
nocents?

SAKURAMARU: What a sentimental one you are. More than mere
wash water, they'll probably need a full tub bath.

YAE: Well, if that's the case, then, this river water will do.

SAKURAMARU: No, wait. It's been raining and the riverbank will
be slippery. If I let you get hurt, things will be . . . ah . . .
rather inconvenient for us . . . tonight. Bring some of the
water from in front of the shrine.

YAE: But . . . well . . . somehow that seems wrong.[7]

SAKURAMARU: Don't worry, don't worry. As the saying goes, "Ten
virtues has the sovereign, nine the gods."[8] So, since the
Prince is the Emperor's younger brother, he has nine virtues and a half. Now go and get the water.

NARRATOR: Thus urged, off to the shrine
Heads his wife to dip the water.
Alone now, Sakuramaru
Is about to relax and doze off,
When in rush Miyoshi no Kiyotsura
And a company of his men,
Truncheons in hand, sleeves rolled back.

---

[7] Because the water is there for worshipers to purify themselves. The sexual over-
tones in these lines having to do with water would surely have delighted a contemporary audience. The wash water for Kariya and Prince Tokiyo that Sakuramaru refers to would be for ablutions following sexual intercourse. The love-
making in the carriage has aroused Sakuramaru; hence, his concern for Yae on
the slippery riverbank, where some accident might interfere with his own intended advances toward her later in the evening.

[8] The proverb means essentially that the sovereign, partly by virtue of his mas-
culinity, partly as a result of his preservation of Buddhist laws in previous exis-
tences, possesses greater virtue even than the gods.

(act 1, scene 2)

NARRATOR: Beckoned by love,
Traversing grasses moist with dew,
Forward comes the gentle Lady Kariya,
Daughter of Lord Sugawara.
In the tender bloom of maidenhood,
A picture of loveliness . . .

(Mareyo) (act 1, scene 3)

NARRATOR: For the forthcoming transmission
Of the calligraphic secrets;
Quote willfully has he set his mind
That already has he been
Selected for that honor.

SAKURAMARU: Saaa, saaa, come children, (act 2, scene 1)
Come and buy, come and buy.
Candy birds have I,
Sweet birds made of candy.

(act 2, scene 3)

TARŌ: Lady Kariya's high position puts me in the shade. I've only heard
her name. She sure is a beauty. I can see why Tokiyo or whatever
his name is went and lost his head over her.

(act 3, scene 1)

UMEŌMARU: What! Sakuramaru, did you hear that? It's the minister
   Shihei, who's caused all the trouble for Prince Tokiyo and Lord
   Sugawara. We couldn't have asked for anything better . . .

(act 3, scene 1)

MATSUŌMARU: Wait! Wait! WAIT, I say!

(Yae, Shiradayū) (act 3, scene 2)

SHIRADAYŪ: Did you hear that, daughter? People nowadays are sly ones. He saw through my little economy trick. Come over for a nightcap, he says. Ha ha ha ha ha.

(Shiradayū, Sugawara) (act 4, scene 1)

NARRATOR: To this field and mountain landscape
With spring-like sky, comes Lord Sugawara
Astride an ox released to paddock.

(act 4, scene 1)

SUGAWARA: I swear an oath to Bonten, to Taishakuten and King Emma, and my ghost will become chief of the one hundred sixty-eight thousand rumbling thunders that reverberate through the heavens.

(here the mask has been removed.)

(Chiyo, Genzō)

GENZŌ: What . . . is this?

NARRATOR: In his consternation,
The barb of his attack is dulled,
It seems he cannot press on.

KIYOTSURA: Aha, there you are Sakuramaru. Word has it that you
took Prince Tokiyo off before the services at the shrine were
over. Where did you go with him? Come on, out with it!

NARRATOR: He begins to press him.

SAKURAMARU: I haven't the slightest idea. Those of low station
don't know the affairs of their betters. You'd do better to ask
the Prince himself.

NARRATOR: No sooner has he spoken than . . .

KIYOTSURA: Enough of your effrontery. For some time now I've
been hearing of suspicious things you've had a hand in. And
especially today. If anyone has defiled the precincts where
services are being held for the recovery of His Majesty,[9] I
don't care if it is the Prince or the Crown Prince, he'll surely
be arrested and punished. If you don't tell us the whole truth,
we'll drag you off and torture it out of you. Men, tie him
up!

NARRATOR: A command, and Kiyotsura's minions
Scatter and surround Sakuramaru,
Who braces himself to confront them.

SAKURAMARU: If I say I don't know, then by all that's deep in hell
or high in heaven, I don't know! Show me any insolence
and I'll kick the whole lot of you around like a football! I'll
kick you and then I'll trample on you! Shall I show you some
of my footwork?

NARRATOR: Both feet lunging forth,
This show of strength—
Sturdy as an ancient tree—
Belies his gentle face.

KIYOTSURA: Pshaw! The wretch puts on a fine show of impudence! From what I saw a little while ago, there's someone

---

[9] Sexual intercourse in the precincts of a Shinto shrine, such as the Kamo Shrine
in this scene, would have c␣nstituted a defilement that would call for some sort
of ritual cleansing or exorcism of the area.

in that carriage. Tear off the blinds, men, and take a look.

NARRATOR: As henchmen follow orders and advance,
Sakuramaru grabs first one by the neck
And then another, hurling them aside.

SAKURAMARU: We grooms have charge of carriages. Come on and
try, if you've got the nerve.

NARRATOR: He kicks aside and sends aflying
Those who charge upon him,
Wrenching truncheons from their hands.
Driving all before him,
Off he dashes in pursuit.
In the intervening lull,
Both the Prince and Lady Kariya realize
They must be seen by no one.
Hurriedly,
From the carriage they alight, alight.
Their hearts, as it is with youth,
Are bent on but a single course:
For them, escape. And thus do they embark,
Dressed yet in their courtly robes,
Upon a journey transitory,
To a destination not yet known.
Grasping an opportunity
Kiyotsura returns to the scene.
He opens the carriage blinds and peers in,
But it is empty.

KIYOTSURA: Good heavens! I've made a mistake! There'll be hell
to pay if that groom comes back.

NARRATOR: So saying, he escapes by a hidden path.
No sooner has he gone
Than in runs Sakuramaru.
Alarmed to find the noble couple gone,

He looks into the carriage
And sees a note left by the Prince.

SAKURAMARU *(reading note):* Let's see now. . . . "Rather than be disgraced by discovery here, we have fled."

NARRATOR: Reading aloud the letter,
     His mind is in consternation,
     His breast as rigid as a plank.

SAKURAMARU: I must go after them and help.

NARRATOR: He is set to dash off after them
     When Yae, his wife, appears.

YAE: Oh, here, I've brought the water.

NARRATOR: She shows him, but he thrusts it aside.

SAKURAMARU: What? The devil with the water! That miserable Kiyotsura came to investigate the carriage, and so the Prince and Lady Kariya, afraid they'd be discovered, have fled to who knows where.

YAE: What! Why that's . . . Are you sure?

NARRATOR: Thunderstruck, his wife
     Lets the bucket fall with a clatter.

YAE: Well then, . . . where are you off to?

SAKURAMARU: Where? Well, to begin with, the lady is the adopted daughter of Lord Sugawara. Her real mother is Lord Sugawara's aunt who lives in the village of Haji in Kawachi Province.[10] That's probably the first place they'll go, so I'll follow them. You take the carriage back to the Prince's palace. If it's left here there'll be trouble later.

YAE: I understand. Then, I'll masquerade as you and take it there. Give me your cloak. *(Sakuramaru hands her his white tunic.)* Go along now and don't worry about me.

---

[10] In the vicinity of Fujiidera City, in the southern portion of modern metropolitan Osaka.

SAKURAMARU: All right.

NARRATOR: Kicking up white sand beneath his feet,
    Off he dashes as if flying.
    Yae throws the cloak about her shoulders,
    Disguising herself as her husband.
    She pulls at the carriage ox,
    Pulls with all her strength,
    Giving the ox commands:
    "To the left, now to the right."
    Hard she tugs, but slow the ox's feet.

YAE: Stupid beast!

NARRATOR: Now she pushes from behind,
    And round the wheels begin to move,
    As through the heavens
    Wheel the moon and sun.
    Is this diurnal round
    One of the almanac's ill-fated days?
    For the lovers a time of disaster?
    For her man a day of dark portent?
    She shoves against the creaking cart—
    So fateful for lovers' nuptials—
    And prays for heaven's pardon,
    Begs the gods that all ends well.
    The fruitless and bewildering search within her heart
        to see
    If this lone day is one of fortune's respite
    Among the time-chart's cycles of ill-luck—
    Like seeking out some special mark
    Within the random mottling on the bull
    She drives before her,
            Homeward bound.

Scene 3. The Transmission of the Secrets

(The scene is a large room in Sugawara's residence, the sides at right and left covered by sliding doors, the central portion of the stage open revealing the interior of a large room at the back of which is a facade of sliding panels decorated with a painting of a stylized tree spotted with lichens and abloom with red flowers. At center, seated at a low table and practicing his calligraphy, is Mareyo, one of Sugawara's senior disciples.)

NARRATOR: Perseverance and practice
    And fondness for the subject—
    That of those three
    Fondness alone most makes for skill,
    Is for those who pursue the arts
    A precept wrought in gold.
    Impelled by his love of calligraphy,
    Michizane studies from dawn till dark,
    During lulls in the business of state.
    From those ranked high and low
    Among the nobles of the court,
    To warrior and townsman alike,
    The number of his disciples knows no end.
    Among them, his lordship Mareyo,
    A senior disciple,
    Long a student of the writing art.
    For the forthcoming transmission

Of the calligraphic secrets,
Quite willfully has he set his mind
That already has he been
Selected for that honor.
Since the darkling hours of the morn,
Mareyo has been at his writing desk within the palace,
Calling boisterously now for tobacco, now for tea.

(Mareyo claps his hands. Tsubone enters from the SR sliding doors.
She beckons to Katsuno who enters from the same SR doors and
kneels next to Tsubone.)

NARRATOR: Tsubone, chief lady in waiting,
Chides the other maid
For being out of earshot at a summons.

TSUBONE: Is no one there in the next room? Master Mareyo is
calling.

NARRATOR: Mareyo turns his complaints upon Tsubone.

MAREYO: I've been clapping my hands till they're smarting, but
everyone pretends not to hear. Oh, I see. Can it be that my
coming here every day is a bother to you and you've both
decided to get the better of me by not answering? I've been
practicing my writing for seven days now, but let me tell
you it's not for my own benefit alone. The master's son Kan
Shūsai is a bare seven years old, not yet of an age to receive
the secrets of calligraphy. So I, Mareyo, will receive the secrets. Then, when Kan Shūsai has attained manhood, he
will receive them from me, so I'm only performing my duties for my master. You're supposed to move quickly when
I call you, but you're all too sluggish.

TSUBONE: There, Katsuno, take heed of what you hear. If you
are not at hand when needed, then it makes trouble for me.
No matter what is said to you here, you just answer "Yes
sir, yes sir." Isn't that right, Master Mareyo?

MAREYO: That's right, just as you say. You understand things quite well. Devoting myself to calligraphy like this every day is for the sake of the house of Sugawara. Now, I want you to show Lord Sugawara this specimen I've just written.

NARRATOR: He holds it out to her.

TSUBONE: Oh no, please let me off today.

MAREYO: Let you off? Why?

TSUBONE: Well, however many times he sees them, Lord Sugawara is displeased. It's probably not due to your calligraphic efforts but rather that I present them poorly. Let Katsuno do it today instead of me.

MAREYO: No, that won't do at all. The transmission of the calligraphic arts is a solemn and secret affair. Can't you see the sacred rope placed before the study? I can't send in such a sensual and enticing young woman as her. Up to yesterday Lord Sugawara may not have liked my writing, but this example is quite exceptional. Strength has flowed to the tip of my brush. It's a superb example of the very soul of calligraphy. The calligraphic secrets are as good as mine. I want you to take it to him proudly.

NARRATOR: At such insistence here is no choice:
      She must take it to Lord Sugawara.

(Tsubone exits through the SL sliding doors.)

MAREYO: Well, Katsuno. You understand what Tsubone said, that you're to do what I ask?

KATSUNO: Yes, I understand.

MAREYO: Eh, that's fine. Fortunately, there's nobody around. This is the best luck I've had in years. Let's go behind that screen and I'll show you how much I love you.

NARRATOR: She tears herself from his grasp.

KATSUNO: Oh! Get away from me! If you try anything outrageous I'll scream. You understand?

MAREYO: Oh, I understand. *(Grabs Katsuno's sleeve.)* Go on, say
I'm afraid of your calling for help, but do you think I can
control my feelings once they're aroused? Come, my sweet,
do as I say.

NARRATOR: Quickly he grabs her
And pulls her toward the screen.

KATSUNO: Oh, Help! *(She slips away, but he grabs her again.)*

MAREYO: Go on, call for help. Who's going to hear you?

KATSUNO: Help, Lady Sugawara! Young Master!

NARRATOR: Have her cries for help been heard?
Lord Sugawara's wife appears,
(Lady Sugawara enters from SL.)
Leading her son by the hand.
Mareyo is most taken aback.

MAREYO: Oh, well, well. You've . . . ah . . . come at a rather
awkward time. . . . Ah, . . . welcome.

NARRATOR: Having now released Katsuno,
His hands fumble gawkily about,
As he lamely tries to save the situation.

MAREYO: Katsuno asked me to cure her heartburn, and I was just
beginning the treatment, as you can see. As your ladyship
knows, I am expert in almost everything. I'm a clever fellow
quite rare in this world. That's why my parents, in their pride,
named me Mareyo, which means "marvel of the world."
The young master here is another example, quite wise beyond his years. In naming him Kan Shūsai you took *shū*,
the character that means "excel," and *sai*, which means
"intelligence," and since he is the honorable son of the house
of Sugawara, or Kan—thus you named him Kan Shūsai.[11]

---

[11] Mareyo's glib etymology of the name to the contrary, the term *shūsai* in the
Heian period meant a university student. It is used, however, as the name of
Sugawara's son throughout the play.

Well, put briefly, it works that way. Oh, I'm just too clever. But, for Katsuno, I suppose it's a case of a masseur whose treatment hasn't worked. Now, if my lady is thinking . . .

LADY SUGAWARA: There's no need for any explanation, Mareyo. I am aware of your usual behavior. How could you have any doubts!

NARRATOR: Her greeting is gracefully noncommittal.

MAREYO: Ah, I am relieved to hear that. But, apart from the immediate circumstances, there is something I'd like to ask about. *(He sidles up beside Lady Sugawara.)* There's a rumor that there has been something going on between your daughter Lady Kariya and Prince Tokiyo. As of today I have been in attendance here for seven days, but there has been no word about it here in your residence. I thought it was just groundless talk, but Lady Kariya's residence is empty. Does the fact that no search has been made mean perhaps that their parents have let them run off together?

NARRATOR: Such is Lady Sugawara's distress,
    For a moment she cannot reply.
(She suppresses her tears with her left sleeve.)

LADY SUGAWARA: I've tried to keep it secret, but this has been impossible. It was inevitable that Kariya would be criticized by unfeeling gossips. *(Mareyo is still making gestures to Katsuno, but she ignores him.)* But Prince Tokiyo is far more important. They met together in secret, a lovers' tryst in a carriage traveling along the road of love, then hastily they parted. Now the Prince is embarrassed that the matter will become known. He hasn't returned to his palace, and since he is not just an ordinary personage, his attendants are not likely merely to leave things as they now stand. As for my daughter—this you know, Mareyo—her real mother is my husband's aunt Kakuju who lives at the village of Haji in

Kawachi Province. Before Kan Shūsai was born we adopted her as our own daughter. She hasn't returned home here, so I think she may have gone to our aunt's house. I've secretly sent a man there to inquire. *(Again Mareyo covertly attempts to induce Katsuno to come to him. She makes reproving gestures and remains seated.)* Until today I have purposely kept all this from her father because, by imperial command, he has closeted himself for seven days to prepare for the transmission of his calligraphic secrets. During this time he has not been in attendance at the Emperor's palace, and he has heard none of these rumors. After the secrets have been conferred and he finds out, he is sure to be upset. I've racked my mind as to what to do, so please bear with me.

NARRATOR: In telling the story, small wonder her concern.
(She again suppresses tears with her sleeve.)
> Now from the neighbor room a keeper of the inner gate
> Comes in and bows respectfully.
(Gatekeeper enters from SR sliding doors.)
GATEKEEPER: As you ordered, madam, a search has been made for Takebe Genzō, formerly employed in this household. We have pursued the matter in every direction. At last, both Genzō and his wife have been found and they have just now arrived. Shall I conduct them here?
LADY SUGAWARA: Oh, Genzō and his wife! I've been waiting anxiously for them. Quickly, tell them to come here. Kan Shūsai, it won't be any fun for you to be here while I talk with Genzō. Run along and play with Katsuno. Mareyo, if you don't mind. . . .
MAREYO: Well, if I'm going to be in the way here, I'll go elsewhere. *(Follows Katsuno and Kan Shūsai off through the SR doors. As he goes, he taps Katsuno on the shoulder, making further advances. She ignores him.)*

NARRATOR: All depart, one by one,
    To other parts of the palace.
*(During the following recitative, Genzō and Tonami enter through
the downstage right sliding doors. Genzō enters hesitantly, Tonami following and carrying his two swords. As soon as they enter
they kneel and bow deeply.)*
    That in secret Genzō and Tonami loved,
    A love unknown to the world,
    Became the seed that brought upon them
    The anger of Lord Sugawara—
    A master due trust as though a parent.
    The ties of man and wife will linger on
    Through this and one more life;
    Yet more enduring, through three lives,
    The bond uniting master to disciple.
    But heedless was the couple of this greater tie,
    And for their wrongful liaison,
    From their master's house were they cast.
    Now a cold and shabby life they lead,
    And Genzō is a beggarly and masterless man.
    For Genzō and Tonami,
    As poorly garbed as birds bereft of plumage,
    The summons of this day,
    Like the wondrous blooming of the *udonge* flower, [12]
    Brightens and opens their hearts,
    As the doors are opened for them.
    They cannot forget what befell them
    Within and without their former master's house;
    But mindful of their past offenses,
    They are hesitant and fearful
    And their legs tremble beneath them.

[12] A fabulous flower of India said to bloom only once in 3,000 years, at which
time a Buddha would appear.

No sooner do they glimpse
Their former mistress at her seat
Than low they bow in deep obeisance.

LADY SUGAWARA: Genzō, Tonami. It has been such a long time. I've counted them up: four years it has been now since you incurred my husband's displeasure and were banished from this house. My lord looks down on no man; he is as compassionate as ever . . . and as stern. It is his way that once his mind is made up it does not change. I had thought nothing could be done, and then suddenly he summons you here on some business. I have no idea what the matter concerns, but I'm sure you need have no apprehensions. Surely it will be pleasant news. But there, I'm doing all the talking. You must be impatient to learn why he has called you. *(Calling out.)* Someone inform Lord Sugawara that Genzō and his wife have arrived. Now, both of you, rise and come closer so we can talk more easily. You needn't be so formal. Come closer, come closer. These long years you've been away from here, has life been hard for you? How you've changed from what I used to know. The clothes you're wearing, Genzō, they're the coarse stuff of the common people. But, Tonami, your embroidered gown is lovely. I should have expected as much, shouldn't I? Has there been a child between the two of you yet?

(Genzō remains bowing; Tonami is weeping into her sleeve.)

NARRATOR: Tonami replies in tearful gratitude.

TONAMI: We do not deserve these most gracious words. For deceiving our master we have been punished, and life since then has been hard for us. We sold off first one of our robes, then another and another until all have, as it were, gone up as smoke to cook our morning and evening meals. In the end this gown alone *(holds out a sleeve)* has been kept, as I could not forget your kindness in giving it to me. All too soon my fine tortoiseshell hair ornaments *(touches her hair)* also were exchanged for more commonplace ones of banyan wood as side by side we've had to work. Even the poorly starched formal clothes my husband has on were rented just for this day. Oh, look at that. How embarrassing! *(Tonami giggles embarrassedly and takes from the back of Genzō's collar a pin with a rental tag attached.)* But it is not right to bother you with all these things. Our shame has been our own doing, as a sword poorly kept will surely rust. It must be because the gods watch over warriors that Genzō's sword, though rusted, has still not passed into another's hands.

GENZŌ: As my wife says, having sunk to our present circumstances, all the more do I feel ashamed at how headstrong and disloyal we were in the past. When I think back upon the punishment accorded us by my lord, I am filled with deep regret. *(Bows deeply.)*

NARRATOR: Both husband and wife succumb to helpless tears.

Tsubone now emerges from within.

(Tsubone enters from SL.)

TSUBONE: The Master wishes to see Genzō alone in the study. He has issued instructions that no one, not even Lady Sugawara, is to enter until the interview is over.

LADY SUGAWARA: Yes, of course, I understand. Genzō, go with Tsubone. Tonami come with me.

(As all exit, the sliding panels at centerstage rear close. They reopen shortly revealing a section obscured by a bamboo blind. Genzō is admitted through downstage SR sliding panels. He enters hesitantly, bows, and remains in this attitude for some time during the beginning of the scene. Tsubone enters through the SR sliding panels, goes to the blind and, bowing, announces Genzō's ar-

rival. As the blind rises, she withdraws. Behind the blind, Suga-wara is seated before a writing table; a calligraphic hanging adorns the wall behind him.)

NARRATOR: Joy mingles with fear in Genzō's heart
As he is summoned by his former lord.
He enters through the sliding panels
Opened by Tsubone, who then announces him.
A sacred rope has reverently been hung within,
And Sugawara is seated, smiling,
Behind a simple desk of plain unpainted wood.
Awed by Sugawara's gaze,
Genzō is so bathed in sweat
It soaks into the shoulders of his mantle.
A pause, and Sugawara speaks.

SUGAWARA: I have been searching for you because of an urgent matter that has come up, but no one knew where you lived. Finally, only yesterday, I learned of your whereabouts. I am most pleased now to see you before me. From the time when you were but a youth you served me, and it was precisely because you loved the way of the brush that you excelled, because you studied hard that you learned. You surpassed my other disciples of long standing, and I thought surely that you would become a splendid calligrapher. Then, so unexpectedly, came an end to our relationship of lord and servant. Perhaps you've even forgotten how to hold a brush.

NARRATOR: At his words, Genzō feels even more gratitude.

GENZŌ: Your kind words put me at a loss for a reply. Since I was young and still had forelocks on my head,[13] you had me in your close service. You always had me write and learn, say-

---

[13] That is, had not yet gone through the ceremony of coming of age, at which time the forelocks were shaved off, youthful name and style of dress were changed, etc. This usually occurred between the ages of eleven and sixteen.

ing that to write with a skilled hand was the highest of all the arts. To say that I learned to write during my spare moments while I served you would be ill-mannered, but I remember you told me that skill in an art is a lifelong benefit, even though the characters I write now sprawl like the writhings of a worm. These things I remember as I earn a meager livelihood gathering together school children in Narutaki village and teaching them to write. Until today my wife and I have had our lives supported by the hairs of the brush. Each day I write corrections of my pupil's calligraphy, but my hand shows no improvement. That you should be so gracious as to inquire about me makes me regret sorely my own clumsiness and my dismissal from your service.

NARRATOR: Sugawara listens attentively to this contrition.

SUGAWARA: Instructing children is no ignoble profession. Calligraphy has the blessings of the deities, art is a virtue. If you have been doing as you say, then it is unlikely that your skill with the brush has declined. There is hardly need to examine you, but nevertheless I would like for you to write something. Afterward I will explain to you my reasons. For your copy book take these two poems, one written in Chinese, the other in the Japanese script, and write them out.

NARRATOR: The master, with his own hands,
　　　　　Holds out a plain wooden writing desk,
　　　　　But Genzō, bowing and shrinking back in awe,
　　　　　Will not advance.

(Sugawara places the writing desk in front of himself.)
　　　　　Abruptly from the shadows
　　　　　The devious Mareyo steps forth.

MAREYO: Well now, Genzō. I've overheard everything from over here. The master may, of course, say what he pleases, but

you should beg his leave to decline this proposal and withdraw. Yet you just remain there bowing and blinking your
eyes, looking for all the world like a toad. Does this mean
you actually intend to accept his generous offer and write?
You are too presumptuous!

GENZŌ: I am honored, Mareyo, that you should remember me.
What you say is true; I can serve no use here. But I am
hardly unaware of my present position. At the moment I
am unsure whether or not I should write from the copy book
handed me. Living in the country as I have for the past four
years, using crude ink sticks and the cheapest of brushes,
writing on the backs of bills and waste paper, I cannot help
but hesitate right now. At such a fine desk, and with such
excellent ink and brushes and paper as these, how can I write
a single character, even make a mark?

MAREYO: There, you've got the idea. Well, if you see that it's
impossible, why don't you take your leave?

GENZŌ: Well, that's just it. As you know, I have been banished
from this house. I had hoped I might seek, through your
good offices, to restore myself in my master's favor. *(Bows
to Mareyo.)*

MAREYO: Hmmm, I see. I might make apologies on your behalf,
but I'm afraid it's too late now. Let me sum up the situation
for you. Our Emperor has said that one is unsure in this
world how long he may live. Though life and death know
no distinction between old or young, in the normal course
of things death comes first to the aged. This year Lord Sugawara is fifty-two. He is past that age of fifty when, as they
say, one knows the will of heaven. His Majesty has de-
plored the fact that age comes and the years go by, and that
no disciple has been chosen to whom could be handed on
the calligraphic teachings of Lord Sugawara, whose artistry

is praised even in China. It would be unfortunate should it
end with one generation. It has been the imperial wish that
a worthy disciple be selected and given the calligraphic secrets. Thus the master has for seven days been fasting in
strict preparation for the transmission. After all of this is settled, I'll speak to him on your behalf.

GENZŌ: Ah, having heard this, I can see it is a most gratifying
wish of the Emperor.

MAREYO: Well, the imperial command and the great joy it brings
around here are all quite well known without your saying
so. Now, quickly, be on your way. *(He takes Genzō's arm.)*

NARRATOR: He presses Genzō to leave.

SUGAWARA: No, do not leave, Genzō! Write as I have asked you.
*(Genzō bows, goes before Sugawara and reverently accepts the
writing desk, taking it back to his place at SR.)*

NARRATOR: The words bring joy to Genzo
But only anger the self-opinionated Mareyo,
Who glares at his rival.

MAREYO *(advancing on Genzō)*: You dare to think of writing
without deferring to me, your senior among the disciples? [14]

GENZŌ: Though you may laugh at my efforts, I will not be
ashamed of them. Please excuse me.

NARRATOR: He sets himself before the desk,
Takes the copy book,
Lifts it up, and bows in reverence.
He mixes well the ink—
So fragrant,
So rich in hue.

---

[14] This apparent countermanding of Sugawara's orders by Mareyo, apart from
further establishing Mareyo's supercilious insolence, may be explained by the earlier
observation (act 1, scene 1) by Sugawara that Mareyo is his senior at court even
though he is Sugawara's disciple in the study of calligraphy.

What heavenly grace attends
The hand that wields the brush.
Mareyo edges up to Genzō.

MAREYO: I wouldn't put it past a tricky rascal like you to use the nearly transparent paper you have to trace from that copy book. Well, I'll see that you don't practice such deception. How shameful. Are you unaware of your disgraceful appearance? Sitting there before the desk, wearing your dirty trousers over a dressing gown, why you look exactly like one of those priests at a poor country temple who merely list the offerings brought by pilgrims. Be sure you don't write everything out in the wrong order now!

NARRATOR: Foul-mouthed the abuse
That Mareyo pours on Genzō.
Feigning a stumble,
He jars the writing table,
And nudges his rival with his elbow.

(Genzō grabs Mareyo by the arm, pins him beneath his right knee and goes on writing despite the struggling Mareyo.)

But the patient Genzō
Shows no mark of reproach,
As from the writing book
He calmly copies out the poems.
Concluding his task,
He places desk and writings
Back before his master,
Withdraws,
And bows in humble reverence.
Sugawara takes up the finished copy.

SUGAWARA *(reading the first poem)*:
A scant few inches has the grass pushed up through the sands of the beach;

But a few feet do the mists of spring trail above the
branches of the trees.

This is a poem I wrote in Chinese.

Only yesterday
I bade the old year farewell,
And yet today
How quickly rise the mists of spring
Around Mount Kasuga.

This other was composed by Hitomaro.[15] Both poems capture well the feeling of early spring. There can hardly be
any better form than the way you have written the characters, both our Japanese script and that of China. Excellent,
Genzō, splendidly done! In transmitting the laws of calligraphy, one must consider the eight master strokes and the
sixteen points of brush technique, but I need not name each
one. People know them. The Sugawara style is a tradition
in which the sacred secrets transmit the very soul of the art.
On this day that completes my seven days of abstinence, the
gods have shown their divine will, Genzō. To you will be
passed the secrets of my art.

NARRATOR: Sugawara's joy knows no bounds.

GENZŌ: Thank you, I am so grateful. *(Wipes away tears.)* Now,
since the secrets are to be transmitted to me, might I also
be pardoned, and once again as before call you my master?

SUGAWARA: Master? Whom do you call master? Transmission of
the secrets is one thing, banishment is another matter. It
was a special command of the Emperor that I hand on these
secrets, so I could not ignore so excellent a calligrapher as
you, even though you had been reckless in the past. My

[15] Hitomaro was a famous poet who flourished from the end of the seventh century into the early years of the eighth century. Authorship of the poem quoted
here, however, is disputed. See Yokoyama, *Jōruri Shū*, p. 515, n. 20.

own feeling of displeasure remains. As for the transmission of the secrets, it will assure the perpetuation of the way of the brush. I am sure that when the justice of my decision is reported to the Emperor, he will see there has been no partiality. Nor can Mareyo doubt it. Your banishment, Genzō, is the same as before; I am not your master, you are not my servant. Henceforth, I will allow no further interviews.

(Mareyo shows his pleasure at this.)

NARRATOR: Like a red-hot blade his sharp words pierce Genzō.

GENZŌ: The logic of your words is indisputable, but forgive me if I say that I would prefer that you pass on the secrets to someone else *(glances at Mareyo)* and pardon my past transgression.

NARRATOR: With tears in his eyes he begs.

MAREYO: You have my sympathies, Genzō. If you are not forgiven, then there's little glory in being given the secrets. I think it would be a better idea if you were pardoned and I were given the secrets. This would satisfy both our desires. *(Fidgetting with his fan, he looks toward Sugawara and bows.)*

NARRATOR: Just as Mareyo finishes, a guard enters.

(Guard enters from SR sliding doors.)

GUARD: An official of the Imperial Court has arrived with a message. The Emperor sends an urgent request for Lord Sugawara to present himself at the Court immediately.

NARRATOR: A questioning look crosses Sugawara's face.

SUGAWARA: What can this request mean when my seven days of fasting are not yet finished? Have an escort and footmen prepare to accompany me.

NARRATOR: Having issued his command, Sugawara withdraws
         To change into his courtly robes.

(The bamboo blind descends.)

At word of her husband's departure for the court,
Lady Sugawara appears, avoiding others' glances
(Lady Sugawara enters from SL.)
As beneath her long and flowing robe
She conceals Tonami, to give her from afar
One final glimpse of her lord's face.
Considerate of Mareyo's feelings,
Lady Sugawara speaks.

LADY SUGAWARA: I have heard about the transmission of the secrets, Mareyo, and I must sympathize with you. The fortunate one is Genzō. *(Turns to Genzō.)* And yet, I understand that your banishment was not forgiven. Today may be the last time you will enter this house. My heart goes out to you, Genzō. When you say farewell to Lord Sugawara as he departs for Court, . . . that will be the end, that will be the end.

NARRATOR: With her eyes she indicates to Genzō
Where Tonami hides beneath her robe
The couple's hearts swell with thanks,
And for their lady's warm compassion
Flow tears of gratitude.
Regaled in his robes of state,
Sugawara emerges from within.
To Genzō he hands a single scroll,
The sacred secrets of his calligraphic art.
(Genzō comes forward, opens his fan and, holding it horizontally, receives the scroll upon it.)
For Genzō, a moment of glory.
And be it known that from this time begin
The village schools which honor
And hand down to far off generations
The memory of Sugawara,
The style of his writing art.

(Genzō places the scroll in the kimono fold at his breast. Mareyo, who has missed this action, now sees the empty fan and begins to look perplexedly around the room.)

SUGAWARA: I have carried out my duty. Our interview is now ended. You must take your leave. Now go.

NARRATOR: Words to hasten him on.

MAREYO: All right, Genzō. Enough of your weeping face! If you can't find your legs and get up and leave, I'll happily drag you out.

NARRATOR: Mareyo moves toward Genzō.

(He grabs Genzō's arm.)

LADY SUGAWARA: No, Mareyo, don't be harsh with him. For Genzō this is the final end of all association with his lord. You must realize his grief and his reluctance to leave. Genzō, cease your tears and prepare to go. Tonami, look for a last time upon your lord.

NARRATOR: She allows Tonami to peer out
From beneath the hem of her robe.
Though aware of her gaze,
Sugawara feigns indifference
As he prepares for his departure.
Suddenly, for no apparent reason,
The tall court hat he wears falls from his head.
He catches it in his hand.

SUGAWARA: Haaah! My hat, though touched by nothing, falls from my head. What can this portend?

NARRATOR: His mind is ill at ease.

LADY SUGAWARA: Ah, I know. Genzō's request was denied, and so his tears fall. Thus, as a sign of his grief, your hat too falls. It can be nothing more than that.

SUGAWARA: No no, it can hardly be that. Well, I will know the meaning after my audience at Court. Quickly now, have Genzō leave at once.

NARRATOR: He restores his hat to his head
           And departs for the Court.
           With groveling timidity
           Mareyo sees his master off.
(Both exit SR.)
           But, heart-stricken in his banishment,
(Mareyo returns.)
           Genzō is rooted to the spot,
           Only stealing a glance
           At the back of his departing lord,
           Until a hanging screen occludes his view—
           This too, heaven's scourge, he feels.
(Genzō rises, is about to try and go to see Sugawara off. Mareyo
flutters about blocking his way.)
           Down he casts himself
           Enveloped in manly tears.
           Tonami's grief,
           A hundred-fold her husband's.
(Tonami sinks to the floor in tears.)
TONAMI: Our lord spoke to you, and you were able to look upon
        him directly; but in the end, hidden as I was behind my
        lady, I hardly had a glimpse. You indulge yourself in soli-
        tary grief and give no thought to your wife's feelings. Though
        our offense is the same, you are fortunate. Why do they say
        that a woman's guilt is always greater? [16] Why should it be
        greater? How miserable to have been born a senseless woman!
NARRATOR: How touching Tonami's endless tears,
           As she weeps, heedless even of
           The lofty presence of Lady Sugawara.
           Calmly, Mareyo now comes forward.

[16] A reflection of the (largely Buddhist inspired) bias against women, who were
said to be variously users of abusive language, verbose, jealous, deceitful, and so
forth.

MAREYO: Lady Sugawara, you will be remiss in your duties if you do not have Genzō leave. Our master ordered repeatedly that he be driven away without a moment's delay. But I'll let you off a bit, Genzō, if you will just let me hold in my hands for a moment the scroll with the calligraphic secrets. Mind you, I have no desire to read it. I merely want to hold it in my hands so that my own writing efforts may be blessed by the gods.

NARRATOR: For Genzō there is little choice
But from his breast to draw the scroll,
Whereupon Mareyo snatches it
And tries nimbly to dash away.

GENZŌ: Oh! Not so quickly Mareyo!

NARRATOR: Genzō leaps in hot pursuit,
Grabs Mareyo by the collar, and pulls him back,
Measuring his length on the floor
With a shoulder throw, as though
A giant were merely blowing a bubble about.
He retrieves the scroll.

(With his left knee Genzō pins Mareyo to the floor.)

GENZŌ: Try to steal it, will you! You're nothing but a common daytime sneak thief in fine clothing! Just move an inch and I'll kill you!

(Tonami hands Genzō his long sword.)

NARRATOR: A little from its scabbard
Genzō draws his sword.

LADY SUGAWARA: Wait, Genzō, stop! Tonami, don't let him do anything rash.

GENZŌ *(growling in rage at Mareyo)*: You . . . . You . . . . . Haaaa, too bad you are to be spared! *(Checking his anger, Genzō returns the sword to Tonami.)* But I'll use this desk to punish you as we do unruly children in our school. Come over here, Tonami.

(He smears writing ink on Mareyo's face.)

NARRATOR: Quickly from Tonami he takes the writing desk
   And puts it on Mareyo's back.
   He jerks off the culprit's sash,
   And to a leg of the desk
   He tightly ties his arms, spreading them wide
   Like geese flying in formation.

GENZŌ: Instead of spanking you with the bamboo paddle a schoolteacher uses on thieving children, I'll just use the end of my fan to leave a few marks on your cheeks for others to see later.

NARRATOR: Again and again Genzō strikes him,
   Then sends him flying with a kick.
   For Mareyo, pain and chagrin
   In exchange for his life.
   Bearing both desk and shame,
   He retreats from his tormentor.

(Thoroughly trussed and hopping on one leg, Mareyo runs off at SR.)

   Genzō and Tonami turn now
   And bow to Lady Sugawara.

GENZŌ: I would have liked to stay until news is received from the forbidden precincts of the palace, but I must ask your pardon for having tarried here so long.

TONAMI: My lady, now that things have thus come to pass, I hope you will not forget us.

LADY SUGAWARA: To be sure, my dear, of course. But I must harden myself to your leaving. I regret that I cannot even offer you a night's lodging. But while there is life there is hope. Our relationship has not been severed entirely; we shall meet again. And now, must you go?

TONAMI: Yes, we must go.

NARRATOR: Tonami's tears flow forth,

Full as the swelling tide.
They dry but for a moment,
Then quickly once again
Her sleeve becomes a sea,
Like the sea-tangle growing ocean.
Piteous it is to watch
This saddened man and wife
Depart the gate.
(With many backward glances, the couple exit at SR.)

Scene 4. Before the Gate

(The scene is outside the gate of Lord Sugawara's mansion. A yellow stucco wall surmounted by curved roof tiles reaches across the stage. In the middle of the wall is a large gate with a heavy curving roof, a lattice beneath, then wooden doors reinforced with black iron straps. Umeōmaru rushes in from SR.)

NARRATOR: Returning by a different route than Genzō,
> In runs Umeōmaru,
> Puffing and choking for breath.
> On the high threshhold of Sugawara's gate
> He stumbles and falls, picks himself up,
> And calls out in excitement.

UMEŌMARU: Quickly, everyone, quickly! Something terrible has happened! I don't know what the charges are, but police officials have seized Lord Sugawara, and they are all headed this way, waving iron poles and staffs of split bamboo. Report this at once to Lady Sugawara!

NARRATOR: Uproar consumes the mansion.
> Outside the gate, the armed escort arrives,

(Escort arrives from SR.)

> Brandishing rods of iron,
> Surrounding Lord Sugawara,
> Denied even his palanquin.
> In the lead: Miyoshi no Kiyotsura,
> Minion of Shihei.
> He faces toward the gate.

(All enter from SR. Kiyotsura crosses the stage and seats himself at SL. One guard carries a long iron rod, the other a club of split bamboo.)

KIYOTSURA: Prince Tokiyo and Lady Kariya have disappeared from the banks of the Kamo River. After a detailed investigation, it has been determined that, with the foreknowledge and connivance of Lord Sugawara, it was planned that the Prince would ascend the imperial throne and make Lady Kariya his empress. The penalty for such a crime is exile. The place of exile is to be announced later. Until then, he is hereby placed under house arrest. All entrances are to be locked and barred. As guard at the gate, I assign my retainer Arashima Chikara.

NARRATOR: So stricken by this news,
　　Lady Sugawara dashes forth,
　　Heedless of decorum before the guards.

LADY SUGAWARA: Lord Michizane, what in the world has happened? Why didn't you explain that this thing took place while you were fasting in seclusion, that you knew nothing of Kariya's doings? I cannot understand the reason for this exile of one who is guiltless. What bitter things have come to pass.

SUGAWARA: Do not make yourself seem foolish. Though the charge against me is false, I feel no rancor against the Emperor. The command that I, now declining in years, should pass on my humble art came because of the Emperor's esteem. Until yesterday I basked in His Majesty's favor; today I incur his anger. It is all the will of heaven. When my hat fell from my head a little while ago, it was a sign that my name was to be stricken from the court lists, that I was to become a man without rank, without office. I have no regrets now.

It is not as though I were going to my place of exile at once.
Come, it is unbecoming; do not grieve for me.
NARRATOR: He frees himself from his wife
       As Mareyo returns.
(Mareyo enters from SR.)
MAREYO: Ah, Master Kiyotsura, many thanks to you for a job well
    done. I've heard all about this fellow you have here under
    guard. As his pupil, I turn the teacher over to you. Hence-
    forth, it is Lord Shihei whom I'll call my master. I hope
    you will use your good offices to report to him that I am
    unconnected with Lord Sugawara.
KIYOTSURA: You need have no worry. I understand. *(To his
    guards):* Now, in accordance with the regulations, drive Lord
    Sugawara into the house and nail shut the gate!
CHIKARA: Yes sir.
NARRATOR: Arashima Chikara advances upon Sugawara,
       Brandishing his bamboo staff.
MAREYO: Wait! I, Mareyo, will perform that task for you.
NARRATOR: He takes the bamboo staff.
MAREYO: Well, Master Conspirator. Now our situations are dif-
    ferent. To show you my ability, now that I've changed my
    loyalty to Lord Shihei, I'll use this bamboo staff on you.
NARRATOR: As he lifts the staff to strike,
       Hot-tempered Umeō suddenly dashes out the gate.
       A savage push sends Mareyo reeling.
MAREYO: Insolent underling! You must be bent on suicide to in-
    terfere like this!
UMEŌMARU: I need hardly be told that I'm low-born. But to hear
    the word "insolent" from *your* mouth—ha ha ha ha! It's
    enough to convulse a person with laughter. Waving that staff
    around, who do you think you're going to strike?!

MAREYO: This conspirator Michizane, that's who.

UMEŌMARU: Conspirator!? Who's a conspirator, you ungrateful swine? If Lord Sugawara won't raise his hand against you, then punishing you falls to me!

NARRATOR: Umeō is set to pounce again,
But Sugawara stretches forth his hand
And pulls him back.

SUGAWARA: Wait, Umeō! You are being impertinent. *(Umeō kneels and bows.)* Michizane is as you see him because of an imperial order. Mareyo's actions aside, whoever offers resistance will be giving affront to the Emperor himself. Should any person in my household fail to comply with my orders—and this includes you, Umeō—he will be banished for all time!

NARRATOR: Hearing this, Mareyo recovers from his fright.

MAREYO: Well, Umeō, aren't you going to do as you said? You scum. You're all talk with nothing to back it up.

NARRATOR: Such browbeating Umeō must endure,
And hold his wrath in silence.
Now Arashima and his minions,
Showing neither justice nor mercy,
Force the dispirited Sugawara
Into the confines of his house.
A piteous spectacle it is to behold.
"Now then," shouts Kiyotsura,
"On with the bars and locks we brought."
And to the front and rear he sends his men.
Swiftly set are the barricades
At the low wall-gate,
Even on the water sluice.
What a bitter thing for all who watch.
Kiyotsura surveys his handiwork.

(After Sugawara has entered the gate, bamboo poles are set up in the pattern of an "X" across the entrance.)

KIYOTSURA: There, it serves him right. Well, all the exits seem secure, but they may try to climb over the wall. Keep a sharp eye, Chikara! It's getting dark, Mareyo. Shall we be going?

NARRATOR: But a few feet have they walked together,
    When from his waiting place amid the shadows of the
     wall
    Takebe Genzō abruptly steps forth.
    With a blow he knocks Mareyo senseless,
    Then throws befuddled Kiyotsura to the ground.

(Genzō enters from SR. He has pulled down the upper part of his dark kimono and tucked up the skirt into his sash. A white kerchief covers his head and is tied beneath his chin. Tonami follows, carrying her former long robe in her right hand.)

GUARDS: A trespasser! Knock him down! Kill him! Tie him up!

NARRATOR: Guards run about in bedlam!
    Genzō gives his short sword to Tonami,
    And together they fend off those who would approach.
    Soon Mareyo, his wits regained, stands up.

MAREYO: It's that wretch Genzō! Not once but twice you've made trouble today! If the outrages you commit are attributed to Lord Sugawara, his sentence of exile may be changed to death.

NARRATOR: Hardly has he spoken
    Then Genzō laughs aloud.

GENZŌ: Ha ha ha. Listen to him, wife. The short-memoried Master Blockhead! I may have received the secret teachings of calligraphy, but my banishment was not forgiven. Genzō has no master. Umeō has a master, and he can't lay a hand on you without being disobedient. It was so pitiful to see him endure your insolence that I have acted for him and

given you a drubbing. Next, I'll be his second and mow down
the whole lot of you!

NARRATOR: Genzō and wife, side by side,
Unsheath their swords.
In the wind of their blades
That rain down blow upon blow,
The rice-chaff underlings
And sawdust lords
Are blown about pell mell
And scattered away in flight.

(Genzō sheaths his sword.)
Their foes dispersed,
Now as the twilight deepens,
Genzō cannot bear to leave.
He knocks upon the gate,
Tap, tap, tap.
From within a voice of challenge calls.

GENZŌ: I know that voice. Is it Umeō?

*(After Genzō knocks at the gate, Umeōmaru appears above the
wall to the left of the gate, Genzō at SR and Tonami at SL both
look up at Umeōmaru as he responds to the knocking.)*

UMEŌMARU: Is that master Takebe Genzō?

GENZŌ: What do you mean "master"? This is no time for young-
sters like yourself to be so dull-witted. Look, it would be
easy enough to kick the gate off its fastenings and escort our
lord away from here. But you heard what Lord Sugawara
said, and you know how strictly he observes the rules of
proper conduct. I fear that the slanderers of our lord are
plotting the destruction of the whole house of Sugawara.
Here's my plan, Umeō. Let my wife and me take the young
lord Kan Shūsai to safety. Pass him to us secretly over the
wall.

UMEŌMARU: Excellent, good idea Genzō. If we were to ask the

Emperor for Kan Shūsai's release, it would surely be refused. Spiriting him away like this is for the sake of the house of Sugawara.

GENZŌ: You're right. I want to get the lad away from here as quickly as possible. Hurry!

NARRATOR: Before a moment passes,
    Uemō appears atop the wall,
    Heart racing with exceitement.
    Against Umeō's darksome face,
    Fair the features of the child he bears—
    Young Kan Shūsai,
    Handsome as a full-hued flower
    Early in the bloom.

UMEŌMARU: Our precious young lord, Genzō. Take good care of him.

GENZŌ: I will, I will.

NARRATOR: So high the roof that tops the wall,
    That stretch as he will
    Genzō cannot reach.
    Casting about for a way,
    He clasps Tonami, lifts her up.
    Her hands reach to the eaves.
    The child is hers,
    Lowered in her embrace.
    Outside the wall and within,
    Two loyal servants' hearts
    Open wide with joy,
    Though unopened remains the gate.

(Genzō places Kan Shūsai on Tonami's back, covers him with his cloak and ties his kerchief around the child's head.)
    But sharp-eyed Arashima Chikara has spied them.

(Chikara enters from SR curtain.)

CHIKARA: Look there! Thieves can choose any time to come they say, but the watchman must ever be alert. There's a damn prowler inside the wall helping his confederate on the outside! Sound the alarm! They're taking Kan Shūsai!

NARRATOR: He sets out in pursuit, but Genzō blocks his way.

GENZŌ: Where do you think you're off to? Can't let you go, can I now?

NARRATOR: As Genzō starts to slash away
Chikara also draws his sword.
The combatants cross blades in the melee,
Then disentangle, charge in, retreat.
For Umeō, watching the fray atop the wall,
It is as though he sits in a balcony seat,
Front row before the stage.
Then, even as he watches, Arashima Chikara,
His head split wide, falls dead.

(As Chikara tries to slash at Genzō's legs, Umeō hurls a roof tile at Chikara. Genzō leaps up to avoid the sword. Just as the tile strikes Chikara, Genzō's sword comes down upon his head.)

GENZŌ: No need to give this one the final blow. We'll leave him as he lies.

NARRATOR: Genzō and Tonami begin their flight from danger.
Now Kan Shūsai's future seems secure.

UMEŌMARU: Take good care of the young lord, Genzō and Tonami.

GENZŌ: You watch over our lord and mistress, Umeō.

UMEŌMARU: I will.

NARRATOR: Thus in farewell they beseech each other.
And just as village schools preserve
The skill and art of the writing brush,
So too is handed down
The fame of these three loyal souls
To stand exemplar for all ages.

ACT II

Scene 1. The Journey—
Sweet Words Exchanged

(Rolling green hills appear in the distant background, with yellow rice fields and green dikes in the closer background. A river winds through the landscape at SR off toward a cluster of thatched farm houses. In the immediate foreground at both SR and SL small stands or blossoming cherry trees mingle with pines. On stage is Sakuramaru, disguised as a traveling seller of sweets. His stock of sweets is contained in two unpainted boxes attached to a pole he carries across his shoulder. A pale violet paper parasol is fixed to one of the boxes. The boxes are in reality the hiding places of Prince Tokiyo and Lady Kariya.)[1]

SAKURAMARU: Here here, come children,
Come and buy, come and buy.
Candy birds have I,
Sweet birds made of candy.
And if that suits you not,
Then try rock candy, hard
And cracked off by the chisel.

---

[1] The journey scene, or *michiyuki*, in traditional plays for the puppet theater is a poetic interlude containing much wordplay and often performed mainly as dance. The puns I have tried to incorporate as much as possible into the English text, but I have made no attempt to indicate the complexities of the choreography. In general, dance movements accompany the more poetic passages, while dialogue sequences tend to be performed more realistically.

Or sesame drops
To stop the mouths of crying children.
But, lo, there's more: Hirano sweets,
And *katsurame*, the candy of Katsura Village,
Money candy from Nishinomiya.[2]
For these, go buy them where they're made.
But as for me, come buy
The sugarplums of which I boast,
My round cherry sweets,
Cherry candy, *sakura* candy.

NARRATOR: Though to his wares he gives his name,
His face he hides with a scarf.
His clothing—cap and pants and sleeveless coat—
Are slight in weight, as slight his rank in life;
But loyalty lies heavy in the heart
Of this groomsman Sakuramaru.
Following what came to pass
Beside the Kamo River's dancing wavelets,
Prince Tokiyo and Lady Kariya
Have been obliged to flee;
At length has Sakuramaru
Happened upon them.
For a day or two they may
Conceal themselves from their homes,
"But then what?" have they wondered.
Now have they set their minds
To seek aid from Lord Sugawara's aunt.
No longer as a carriage groom
Does Sakuramaru attend them;
Now does he hide the noble pair,

---

[2] The shrine of Ebisu, the god of wealth, was in Nishinomiya; hence, candy produced there was made in the shape of money.

One in each of the candy chests
He carries on a shoulder pole.
Shunning the eyes of an inconstant world,
The trio make their way to Haji village,
Hawking candy as they go.
Yet Sakuramaru's care-worn heart
Is deeply troubled.
In the depths of night they leave the Capital,
And though they reach Fukakusa,
The inky road is hard to see.
At Gokō Shrine the day dawns,
And they hurry on their way,
Through Serikawa, on past Yodo.
Each time they pass beyond a town
They breathe more easily,
Feel free of prying eyes and wagging tongues.
At Iwashimizu[3]
Sakuramaru lowers his burden.
"Come out," he says, and as he opens the cases,
The stately form of Lady Kariya
Comes forth. For a moment
In the morning sun,
She gazes about with rapture;
But around her, only unfamiliar peaks,
Obscure and unknown hamlets.

KARIYA: When I see such vistas as these, it is as though I have
no cares at all. And you, my prince?

TOKIYO: I was just thinking the same thing. It was after we left

[3] The journey takes the trio from Kyoto, south through Fukakusa, Gokō Shrine, and Serikawa (all in modern Fushimi, the southernmost ward of Kyoto), then further south through Yodo and Iwashimizu. Most of these place names are occasions for puns which, as much as possible, have been incorporated into the translation.

the Capital that your father, Lord Sugawara, through some
misunderstanding, was confined to his home. So, while I
can't be certain, I do feel that the time will come when you
are forgiven. But me, I feel like the candy we sell: as the
sweets are shielded by a parasol from the sun, so must I, an
outcast, hide my face in a rush hat. Oh, will my fears all
someday melt away and let me know peace?

SAKURAMARU: Things are not as bad as you may think. Your very
concealment, with candy on top and my lord hiding beneath, is a lucky sign that you will soon rule this land.[4]

NARRATOR: Yet even more the Prince shrinks back, downcast.
Slowly they make their way
Along the slippery roads,
Across the ricefield footpaths.
The bracken along the way
Thrusts its stems beneath the hem
Of Lady Kariya's robe,
Turning it outward to display
The pattern of its lining.
In the spring fields,
Now sweet scented by fragrance
From the noble lady's gown,
Throng hosts of butterflies.
Should on her sleeve they light,
Dust from their wings might form
A powder for the lady's face,
So long deprived of a mirror.

[4] A play upon the Chinese characters used in the expression here produces two
different meanings. *Ame ga shita* means "beneath the candy." Replacing "candy"
by the character for "heaven" (also read *ame*) alters the meaning to "all beneath
heaven," or "the realm," suggesting that Prince Tokiyo will eventually assume
his role as ruler.

Here is the village of Kariya,[5]
The place perhaps from whence
Her name was drawn.
Now is the time for planting rice
In the seedling beds.
How rare to see for endless vistas
The handiwork of farmers.
Hearing the call of the cranes—
Those emblems of long life—
Returning to their nesting places,
The lovers recall the vows
Made in their sleeping chamber,
Vows their tender passions
Would for a thousand years
Remain unchanged.
From evening had they lain together,
Locked away from others,
Locked in each other's embrace,
Sleeping through the night,
Unmindful that the moon might shine
Or that the sky be cast with clouds.
   With the hand that grabs the pillow
I sleep, my sash undone.
      I stand so deeply in your trust,
      So deeply in your trust.
   With the hand that grabs the pillow
I sleep, my sash undone.
      I stand so deeply in your trust,
      So deeply in your trust.[6]

[5] Kariya Village is now located in the town of Shijō Nawate, northeast of Osaka.
[6] Apparently a contemporary popular song, the source of which is unknown.

Ah, well remembered, that night,
Now but a dream long past.
Must they waken from their reveries
As the breeze of spring blows bracing
Through the warming sky?
A voice comes from the forest up ahead.
Quickly, lest they be discovered,
Their "candy seller" hides them once again.
Then, drum in one hand,
Drumstick in the other,
He strikes up a rhythm
And sings out merrily.

SAKURAMARU: Here, here, here it is!
These are Jimmu sweets,
Created, so 'tis said,
By our own first Emperor, Jimmu.
I too have learned to make
This famous sweetmeat kneaded first
By the candy-loving Emperor Jimmu.
You matrons and young brides,
Tie up your sleeves howe'er you please
With silken cord, red dyed.
And if you think to buy
These rolled and kneaded sweets,
Why, now's the time, the time is now!

NARRATOR: So goes the hawking to draw the children,
And mothers come to purchase little gifts.
As Sakuramaru wraps the sweets,
He listens to the worldly gossiping.

(Two women and several children enter from SR to buy candy and chat.)

WOMAN CUSTOMER: It's a sad thing to hear that Lord Sugawara of

the Capital has been exiled to Tsukushi.[7] So now he's at
Yasui in Settsu Province, while his ship awaits a fair wind.
(She exits SR.)
NARRATOR: So near to Lord Sugawara,
    Yet they did not know!
    The customers gone, the trio is astonished,
    Saddened.
    Prince Tokiyo opens the chest a bit,
    Showing only his face.
TOKIYO: What! They said Michizane has been exiled?
KARIYA: My father is at Yasui? I must at least see his face. Please,
    I beg you, Sakuramaru, take us to Yasui and let me see him
    before the ship sails.
NARRATOR: She breaks into incoherent tears.
    Sakuramaru, fearful
    Lest others hear their voices,
    Conceals the sound with notes from his flute.
    In a moment he has turned from their path,
    And set out bearing his tearful burden,
    Their destination Settsu Province
    And the beach at Yasui.
    But the troubled thoughts
    That now disturb their hearts
    Yet magnify their wretchedness.

[7]Though Tsukushi is often used as the ancient name for all of the island of Kyushu, it more narrowly refers to the two old provinces there named Chikuzen and
Chikugo, more or less the modern Fukuoka Prefecture. Sugawara's place of exile
was Dazaifu, located a few miles southeast of the modern city of Fukuoka.

Scene 2. Yasui Beach: Awaiting the Tide

(Foam-capped blue waves stretch out to the horizon in the far background. In the foreground is a sandy beach, a group of pines standing at SR, a black lighthouse somewhat farther back and near the center. At center stage, resting on a black support, is the plain wood palanquin containing Sugawara, who is not visible. At each side of the palanquin stands a guard. Both guards hold long-bladed halberds. Seated on a stool at SR of the palanquin is Terukuni.)

NARRATOR: As the world moves in disquiet,
>So do winds disturb the face of the sea.
>His ship of exile delayed within the harbor,
>Here waits Lord Sugawara.
>At length, his slanderers' tongues
>Have prevailed,
>And guilty he stands of a crime
>To which he never gave thought.
>The prison ship to bear him into exile
>At Dazaifu in Tsukushi
>Has only now reached Yasui in Settsu Province.[8]
>Chief of his warrior escort
>Is Hangandai Terukuni,
>Long a vassal to the Retired Sovereign.

---

[8] The old province of Settsu surrounded the modern city of Osaka.

His guard posts have been set
At Ausaka and Masui;[9]
And, spears and halberds ready,
The guards are sternly watchful.
While hosts of officials
Surround the party,
There in the shadows of the pines
They have waited, eyes upon the sky,
Seeking fair weather.
Hangandai Terukuni casts his eyes across the sea.
He has had the curtains drawn aside
On Sugawara's prison palanquin,
And now he bows before it.

TERUKUNI: I have checked the sea, my lord, and it appears that
we will not have fair sailing weather for yet a few days. Rather
than remain here, may I suggest that you proceed to Haji
village in Kawachi Province and bid farewell to your aunt,
Lady Kakuju.

NARRATOR: Responding from the window of the palanquin,
Sugawara's careworn face appears.

SUGAWARA: You have served in the Retired Emperor's palace, and
you have learned to be like His Majesty: compassionate to
all, even the lowliest. But should you permit me, prisoner
that I have become, to to go Haji, then your punishment
would surely be worse than mine. What you propose is un-
thinkable.

TERUKUNI: I am most grateful for such unselfish consideration.
Yet, should I incur punishment for assisting so noble a personage as yourself, then, as the saying goes, posthumous
honor does credit to one's posterity. What I have suggested,

---

[9]Both Ausaka and Masui are located within the modern city of Osaka.

however, is not my own idea but that of His Majesty, the Retired Emperor himself. He told me in confidence that he had heard you had an aunt in Haji Village, and that if we found time while waiting in Settsu for fair weather I might allow you to make a farewell visit to her. You need feel no constraint. Please, now, put your mind at rest and go to Haji Village.

NARRATOR: At this urging, Sugawara gazes
　　　　Longingly back toward the Capital.

SUGAWARA: Ah, how fortunate I am for His Majesty's thoughtfulness. "Neither father nor mother has the Son of Heaven" says the proverb,[10] but His Majesty seems a true father to me. Yet it is beyond his power to help, and I am a prisoner. Is this some retribution for a past offence? How transient is this insubstantial world! How wretched is my fate!

NARRATOR: Though well he knows one's karma
　　　　Passes through three generations,
　　　　Sad and touching is he
　　　　As he summons back to mind
　　　　The bitterness of the world.
　　　　The boatman, having watched the sky,
　　　　Comes forward.

BOATMAN: From the looks of the weather this morning, I thought we would be staying here two or three days, but it has cleared up unexpectedly and the wind has died down. So, let's prepare to set sail.

NARRATOR: Terukuni is quick to respond.

TERUKUNI: Be silent! Since weather you thought would not clear
　　　　up has done so, I doubt you'd be aware that good
　　　　weather might turn bad.

---

[10] Meaning that the exalted position of the emperor is such that he owes obeisance to no one, not even the filial piety of a child to parents.

BOATMAN: No, no. The second and eighth months are the most exhausting for us sailors. Why, the weather will change as quick as one can turn over his hand.

TERUKUNI: How you yap away! With an important prisoner in custody, how can we set sail in weather that can change at the flick of a hand?

BOATMAN: Oh no, I'm sure that . . .

TERUKUNI: Flusterhead! There are clouds gathered above the mountain over there. There'll be no sailing weather for a good four or five days. Don't meddle in things that don't concern you!

NARRATOR: At such tongue-lashing,
          The boatman stands astonished.

BOATMAN: Even the best boatman is powerless in the face of such a blast of wind as this.

NARRATOR: Muttering to himself
          And grumbling, he leaves.
          Moved by Terukuni's kindness
          And the Retired Emperor's warmth of heart,
          Sugawara resolves to proceed
          In stately fashion to Kawachi Province.
          In his palanquin
          He rested at this place, they say;
          And so the cursive symbols for the name
          Of Yasui were written down anew,
          From "Tranquil Well"
          To "Tranquil Rest," where stands a shrine [11]
          Whose reverence by ages sequent

[11] The place referred to is the Yasui Tenjin Shrine, located in the modern city of Osaka. Allegedly, the name of the place was originally written with the characters meaning "Tranquil Well," but this was changed to "Tranquil Rest" (the pronunciation remaining the same) because Michizane stopped there on his way into exile.

Shows the grandeur
And the virtue of its god.
Just then, Sakuramaru,
Accompanying the Prince and Lady Kariya,
Dashes in ahead of his party.

(Sakuramaru enters from SR. Offstage drums heighten the excitement of his arrival.)

SAKURAMARU: We have heard that Lord Sugawara has been sentenced to exile, and there are those connected with him who beg to say farewell. One thing more: I would appreciate hearing directly from you, sir, the circumstances of the crime.

NARRATOR: At his approach, guards move around him shouting.

1st GUARD: A direct conversation? What an insolent fellow!

2nd GUARD: Bidding farewell? Outrageous wretch!

3rd GUARD: Keep an eye on him.

NARRATOR: Noting his guards' actions, Terukuni quiets them.

TERUKUNI: Wait, we'll have no rash behavior! If he wants to hear about the offense, I'll tell him. The Emperor cleared Lord Sugawara of several other charges. But as His Majesty could not explain the illicit affair between Prince Tokiyo and Lady Kariya, he was unable to save him on that account. There was no way to prevent Lord Sugawara's conviction for that offense.

NARRATOR: Saddened at these words,
Both Lady Kariya
And the Prince rush forth.

(Prince Tokiyo and Lady Kariya enter from SR.)

TOKIYO: What is this? You say he was arrested because of us? How terrible, how shameful. An illicit affair is an offense of the two of us alone. Let *us* be punished by exile or even death, but spare Lord Sugawara!

KARIYA: Let me see my father! Please help him!

TOKIYO: Let us see him!

NARRATOR: Loud is their weeping and wailing.
>   Terukuni withdraws a distance
>   And bows his head.

TERUKUNI (*having recognized the prince*): Your forgiveness, my lord, but if you speak to Lord Sugawara it can only mean that his punishment will become more severe. All of this had its beginning just the other day. It was Lord Sugawara's suggestion that you take the place of the Emperor and have your portrait painted by the Chinese priest. It was Lord Sugawara's black scheme, say those who have slandered him, to have it believed, all the way to China, that you were the real emperor. He would then, they said, set up his own daughter as empress, and thus through her have a direct relationship to the throne. Then, while such insinuations were making their rounds, you, my lord, ran off with Lady Kariya. Thus, when the accusations finally reached the ears of the Emperor they appeared to be true. And so, Lord Sugawara has been convicted of a crime he did not commit. Since the lady is his daughter, she especially cannot possibly see him, as I fear this might be taken as disrespect to the Emperor. In any case, as things now stand, if you wish to do something on Lord Sugawara's behalf, you should sever all ties with Lady Kariya, return to the Imperial Palace, and clear yourself of the charges of conspiracy. Then make a plea that Lord Sugawara be permitted to return to the Capital.

TOKIYO: Sad it is to learn that because of me he was convicted. Yet how can I cast aside the vows I have made to Lady Kariya, for she has pledged her love to me and accompanied me here.

NARRATOR: He laments his plight,
>   And the lady adds her grief.

KARIYA: For the sake of my father, to whom I've now become an enemy, punish me, and pardon his sentence of exile. I beg you all!

NARRATOR: Down she falls, dissolved in tears,
Weeping as though to die.
Sakuramaru, now in bitter agony
For having stood as go-between,
Senses anguish tearing
Through his very bones, his flesh.

SAKURAMARU: Now I see. Who but I would have served as intermediary for this love? The one to blame is none other than myself.

NARRATOR: Though he mourns the tragedy,
There is no help.
His tears flow forth;
He finds no fitting words to speak.
Recovering his composure,
He moves to the Prince's side and bows.

SAKURAMARU: In the beginning, my lord, I was but the son of a poor dirt farmer. It has all been thanks to Lord Sugawara that I received a stipend and became your lordship's groom. I cannot stand shamelessly by and watch my benefactor sent into exile. And yet, there is nothing that one such as I can do. Please do as Master Terukuni says, and sever your ties with Lady Kariya. If you plead your case as one not related to Lord Sugawara, it is not beyond hope that your request may be granted. After Lord Sugawara has returned once again to the Capital, you can openly marry the lady. For a while, please part with her.

NARRATOR: Tormented by the thought
That he has been the cause of all this woe,

Sakuramaru throws himself to the ground
In supplication.
Prince Tokiyo begins again to weep.

TOKIYO: To have left home once is shame enough; to go back again will only add to my disgrace.

TERUKUNI: You need not return to your mansion. It would be even better if you went to the Retired Emperor's palace, and made your plea. I hope you will take this course.

NARRATOR: Thus pressed,
Prince Tokiyo, still choked with tears,
Turns to Lady Kariya.

TOKIYO: If I am blinded by my love for you, and should I fail to petition for Lord Sugawara's return to the Capital, the gods of heaven will surely be angered. My vows to you are everlasting and will not change. But let us part, Lady Kariya, remembering that it is for your father's sake.

NARRATOR: The words come forth through tears.

KARIYA: It is all more than I deserve, since I am the cause of your grief. Had I rather died of longing for you, there would not be this sadness I now feel. I am heart-sick at this parting.

NARRATOR: Teardrops fill her eyes
As she beholds her Prince.
And in the eyes of him beheld,
More tears.

TOKIYO: Until we meet again, take care, my dearest.

KARIYA: And you, my love, be of good spirit.

NARRATOR: The rest, a tearful clinging to each other,
As though each would perish.
Upon this scene arrives an unknown woman,
Borne in a palanquin.

(Woman enters from SR.)
> Boldly, without a trace of fear,
> She faces Terukuni.

WOMAN: My name is Tatsuta from Haji Village. I am the daughter of Lord Sugawara's aunt.

NARRATOR: At this, the Lady Kariya is elated.

KARIYA: My sister! Is it Tatsuta?

NARRATOR: She tries to cling to her sister,
> But Tatsuta pushes her away,
> Brushes her aside.

TATSUTA: My mother Kakuju has heard of Lord Sugawara's exile. She is too old and distressed to come here herself, and in this she begs your indulgence.

NARRATOR: At her words, once more
> Lady Kariya grasps at her sister.

KARIYA: Her grief is all the more misery for me.

NARRATOR: From the weeping Kariya
> Tatsuta tears herself.

TATSUTA *(to Terukuni)*: Please, my mother hopes that you might spend a night in Haji Village while waiting for clear weather. This will permit her to bid Lord Sugawara an appropriate farewell. I realize it is an unreasonable request, but I should like to relieve the grief of an aged lady who can hardly be certain of the morrow. My husband, Sukune Tarō, was to come here with me, but he hesitated at the thought of putting aside the duties of his office. We women are by nature lacking in manners but, ignoring the rashness of my conduct, I have come here with this request. I most earnestly entreat you, sir, to give my proposal your consideration.

TERUKUNI: No, I cannot entertain such a request from a member of the same family. And yet, I must admit I do not feel easy about having so important a prisoner pass nights here on the beach. Then—merely for the sake of security, mind you—we will go to Haji Village and lodge at Lady Kakuju's house.

NARRATOR: Tatsuta is pleased at this response.

TATSUTA: Oh, that is . . . ah . . . an excellent precaution.

NARRATOR: Grasping her sleeve, Lady Kariya
Holds back the elated Tatsuta.

KARIYA: Oh please, I do so much long to see my father.

NARRATOR: Tatsuta pulls away the sleeve
To which the lady clings.

TATSUTA: What a dreadful thing for you to ask! What sort of face do you expect me to put on when I confront Lord Sugawara? When you were just born to mother, and before Kan Shūsai was born, you were adopted by Lord Sugawara. You are my younger sister, but you're now a noble lady in the house of Sugawara. Improper though it was, you went and fell in love with the Prince, and that is what has brought on this crisis, isn't it? Love and reason do not go hand in hand, they say; but you have gone too far. Even I, your sister, I'm embarrassed to face the world. What shame I feel.

NARRATOR: And yet, the heart that chastises
But shows the warmth of sisterly affection.
Within his palanquin,
Lord Sugawara of a purpose
Holds to silence.
It is Hangandai Terukuni
Who takes the matter in hand.

TERUNKUNI: Be patient, Lady Tatsuta. Your opinions serve no purpose now. You there, Sakuramaru, what are you daydreaming about? Escort the Prince at once to the Retired Emperor's palace. And you, Lady Tatsuta, are forbidden to accompany Lady Kariya as a traveling companion. Is that

understood? However, . . . I place her in your strict cus-
tody to go to your mother's residence at Haji Village.
NARRATOR: Sympathetic in his heart,
    Terukuni arranges a plausible reason
    That they may travel together.
    In the palanquin brought by Tatsuta
    He places Lord Sugawara.
    At rear and front an escort is installed,
    And gently is the litter borne,
    Terukuni following close at hand,
    As like some ordinary entourage
    They hasten off to Haji Village.
(Two bearers carry the palanquin and the party exits SR.)
KARIYA: Oh, father!
TOKIYO: My Lord!
NARRATOR: As the couple seeks to follow
    The departing Lord Sugawara,
    Sakuramaru stops the Prince,
    Tatsuta restrains Lady Kariya,
    And the pair are drawn apart.
    Thus the lovers' parting,
    Their farewells incomplete,
    Not even a keepsake fan exchanged.
    Surely Kariya's gentle-hearted sister
    Will arrange for them to meet again.
    More and more their longing
    For each other grows.
    Their eyes, swollen now with tears,
    Are red as are the waters of Akai.[12]

---

[12] Akai refers to a stream by that name in the precincts of the Temple of the Four
Heavenly Kings (Shitennōji) in Osaka. There is a pun here: "Their eyes, swollen
now with tears, are red *(akai)* as are the waters of Akai."

When, oh when, their hearts at peace,
Are they to meet again?
Brief this tearful parting,
Fleeting as the foam
That floats upon the waters
At Yasui and Meeting Hill,[13]
Until all that remains
Are echoes of their voices calling out,
"Farewell, farewell."

[13] "Meeting Hill" is a translation of Ausaka, already mentioned in note 9. Here, however, there is a pun on the two place names: "When, oh when, their hearts at peace (*yasui*), are they to meet (the *au* of Ausaka) again?"

Scene 3. The Chastising

(The scene is a large room in the house of Kakuju, Sugawara's aunt. Into walls decorated with stylized cloud patterns against a white ground are set two openings: one at extreme SR has no doors and represents the entrance to a corridor; the larger one at center stage has six sliding panels closed across it. The panels are painted with a mountain landscape scene. At SL is a small room enclosed by shōji panels, three facing the audience, two others facing toward center stage. As the narration begins, no characters are on stage.)

NARRATOR: At Kakuju's request
        For a farewell meeting
        With Lord Sugawara,
        Hangandai Terukuni
        Has permitted the exile
        To go to her villa in Kawachi.
        The aged lady's joy knows no bounds.
        The welcome for her visitor
        Has kept her household staff
        So busily employed
        They scarcely know day from night.

(Tatsuta enters from the SR corridor opening. She looks furtively about, then moves to the center stage sliding panels.)

        Quite by chance has Lady Tatsuta
        Met her sister Lady Kariya

At the vessel landing.
And since most secretly
Has she brought her sister home,
Most people in her household
Know not of the lady's presence.
Softly now, Tatsuta
Slides open the door
Of the little room in which
Lady Kariya has been hidden.
*(Tatsuta opens the four center panels, again looks furtively about,
then summons forth Kariya from within.)*

TATSUTA: How tired and lonely you must be. I've wanted to come
and keep you company, but with so much going on here I
haven't been able to leave mother's side. Since nobody was
around, now seemed a good chance. Come on out and relax.

NARRATOR: Prompted by her sister's gentle concern,
Lady Kariya emerges from the room,
But still her eyes are brimmed with tears.

KARIYA *(wipes her eyes with her sleeve)*: You've been so kind to
me since I parted with Prince Tokiyo. How I wish I could
see my father and beg his forgiveness for all the unfilial things
I have done. If that's not possible, I ought to resign myself
to death. Yet I can't help thinking of my real mother Kakuju and my foster mother Lady Sugawara, of Kan Shūsai
and the Prince in the Capital. Please understand how I feel.

NARRATOR: To her grieving,
Tatsuta now adds her tears.

TATSUTA: No wonder you are so unhappy, no wonder. But, please
don't lose patience because you can't see Lord Sugawara.
My mother's request was granted, and he is now staying in
this house. I thought I might look for a good opportunity to

tell mother about your being here, and ask for her advice. If I could just find out her feelings, in some casual way. But that won't work. Mother is very strict, no different in her sense of proper behavior than my late father, the county magistrate. Though she is your real mother, she gave you out for adoption; she regards those who adopted you as your parents, and herself as an outsider. To go on thinking of each other as parent and daughter, she says, would be like pampering some naive child of a farmer or townsman. It's no use asking something of her when we know all along that she won't agree. We've kept your presence here a secret from her up to now, but we cannot leave matters as they are. Today is the third day of Lord Sugawara's stay. Word has come from the landing that the stormy weather has passed. There will be good sailing weather now for the boat to Kyushu. Terukuni has sent word that they will leave at dawn tomorrow, so preparations are being made for Lord Sugawara's departure. I had hoped to have you see your father before this, but now things have gone wrong.

(Tarō saunters in from the corridor, sees the two women, checks his approach. He then leans nonchalantly against a post, listening to their conversation.)

This makes it all very difficult. What can we do? When at a loss, consult someone, they say. Don't weep; help me think of something.

NARRATOR: Fumbling about without resolve,
      They are sunk in rumination,
      When suddenly from behind them
      Sukune Tarō appears.

(Tarō is ruddy faced, somewhat fat.)

TARŌ (boisterously): Here's a person just full of ideas!

TATSUTA: Oh, Tarō! You caught me unawares.

TARŌ: What do you mean, unawares? Look here, Tatsuta, it's disgraceful your hiding someone like this behind your husband's back and carrying on secret conversations. I know that Lady Kariya is your younger sister and that she was given out for adoption right after she was born, but Kawachi is a far cry from the Capital, and there's quite a status difference between a warrior's house and that of a nobleman. I could make some pretensions, basking in the prestige of Lord Sugawara's aunt; but it's no use boasting that I am Kakuju's son-in-law. Lady Kariya's high position puts me in the shade. I've only heard her name. This is the first time we've met. She sure is a beauty. I can see why Tokiyo or whatever his name is went and lost his head over her. *(Turning to Tatsuta.)* Before I saw the lady's face, I thought you were a regular Yang Kuei-fei, but in comparison I see you're hardly a Yang Kuei-fei.[14] I'll just have to change your name.

TATSUTA: Oh? And what might you change it to?

TARŌ: Why, it's obvious. Lady Second Best. *(Pats Tatsuta on the shoulder.)*

TATSUTA *(good-naturedly)*: Well, you certainly don't mince your words. Listen, Lady Kariya's presence here is still a secret from mother. Please, don't say a word about it.

TARŌ: Oh, don't worry. We've been notified by Terukuni of Lord Sugawara's departure tomorrow. Kakuju has told me to go to Terukuni's lodgings to offer our thanks for this kindness in letting Lord Sugawara stay here, and to tell him to prepare for departure at the first cockcrow. I'm on my way right now. If I get any good ideas I'll come right back and tell you . . . Lady Second Best.

[14] One of the famous beauties of Chinese history, Yang Kuei-fei was the concubine of T'ang emperor Ming Huang (r. 712–756). She was a ruinous influence upon the government during the time she was at court, and the emperor was eventually obliged, with much sadness, to have her executed in 755.

TATSUTA: Oh, there you go prattling and joking still. *(Playfully pretends to strike him.)*

TARŌ: All right, I'll be quiet. Be back later. *(Exits through corridor at SL.)*

NARRATOR: Off he goes to the front of the house.

Lady Kariya watches him leave.

KARIYA: Was that your husband? I was so taken up with my own troubles I wasn't able to greet him properly.

TATSUTA: Oh, you can pay your respects at any time. We cannot delay any longer. Oh, if only there were some way you could see your father.

NARRATOR: Anxiety fills her thoughts.

TATSUTA: Oh, I have it! *(Strikes her knee.)* Look, we know that if we ask mother she won't agree. My husband is away, and mother is not with Lord Sugawara now, so I'll take you to him. I may be punished for this, but we'll leave that for later. Come, this way.

NARRATOR: She takes her sister's hand,

But then, from behind them . . .

KAKUJU *(emotionally, to Kariya)*: Undutiful girl! Where are you going?

NARRATOR: At the sound of a sliding door,

Kakuju appears.

(Kakuju carries a long unpainted wooden staff with a short bar across its top, forming a "T".)

Brandishing high her staff,

She moves toward Lady Kariya.

Quickly the startled Tatsuta

Holds her angry mother back.

TATSUTA: If you are angry that Kariya was hidden here and you were not told of her presence, then strike me, beat me! Didn't you say it yourself the other day? When one lets her child be adopted by another, it is no longer her child. Having said that, mother, it isn't right to punish Kariya! Is it right to use your staff on the cherished daughter of Lord Sugawara? Strike me instead, punish me!

NARRATOR: Heedless of herself,

She takes her sister's place.

KARIYA: No! You have done nothing wrong! I am the undutiful one! Strike me!

NARRATOR: She pushes Tatsuta aside,

Puts herself beneath the staff.

(Kakuju is brandishing the staff above her head.)

TATSUTA: No no! I won't let you be punished!

KARIYA: And I will not let you!

NARRATOR: Deep flows the sisterly love,

As they struggle, each to spare the other.

But the aged woman's anger only mounts

And shows upon her face.

KAKUJU: Tatsuta! I punish no stranger! *(Points at Kariya with her staff.)* Lord Sugawara, to whom I gave her in adoption, is my nephew. She is thus my niece. Now that she has carried on an illicit affair that no parent would permit, who has brought on the banishment of my esteemed nephew? *(To Kariya.)* Despicable creature! I can make no apology to Lord Sugawara unless I break this staff in punishing you. I am past sixty, and my hair is white. When my husband died I should have cut off my hair and become a nun. But Tatsuta here stopped me, saying she would be so lonely and helpless. So I only assumed my holy name and called myself Kakuju. This white hair I have so long thought a hinderance, this very day it stands me in good stead. Had I shorn my head and put on the holy robes, I could not now wield this chastising staff. You too are guilty, Tatsuta. I will begin with you.

NARRATOR: She rushes at them,
    And as she rains down blow on blow,
(First on Tatsuta, then Kariya.)
    Grievous the tears
    That fill the eyes of all,
    Both chastened and chastiser.
(Weakened, emotionally spent, Kakuju thrusts the staff in front of her and leans on it.)

SUGAWARA *(speaking from offstage)*: Wait, wait! My dear aunt, do not punish them so severely. Prince Tokiyo loves my daughter. Do not harm her. She has come here out of longing for her father. *(All three women fall down weeping.)* I will see her. Bring her to me.

NARRATOR: Hearing the voice of Lord Sugawara,
    Resonant from beyond the sliding doors,
    Kakuju throws down her staff,
    And prostrates herself in tears.
    For a space, no word escapes her.
    Then . . .

KAKUJU: The true parent's punishment of her child fulfills her obligation to the foster parent. The foster parent performs his obligation to the true parent by showing compassion. Both soft words and punishment show the blind love of a parent for a child. Your willingness to see Kariya gives greater joy to me than to her. I cannot express my gratitude. Kariya, what a splendid father you have, a splendid father indeed!

NARRATOR: Tears brim her eyes
    And choke off her voice.
    Both of the daughters

Can only sob out their gratitude
For such forgiving hearts.

KAKUJU: Now now, don't offer your thanks from here. He said to
come, so go to him child.

*(Kariya goes to the SL room and slides open the shōji facing the
stage. Stage hands also slide aside the panels facing the audience.)*

NARRATOR: But when the Kariya opens the door
From whence came the voice,
Nowhere in sight is Lord Sugawara.
All that may be seen is a wooden statue
Carved by the lord in his own likeness
During his sojourn.
"What can this be?"
Gasps the bewildered Kariya.

KARIYA: He must have said he would see me in order to stop my
mother's punishment. Can it be he will not see me because
I have been so unfilial? The one who spoke just now was
surely my father. Yet, can a wooden image of my father
speak? Or is he perhaps hiding from me somewhere?

NARRATOR: She wanders in confusion,
Looking first one place
And then another.

KAKUJU: Calm yourself, Kariya! While Lord Sugawara has been
in this house, I have provided him with one of the inner
chambers, which is quite some rooms away from here. When
I heard his voice a moment ago, I wondered why he had
come over here, but I was so happy that I gave it no thought
when I first saw just this statue. Now, however, let me tell
you of something. I asked your father while he was here to
make for me a painting or a carving of himself that I might
have it for a keepsake. He set to work at once. The first statue

he made he broke and threw away. Likewise, he destroyed the second. Upon completing this third statue, he said to me, "The first two possessed the outer form alone. They were merely wooden carvings devoid of any spirit. This one is a keepsake that embodies my very soul." Since it is in Lord Sugawara's form, perhaps one cannot say for certain that it did not speak. He told me that he wanted very much to talk with you but he could not, as it might be disrespect to His Majesty. Do not think of this as an image of wood, Princess Kariya. Surely you must be happy that you have heard your father's voice. Your mother too has realized a cherished wish.

NARRATOR: Upon this joyous scene
Of the mother and her daughters,
Leisurely saunters in
The father of Sukune Tarō,
Haji no Hyōe.

(Both Tarō and Hyōe enter from the corridor at SR.)

HYŌE: Ah, you're here, Kakuju. Your guest's departure is set for tomorrow morning, so you must be quite busy with the preparations. It's unlikely I will be of any use, but I thought as I was making the rounds that I would offer my assistance. On the way, I stopped by to deliver a gift at Terukuni's lodging, and fortunately my son was there. I heard from him that the preparations for the departure are mostly completed. I congratulate you on your handling of things. Now, it has grown late. I thought I might first return home, and then come back at the time of Lord Sugawara's departure. But these legs of mine are old, so if it is no great bother for you, perhaps I'll stay here for the night. Please don't trouble yourself about me.

KAKUJU: You are most considerate, Hyōe. But the house of your daughter-in-law is the same as your own, so why should there

be any need for such protestations? Please, do not hesitate
to call for anything you may need. Tatsuta, prepare a bed-
room for Hyōe in your wing of the house. Hyōe, I will be
seeing you later on.

NARRATOR: As Kakuju leads Kariya away,

Hyōe and son slip into hushed voices.

(Hyōe moves close to Tarō and whispers in his ear.)

HYŌE: Listen, Tarō. As we said on the way over here, there must
be no mistakes.

TARŌ *(nodding)*: Don't worry about it, father.

NARRATOR: Then, one to the inner quarters,

The other to his chamber,

They go their separate ways.

(Hyōe leaves by the center sliding door, Taro by the SR corridor.)

From every apartment

Candles glow forth their light,

As this final eve of Sugawara's visit

Is bestir with late night

Preparations for a feast.

Scene 4. The Crowing of the Cock

(The scene shifts to the spacious inner courtyard of Kakuju's villa. In the distant background are gray mountains with forests at their foot. In the nearer background is the rush fence that encloses the courtyard. It connects to buildings seen at SL rear. Within the courtyard several green mounds are topped with pines. In the foreground at SL is a pond; at SR a continuation of the rush fence ends at a gate that faces toward center stage. It is a chilly night during the second month.)

NARRATOR: Stealthily, from his chambers

    Creeps Haji no Hyōe.

(Hyōe enters through the gate at SR.)

    Familiar with the garden,

    He moves to the low gate,

    Twists the lock, and pushes it open.

    At his signal, a figure outside

    Hands him a traveling chest.

(Hyōe whistles and a servant bearing a chest enters from SR.)

HYŌE: Now look! When the time comes, be ready as I've told you with the required number of men in proper dress and an enclosed palanquin for Lord Sugawara.

NARRATOR: He sends the man away,

    And clutches at the traveling chest.

    Now, glancing furtively about,

    In the shafts of moonlight

Breaking through the trees,
Comes his partner in the plot.

(Tarō enters stealthily from SR, looking behind to see if he has been followed. He spies Hyōe.)

TARŌ *(boistrously)*: Oh, father, is everything . . .

HYOE: Shhhhhhhh!

TARŌ *(more subdued, again peering furtively around)*: Has it arrived?

HYŌE: Don't worry, son. Here, the "thing" I told you about, it's in this box. I've something important to discuss with you. Come over here.

NARRATOR: In the great courtyard
At the edge of the pond,
Father and son plot in whispers,
Unknowing that from the shadows
Listens Tatsuta.

(Tatsuta enters stealthily from SR, a small candle holder in her hand. She blows out the candle, hides behind the fence near the gate, learning forward to listen.)

Her suspicions earlier this night
Aroused by Tarō's manner,
Constantly has she
Kept him in her sight.

TARŌ: As you heard a while ago, Terukuni is to come for Lord Sugawara before two this morning. Now, the plan for killing Lord Sugawara, as Lord Shihei has requested, is to have a false escort come and pretend to take him away. After we've taken him in custody, then along the way we'll kill him, like this! *(He makes a stabbing motion with his right arm.)* Well, that's the plan. But until the first cock crows, that stubborn old mother-in-law of mine will not hand over Lord Sugawara. She'll just drag out her farewells. Is this a bird that will crow at night before the first cock of the morning does?

NARRATOR: He takes the bird from the chest.

(It is a white rooster with a bright red comb.)

TARŌ: Well, well, this sure is a fine bird! It's pretty late at night now. Give us a crow, bird. Crow to your heart's content. Now, crow. *(He touches the bird; it pecks at him.)* . . . Crow! . . . Come on, crow! . . . Father, why doesn't it crow?

HYŌE: Fool, it won't crow just like that! Its crowing has to be a natural thing. You can't force it. But there is a secret way. You pour some boiling water into a large bamboo, and you put the bird on the bamboo. When it feels the warmth it thinks it's daybreak, and then it crows. I have the bamboo here in this chest. The water must be boiling by now. Go fetch the pot. Quietly now!

TARŌ: Easy enough to fetch the pot, but what if the hot water doesn't work?

HYŌE: Son, you weary me. If the water doesn't work, there is another way.

NARRATOR: Thus the plotters scheme.

(Whispering to each other.)

    "By all that's holy!" thinks Tatsuta,
    "This is monstrous!
    I must go and tell mother"

(Tatsuta starts to go, stops.)

    "No, if I do . . .
    Yet, if I do not, then I . . .
    Should I not tell, then they . . .
    I . . ."

(Repeatedly Tatsuta starts to leave, then stops, strokes her breast in consternation.)

Bewildered,
She struggles with her heart,
Then calms herself and speaks.

TATSUTA *(as she enters the gate)*: Sukune! Where are you Tarō?

NARRATOR: Startled at her voice,
The pair are panic stricken.
In a flurry of confusion,
They hide the cock within the chest,
Close the lid,
And try to feign innocence.

(Hurriedly Tarō puts the bird in the chest, closes it, sits on top. Hyōe moves between Tatsuta and Tarō, holding out his sleeve to prevent her seeing the chest.)

TARŌ: Hey! What is this?—shouting out in such a loud voice. You have some sort of important business? If not, then that's very impertinent of you, bursting in here unannounced. You s-s-scared father and me out of our w-w-wits!

NARRATOR: Tatsuta regards them closely.

TATSUTA: You frightened *me* more than I frightened you, my unprincipled husband and father-in-law. What enmity do you bear against Lord Sugawara that you should arrange a false escort for him and then his murder? Or has Shihei bade you to do this? Out of greed for some reward would you betray your loving wife? Have you given no thought to all that mother has done for you? *(Weeping.)* You may have thrown this all aside, Tarō, but I cannot. Father, give up this dreadful thing. *(She goes to Hyōe, takes his sleeve.)*

NARRATOR: To her father-in-law she pleads,
To her husband he begs.
But she can speak no more,
Choked by remorseful tears
That proclaim the purity

Of a woman's upright heart.
Hyōe winks slyly at Tarō.
(While Tatsuta's face is buried in her sleeve, Hyōe makes signs to Tarō that he should kill her.)
HYŌE: Oh my . . . well . . . ah . . . in the face of so sincere an admonishment, both I and my son can only have a deep sense of disgrace. We . . . ah . . . we will mend our hearts. Now, daughter, you just forget all about this.
TATSUTA: Oh, thank you! *(She drops to the ground and bows.)* Such graciousness is more than I deserve. I will dismiss the whole matter from my mind. Since you've agreed to give up the idea, then both in this world and in the world to come I will be a faithful wife and a loyal daughter. Now, the night is chilly. Let us warm ourselves at the fire. I'd like to offer you a cup of warm sake. Come.
NARRATOR: She leads the way.
(Tatsuta starts off to SL ahead of them.)
HYŌE *(whispering to Tarō)*: There! Now's your chance!
NARRATOR *(animatedly)*: Catching his father's signal,
(For a brief moment Tarō hesitates.)
Tarō slashes her through the shoulder.
Though wounded to the quick,
Tasuta turns about
And clutches at Tarō.
(Hyōe watches furtively for any witnesses.)
TATSUTA: Oh! You heartless beast! Ahgh! Coward! Even as a woman, I'm too strong for one of you alone. So you had to trick me to kill me? A woman's loyalty was beyond you! Oh . . . help!
NARRATORY: Her voice is angry in its mockery.
TARŌ: Shut up, you! *(He slashes her shoulder again, she falls. He pins her to the ground beneath his left knee.)*

NARRATOR: Into her mouth
He stuffs the hem of his robe.
Then pinning her to the ground,
With a thrust
He twists the blade home,
Into . . . her . . . heart.
Throughout the struggle
Hyōe has kept watch.

HYŌE (softly): Son, she's not breathing?

TARŌ (excitedly): No worry, father. She's (slowly, and with a faint tinge of remorse) fi-ni-shed. Now, the body, what do we do with it?

(As Tarō tries to rise, Tatsuta's head also rises, her teeth still clenching the hem of his robe. Tarō cuts the cloth, then wipes his blade on Tatsuta's gown.)

HYŌE: Easy. We'll throw it in this pond. Here, put these stones into her sleeves and sash she she won't float. Now, sink her to the bottom.

NARRATOR: As in the pond they cast the corpse,

(Music suggesting water. With his right hand, Tarō clumsily brushes away a tear.)

Crimson stains the water,
A blood-tide red as the autumn maples
Of Tatsuta River,[15]
And like those vaunted leaves of red,
Tatsuta's name shall become
A watchword in this world.

TARŌ: So far so good, father. But we haven't made the cock crow. I'll go and fetch the hot water. (Starts to go.)

HYŌE: No need for that now, Tarō. Leave the bird's crowing to me.

[15] Southwest of the city of Nara, Tatsuta River is famous for its maples.

NARRATOR: From its accustomed place
        In the folds of his robe,
        Hyōe produces a small torch
        To illumine the depths of the pool.
        He inverts the lid of the chest,
        On it places the cock,
        And floats the lid upon the water.
        Then he gives a firm push
        With the tip of his sword sheath.
        As though some nocturnal breeze
        Had rippled the pond's still surface,
        Out a short way floats the lid,
        Riding on soft undulations.
TARŌ: Ha ha ha ha! Father, what in the world are you doing?
        You're playing children's games, making a boat out of the
        lid. That's not very grown up of you. What's the purpose of
        all this? Ha ha ha ha!
HYŌE: My son, how young you are! Since you don't seem to know,
        I'll tell you. When searching for a dead body sunk at the
        bottom of a deep river, if you put a cock on a boat, then
        the bird will crow when it is over the place where the corpse
        is. I just remembered this peculiar characteristic of cocks.
        We're in luck. Here is a convenient way to make good use
        of Tatsuta's sunken body. Look, Taro, it's flapping its wings!
        It must be over the body.
*(By means of an internal mechanism the cock flaps its wings, then
there is the sound of a cock crowing. Hyōe and Tarō dance with
glee.)*
        There! It's crowing! It's sounding the rosy glow of dawn!
NARRATOR: Harsh the lingering chill
        Of the late spring night,
        But crystal clear

The pre-dawn crow of the cock.
Then true to the ancient adage,
"When one cock crows
All others join in song,"
Birds in courtyard roosts
Flap their wings and crow.
Father and son are jubilant,
As though they had caused
The gates of Han Ku to open.[16]

HYŌE: We must be quick now, and hurry the preparations for
Lord Sugawara's escort.

(Rapid beating of drums.)

NARRATOR: Hyōe leaves by the low garden gate.
Sukune Tarō pauses,
Carefully inspecting the scene of their crime,
And finding all in order,
Hurries off.

*(He takes the cord from his sword, uses it to snag the lid bearing
the cock and pulls it to him. He puts the bird into the box and
takes it with him as he leaves.)*

---

[16]The usual signal for the gates at Han Ku Pass to be opened was the crowing
of the cock. Needing to get out before this time, Meng Ch'ang had one of his
men imitate the cock crow, whereupon all other cocks in the neighborhood crowed,
and the gates were opened. The story is related in the *Shih Chi*, the great history
of China completed in the first century BC by Ssu-ma Ch'ien. The appropriate
passage is quoted in Yūda, *Bunraku Jōruri Shū*, p. 373, n. 15.

Scene 5. Sugawara's Farewell

(The scene is an inner apartment of Kakuju's villa. The near fore-
ground is part of the courtyard of the previous scene, a portion of
extreme SL being the pond into which Tatsuta's body had been
thrown. Stretching roughly two-thirds of the way across the stage
from SL is part of Kakuju's villa, a short stairway at its far right
facing toward SR. The building itself consists of two rooms: one,
with low balustrades across the front, is open toward the audi-
ence; the other is framed in an archway, enclosed by shōji panels
and raised slightly above the level of its neighbor room. The open
room is backed by sliding panels covered with gold leaf. The en-
tire facade of the building is beige, decorated with stylized cloud
patterns in gold. At the beginning of the scene, the open room is
closed off by a hanging screen. As the narration commences, the
screen is rolled upward, revealing Kakuju seated at SR, Suga-
wara at SL. Sugawara is dressed completely in white. Between
him and Kakuju are two maids. In front of each maid is a low,
plain wooden stand, one with food, the other with a decoration
of pine boughs. Shortly after the narration begins the maids with-
draw through the sliding panels at the rear.)
NARRATOR: "The time for departure has come!"
> Goes the cry at the sound of the cock.
> For the ceremony of farewell
> Trays are prepared,
> Laden with formal delicacies—

> Lacquered sake bowls and glazeless cups,
> Thin sliced abalone,
> And deep green salted seaweed,
> All brought in by serving maids.
> Into the room comes Kakuju.[17]

KAKUJU *(to Sugawara)*: Should you stay here a hundred days, a thousand nights, there would always be that bitter pain at parting. What we most hope for is an imperial pardon from your exile. Emblems that we long for your return to the Capital are the pine boughs that decorate these trays. With the abalone and salt seaweed we wish you well in what lies ahead. *(Bows.)*

NARRATOR: Lord Sugawara bows in thanks
> For Kakuju's many kindnesses
> Of these recent days.
> Too much for words this sad farewell.
> In comes Sukune Tarō.

(Tarō enters the courtyard from SR, kneels.)

TARŌ: The official escorts have already arrived at the gate. They say that the time of departure has come. Hangandai Teru-kuni has left his lodgings to go and prepare the route of the procession. He has assigned his personal retainers to ac-company the palanquin bearers, and they have now ar-rived.

(He rises, signals the palanquin to enter. Two bearers accompany it.)

NARRATOR: The dubious palanquin
> Is carried in.
> "It is past the time,"
> Say the bearers,

[17] So goes the text, but the production usually has her already on stage at this point.

Hurrying on their charge.
Calmly Lord Sugawara
Comes from the great hall.

(Descends the stairway.)

Until he climbs aboard,
His aunt follows him with her eyes;
But, hesitant in this company,
She shows a smiling face.
Yet, tearless though this parting,
So much more the grief.

(Quickly, Sugawara enters the palanquin, which Tarō hurries on its way off SR.)

Also observing the farewell
Has been Sukune Tarō.
And having seen the escort to the gate
He now returns.

TARŌ: Whew, I'm glad that's over. You must be relieved too, Kakuju. Why don't you go back to bed.

KAKUJU: No, I could not sleep if I wanted to.

TARŌ: What's the matter? Don't you feel well?

KAKUJU: Are you still going on like that? How strange: my son-in-law can find nothing but joy in Lord Sugawara's departure, but Kariya, though she is in the same house, was not even able to bid him farewell. How unhappy she must be. How she must envy those who talked with him. Even Tatsuta, who is no relation to him, I purposely did not call. But why, I wonder, did she not come to wish him well. Somebody go and find Tatsuta. *(Kakuju removes her outer brown robe.)*

NARRATOR: Hearing Kakuju's command,
Sukune Tarō looks uneasily about.
Now the maids of the household return.

MAID: Lady Kariya is the only one inside. Lady Tatsuta is nowhere to be found.

KAKUJU: What? Not here? Where would she go outside this house?
Go and look again. Search every corner, every shadow of
the house!

NARRATOR: She orders a thorough search.

(Maids and servants scurry about, each with a lantern.)

    Paper lanterns in every hand,
    An army of maids and menservants
    Divide the task among themselves
    And look in every place,
    Through the flower garden,
    Around the miniature hill.
    As they search the margin of the pond,
    There upon the grass are found
    Fresh stains of blood.
    'Look! Look!' they shout,

*(Takunai, a servant, holds his lantern up high, looks into the pond,
registers surprise.)*

    "Search the pond, toward which
    The blood stains flow!"

*(Takunai wriggles out of his robe. wearing just his loin cloth, he
dives into the pond.)*

    Those servants who can swim
    Dive deep into the waters,
    And from the bottom of the pool
    They bring up Tatsuta's corpse.

(The body is placed at center stage.)

    Astonishment spreads,
    And throws the house
    Into a very tumult!
    Sukune Tarō stands coolly by.

TARŌ: The villain who killed her is probably still in the house. Close the gate! Let no one out until we've found him!

NARRATOR: As he bawls out his orders,
Kakuju and Kariya enter,
Almost stumbling in their haste.

(The two women enter through the door at center stage, descend into the courtyard.)

KARIYA: Who could have done this thing? She didn't come to me earlier, but I thought she was with mother . . . and now suddenly she lies dead before me. I have parted with my father in life, and now I must part with you, my sister, in death. On the same day, at the very same hour, sorrow and pain both descend upon me. Oh, can there be one so miserable as I! *(She embraces Tatsuta's body as she speaks.)*

(During her lament, Takunai withdraws to SR where he uses a towel to dry off and then puts his robe back on.)

NARRATOR: Clinging to her mother,
She dissolves in mournful tears.

KAKUJU: Alas, my poor child! You thought she was with me, and I thought she was with you. Our mistake has cost Tatsuta her life. How terrible the calamities that befall me!

NARRATOR: Abruptly she sinks down
In distraction born of grief.
Tarō comes to her side.

TARŌ: Tears are no use to a dead person. We'll get the murderer and tear him limb from limb for the repose of Tatsuta's spirit! And we'll start the search right here.

NARRATOR: Hs sits cross-legged on the veranda.

TARŌ: I'll question the whole lot of you, every man and woman, one by one. We'll start with Takunai. Come here, you!

TAKUNAI: Yessir . . . yessir . . . yessir yessir, yessir. *(He comes before Tarō, bows.)*

NARRATOR: He cringes before Tarō.

TAKUNAI: Eh . . . Well sir, I don't know about the others, but you've surely no cause to suspect me. Oh, I know. You've called me to give me a reward for bringing out the lady's body. How grateful I am . . . yessir . . . yessir, yessir, yessir. How grateful.

TARŌ: What! A reward!? Why, you impudent wretch! *(Slowly, showing suspicion.)* How did you know Tatsuta's body was at the bottom of the pond? Come on, out with it!

(As he speaks Kakuju notices the torn place on the hem of Tarō's robe. Her gaze moves to Tatsuta's body, and she registers suspicion.)

TAKUNAI *(in confusion and misunderstanding)*: Ah . . . Oh . . . why, I couldn't see either her head *or* her bottom, sir. You see, from the grass into the depths of the pond there was a trail of blood . . .

TARŌ: Shut up! With nothing but the light from a paper lantern, how could you see it was blood! You killed her and sank her body in the pond! How could anybody else have known about it? That story about the blood, that's no explanation!

TAKUNAI *(in mounting confusion)*: But, master, you're . . . you're being unreasonable. Whether it's an explanation or not, I don't know anything except that the pond there led right into the blood.

TARŌ: What are you talking about, the pond leading into the blood?! *(As he speaks, he thrusts out his foot. Noticing the torn spot on the hem of his robe, Tarō is momentarily rattled.)* The blood's gone to your head, that's what! We'll take you to the interrogation room and use the water torture to make you confess. Take him away!

(Two servants grab Takunai, who struggles vainly against them.)

NARRATOR: He is about to be led away,

Sukune Tarō at his heels,
When Kakuju stops them.

KAKUJU: No, wait! That will not be necessary. While you were conducting your investigation . . . *(she utters a deep sigh)* . . . I am happy to tell you that I have discovered my daughter's murderer.

TARŌ *(leaping down from the room into the courtyard)*: No need to torture him, eh. How perceptive of you to see his guilt. Now, as an offering for my wife's repose, we'll slice the dog from shoulder to waist. Hold out his arms! *(Glaring at Takunai.)*

NARRATOR: Sword in hand,
Sukune approaches his victim.

KAKUJU: Wait! Death by a single blow is for ordinary criminals. Unless the killer is made to suffer, my anger will not be quelled. Against the murderer of my daughter, I her mother will strike the first blow. My son may finish him off. Tarō lend me your sword.

NARRATOR: Resolutely,
She holds her skirt aside,
But not upon the hapless servant
Does she fix her aim.
(Pretending to aim at the quaking Takunai.)
Then she thrusts the blade
Deep into the ribs
Of the unaware Tarō!
Takunai, heart in his throat
At his narrow escape,
Dashes away in flight.
(Takunai disappears off SR.)
Mortally stabbed, Sukune Tarō
Writhes in agony, gasps.

TARŌ: What have I done wrong! You old bitch, you've . . .

NARRATOR: Kakuju cuts short his ranting.

KAKUJU: Don't tell me you don't know! You tried to lay the blame on another; then, tucking your gown up into your sash, you made a great show of punishing him. But there's a piece torn from the hem of your robe. And that scrap of cloth— there, look there, it is stuffed into Tatsuta's mouth to stop her cries.

(Almost reflexively, Tarō raises his left leg, looks at the torn place.)

KAKUJU: What a vile and vicious murder! You forgot that you cut from your robe the piece of cloth she had so tightly clenched in her teeth. Your own crime has exposed you, wretched villain! *(She twists the sword in Tarō's wound.)* Before my daughter's corpse, her mother who has revenged her offers this sword. Has it cut through to your heart, Tarō?

(Tarō writhes in agony as Kakuju leans her weight on the sword.)

NARRATOR: Small wonder may it be
        That aged Kakuju,
        Who killed this hulk of a man,
        Is well remembered
        As her noble husband's widow,
        And as a fitting reminder
        Of our martial arts.

(Kakuju leans her strength onto the sword, forces the still standing Tarō backward.)

        A short pause, and then
        A warrior announces . . .

(Warrior enters from SR.)

WARRIOR: Madam, Hangandai Terukuni has arrived for Lord Sugawara.

KAKUJU: What? Lord Sugawara departed only a short while ago. Who can be coming for him now? Well, I don't understand, but have Terukuni brought in. Kariya, you retire to the inner chamber. I'll let this wretch Tarō suffer a while longer.

NARRATOR: The sword still thrust in his body,

She rudely shoves him aside

(Tarō falls to a seated position on the ground.)

And prepares to greet her guest.

Terukuni quickly presents himself.

(Terukuni enters from SR, bows, enters the room with Kakuju.)

TERUKUNI: The hour of departure has come, madam. If all is ready, I should like to leave quic-. . .

NARRATOR: She interrupts his words.

KAKUJU: What are you talking about, Terukuni? Your men were here only a short while ago to escort Lord Sugawara away. They took him and left about two hours ago.

TERUKUNI: My dear madam, I don't understand what you mean, you handed over Lord Sugawara to my men. Our understanding was that the time for departure would be at the first cockcrow. The cock has just crowed at my lodgings, and I have thus come for Lord Sugawara. If my men came earlier, even if I had come personally, I doubt that you would have released him to us before the appointed time. It was my sympathy for you that led me to allow Lord Sugawara to stay here while his ship awaits good weather. Now that the appointed day has come, I know this parting must be even more painful to you. But, my dear lady, if you imagine that by telling me you have already handed over Lord Sugawara you will keep him from going into exile, then you are taking a most short-sighted view. Indeed, you will only do him harm; it will not serve his interests. Please, no more evasions.

KAKUJU: I assure you, I am not being evasive. There was the crow of the cock in the courtyard, and then there appeared the escort. I most assuredly handed him over . . . But . . . you say you did not take him . . . My daughter's death . . . My son-in-law as you see him there . . . Then, those who came here earlier must have been a false escort.

TERUKUNI: With this disturbance in your household, and these bodies . . . You may be right, my lady. It must be the work of those who would bear false charges against our lord. They have a two-hour start on me. That would give them perhaps seven or eight miles. I must go after them at once and bring them back. (*Throws down his fan, takes a rope from his waist, rushes from the room to the courtyard.*)

NARRATOR In great haste
　　　Terukuni prepares
　　　To dash away.

VOICE OF SUGAWARA (*slowly, with great dignity*): Wait, Hangandai Terukuni, wait. Sugawara no Michizane is here.

(*Terukuni halts. The panels enclosing the SL room open, revealing Sugawara.*)

NARRATOR: The voice emanates
　　　From the nearby room.
　　　Kakuju stands aghast.

KAKUJU: Lord Sugawara! You left only a little while ago. How on earth can you be here?

NARRATOR: Small wonder
　　　Her mystification.
　　　Hangandai Terukuni
　　　Erupts with laughter.

TERUKUNI: Ha ha ha. Oh, my lady, what a convincing face you did put on. For a while I was really taken in by that tale of yours. I am much relieved to see that Lord Sugawara is indeed here. From the looks of things, though, it is quite obvious that you have had serious trouble here, and I only wish that I could hear the circumstances and offer you my assistance. But I am under official orders to escort his lordship. It has grown late. Come let us hasten to depart.

NARRATOR: As he urges their departure,

A gate-keeper enters with news.

GATE-KEEPER: Madam, the escort that was here earlier has returned. They are waiting at the gate.

KAKUJU: What! The escort? Well, they have returned at just the right moment. Here is proof that I was telling no tale. Bring them in. I will show them to Terukuni.

TERUKUNI: Wait! It might be a poor idea for me to meet right away the men who have impersonated me. Let me hide and see what is going on.

NARRATOR: He joins Lord Sugawara

Within the inner room.

Drawing closed the sliding panels.

He hides and watches.

(Kakuju bows toward the SL room, then descends into the court-yard.)

Preceded by the palanquin,

Amid loud voices,

The escort enters.

ESCORT LEADER: Here now, old woman! What kind of mockery of Terukuni's representatives is this! Don't pretend you know nothing about passing off on us this outrageous thing.

KAKUJU: What a disturbance you make! You took Lord Sugawara with you. What is this "outrageous thing" you speak of?

ESCORT LEADER: So, you're still playing innocent, eh. Sugawara is Sugawara, but we've no use for one made of wood. We've brought back your wooden statue to exchange it for the flesh and blood Sugawara. Look here in this palanquin!

NARRATOR: At his words,
   Kakuju perceives what has happened.
   "Ah, how fortunate!" she thinks.
   "Can it be the statue was imbued
   With Lord Sugawara's spirit?
   Could I witness
   More stunning proof than this?"
   Yet she contains the joy,
   Hidden within her heart.
KAKUJU: I do not understand what you are saying. Show me the statue.
ESCORT LEADER: I'll show you the stiff, rough-hewn thing! Look!
NARRATOR: But when he opens
   The palanquin doors,
   No statue sits within,
   Only the stately, handsome form
   Of Lord Sugawara.
   As, smiling, he emerges
   From the palanquin,
   The men of the escort
   Stare at him, mouths agape.
   And Kakuju too,
   Her expectations shattered,
(Kakuju staggers back.)
   Looks in bewilderment,
   First at the sliding doors of the house,
   Then at the form before her.
   Though plagued still by confusion,
   She speaks.
KAKUJU: Oh, thank you, thank you for returning him. I duly accept him back.
ESCORT LEADER: Wait a minute! Where do you think you're going?

For that matter, where do I think *I'm* going? I take Sugawara away, and I find this statue. I see there's been a substitution, so I bring it back, and then it's the real Sugawara
again! Have my eyes gone bad on me? *(Produces eyeglasses,
puts them on and peers about.)* Or has the thing really
changed?

KAKUJU: Whether he changes form or not, you've brought him
back. This way, Lord Sugawara.

NARRATOR: Kakuju approaches him.

ESCORT LEADER: Wait! You've got a lot of nerve!

NARRATOR: He pushes Kakuju aside,
        And forces Lord Sugawara
        Back into the palanquin.
        Slamming closed the door,
        He turns to face his men.

ESCORT LEADER: Men! As you've seen, there are some very strange
goings on here. We can't leave until this matter is cleared
up. Search the house!

NARRATOR: As he rushes into the house,
        He sees before him
        Sukune Tarō,
        Writhing in agony,
        Half dead, half alive.

ESCORT LEADER: By the treasures of Buddha! Tarō has been
wounded! Master, come quickly!

NARRATOR: At his shouts,
        From the escort in rushes
        Hyōe, utterly thoughtless
        He will be discovered.
        He lifts up his son.

HYŌE: What's this! My son! Who . . . who . . . what scoundrel
did this to you? Tell me his name!

NARRATOR: He shouts out in impatience.

KAKUJU: Hyōe! I, Kakuju, have slain him!

HYŌE: What? You stand there proud to have killed your own son-in-law! What has he done that you . . .

KAKUJU: No more deception, Hyōe! When he killed Tatsuta, you helped him, didn't you? Why did you kill my daughter, lord chief of this false escort? It's time to tell the whole story. Now, make a clean breast of it!

HYŌE: Oh, the pity of it all! I was planning for the future of my son here. We joined forces with Lord Shihei and planned to kill Lord Sugawara. My stratagem for making the cock crow almost succeeded, but we've been sniffed out by this rotten old bitch who's killed my son. Prepare to die, Kakuju! *(He draws his sword and starts to attack Kakuju.)*

NARRATOR: He lunges at her, but . . .

TERUKUNI: Yaa! You'll do nothing of the sort!

NARRATOR: And Hangandai Terukuni
Leaps from his hiding place,
And stands in the way
Blocking Hyōe's attack.

HYŌE: I'm not afraid of any of you! My plans have been thwarted. Now, see what feats a desperate man can perform!

NARRATOR: He lunges in to strike,
But Terukuni dodges beneath his sword,
Then tramples the blade to the ground.
Seizing Hyōe's right arm,
He throws him on his back,
And pins him under his foot.
In a mighty voice
Terukuni shouts a command.

TERUKUNI: You men of Terukuni! Bind these imposters, every one! Tie them up!

*(Two retainers carrying poles of split bamboo run out from SR
and begin striking the men of the false escort.)*
NARRATOR: At this command,
> The men of the false escort,
> Bereft of their bravado,
> Flee shamelessly
> Till not a man remains.

(Escort exits pell-mell SR.)
> Now Kakuju,
> Concerned for Lord Sugawara,
> Quickly opens the palanquin door.
> On peering in
> Astonishment possesses her,
> For yet again
> There rests the wooden statue.

(Kakuju draws back in surprise.)
KAKUJU: What . . . what's this!
NARRATOR: Once again she goes
> To the doors of the house,
> And when she slides them open.

*(The open panels reveal the standing Sugawara, now dressed in
a formal robe of state.)*
SUGAWARA: Dear aunt, do not upset yourself.
NARRATOR: At Lord Sugawara's words
> Yet again she stands dumbstruck,
> Bewildered and perplexed.

(Kakuju staggers back toward SR.)
KAKUJU: Which one is the real Lord Sugawara? Come here, Te-
rukuni, and identify him for me.
(Hyōe attempts to escape toward SR, but Terukuni restains him.)
NARRATOR: But both questioner and questioned

Are baffled utterly.

Lord Sugawara speaks again.

SUGAWARA *(first seating himself)*: Since Terukuni's escort was late, I dozed off for a while. Then, hearing a commotion, I awoke and looked out, only to witness Lady Tatsuta's piteous death at the hands of this scheming Hyōe and that murderous Tarō. I could do nothing to help her. How much more deep, my dear aunt, must be your grief. Had I not come here, you would surely have been spared such sorrow.

NARRATOR: His tears of heartbreak

Flow helplessly forth.

KAKUJU: No no! You are more precious than the lives of a hundred daughters. I am only so much more happy that no accident or injury befell you. What cause have I to weep. What cause have I . . . What cause . . .

NARRATOR: Yet tears brim her eyes.

KAKUJU: There, Terukuni, there is the cause of all this evil—that Hyōe. Take your sword and send him to his just reward—and Tarō with him.

NARRATOR: She goes to Tarō,

Grabs him by the hair,

And lifts up his face.

KAKUJU: My deepest wish now is that you and your father see Lord Sugawara alive and well. Perhaps this will ease my daughter's bitter spirit.

NARRATOR: She pulls the sword from his side,

And he breathes his last.

(Tarō clasps his hands in supplication, then collapses forward. Kakuju wipes the blade on Tarō's robe.)

KAKUJU: Though you are loathsome in my sight, this is a wretched way to die. How fleeting and inconstant is this world! By this sword my daughter has died *(cradles the sword on her left sleeve as she gazes sadly at it)* and by the selfsame blade my son-in-law is dead. *(Turns the blade over)*. Now with the same instrument I cut off my white hair, emblem of earthly transgressions.[18]

NARRATOR: Gripping the blade again,

She cuts away a lock of her hair.

(Kakuju collapses in sorrow.)

KAKUJU: I have clung to life beyond my proper span, hoping I might see my first grandchild. Shameful these snowy tresses! Now no grandchild will I know; only bitter sorrow. Now, our roles are turned around: an aged nun, I must pray for my youthful daughter's entry into the land of the Buddha. I will seek the Way of the Buddha through my ties with others linked to me by fate. Namu Amida Butsu. *(For a moment she wilts disconsolately, recovers. She places the lock of her hair upon Tatsuta's body, then takes from her sleeve a Buddhist rosary and prays.)*

NARRATOR: As she prays,

Lord Sugawara too,

His voice filled with tears,

Invokes the sacred prayer

For the peace of Tatsuta's soul.

Hangandai Terukuni is profoundly moved.

TERUKUNI: Lady Kakuju has preceded me in her revenge. Now I follow with my own punishment, you avaricious and inhuman old villain. *(Drags Hyōe off toward SR.)*

NARRATOR: And swift of stroke

He cuts him down.

Kakuju takes the statue in her arms,

---

[18] A symbolic gesture of taking the tonsure: renouncing the world and entering the Buddhist life as a nun.

(Two maids help her take it from the palanquin.)
       And places it with reverence
       At Lord Sugawara's right.

KAKUJU: Hyōe's plot has been exposed, and all now is well. Yet, the mysterious workings of this statue . . . can there be such things as we have seen?

SUGAWARA: As you say, the plot of these villains has been exposed, and I have escaped from danger, but I know nothing of what transpired during the brief time that I slept. As for sculpture and paintings that come to life, there is the story of the horse painted by our famous artist Kose no Kanaoka.[19] Each night the horse would leave its painting and go eat the clover painted on a palace screen. And in China too there is the tale of how the dragon painted by the celebrated Wu Tao-tzu caused the rain to fall.[20] And there are endless stories of how images of the gods and wooden statues of the Buddha have saved people's lives. Three times I carved this statue, so my very soul must have entered into the wood, and thus it came to my rescue. Because of the slander against me, I have been sentenced to exile. But even if I wither and die like some sentinel on a barren seashore, think of this statue as a remembrance of me for later generations.

(They exchange bows.)

NARRATOR: Thus were his words,
       And this rough-chiseled image

---

[19] Noted Japanese painter of the latter part of the ninth century. The legend referred to is noted in *Kokin Chomon Shū* (*kan* 11), quoted in Yūda, *Bunraku Jōruri Shū*, p. 373, n. 18.

[20] A contemporary of the eighth-century emperor Ming Huang, Wu Tao-tzu was perhaps the most famous Chinese painter of the T'ang dynasty. At least one source for the story of his painted dragon causing the rain to fall is *Ruri Tengu* (1807), quoted in *ibid.*, p. 373, n. 19.

Remains at the Dōmyō Temple [21]
In the village of Haji, Kawachi Province,
A grateful reminder of
Lord Sugawara's strength and virtue.
(During this recitation, Kakuju leaves by the sliding doors at center stage rear. Terukuni emerges from SR.)
Terukuni looks about.
TERUKUNI: My lord, these astonishing events have taken much time. It is now fully light. We must leave.
NARRATOR: Again he urges on their farewell.
(Kakuju, now wearing her brown robe, re-enters. Sugawara moves from the SL room to the large one at center stage.)
KAKUJU: I would like to present a small parting gift. *(To the maid):* Bring me the things I have prepared.
(Two maids bring in a large inverted open-work wicker basket. Over it has been draped Kariya's red robe. They place it between Kakuju and Sugawara. Kariya is hiding beneath it.)
NARRATOR: An incense basket [22]
Draped with Kariya's robe
Is brought forth,
And Kakuju bids her maids
Place it close to Sugawara.
KAKUJU: To keep you from the cold on your wave-tossed and windswept journey, please take to your place of exile this robe, a token of your aunt's devotion. I entrust it to you, Terukuni, please guard it.

[21] Dōmyōji, or Temple of the Enlightened Way, located near the city of Fuji-idera in modern metropolitan Osaka, has a long association with Michizane. See Fujino, *Sugawara Denju Tenarai Kagami Hyōkai*, p. 133, n. 410. Until the government order in the Meiji era that Buddhist temples and Shinto shrines be separated, Dōmyōji apparently was both a Buddhist institution and (under the name Dōmyōji Tenmangū) a Shinto shrine.

[22] A large open-work wicker basket inverted on the floor so that incense burned within would perfume robes draped across it.

TERUKUNI: A handsome gift indeed, so fragrantly scented a cloak
to keep out the rain and dew. I will have my men carry it.

NARRATOR: He rises and advances,

Places his hand upon the basket.

Lord Sugawara stops him.

SUGAWARA: One moment, Terukuni. This robe laid over an incense basket bespeaks both a fragrance and my gratitude to
you, dear aunt. But the perfume from within—I do not know
it, yet can its name perhaps be Fuseya . . . or Kariya?[23] I,
Michizane, have received from you a young girl . . . I mean
. . . ah . . . a young girl's cloak; but, alas, I cannot meet
. . . ah . . . it is not meet that I wear it. Still, stooped in
shame though I am, I shall take it with me. Please think of
it as my own cloak, and join with me in offering a litany
for Lady Tatsuta's happiness in the world beyond.

NARRATOR: Such words that have perceived

Kakuju's innermost heart,

Call forth unrestrained

A cry of anguish from Kariya

Concealed beneath the basket.

(The basket moves slightly.)

"Ah, now I see," thinks Terukuni,

As sadly now he understands

What moves poor Kakuju's heart.

And out to the hidden Kariya

Goes Kakuju's compassion.

*(Kakuju stands, controlling her tears. She places her hand on the
basket.)*

KAKUJU: My tears are more for Kariya. Please, your aunt begs you,
see her just once before you leave.

---

[23] Fuseya is the name of an incense; similarly, so would be such a name as Kariya, though Michizane is using it here to hint at the presence of his daughter.

NARRATOR: She goes to Lord Sugawara
    And tugs upon his sleeve.
(Very gently, Sugawara restrains her.)
SUGAWARA: Has age perhaps dulled these ears of mine? I was certain it was a bird that just now cried out. It was the sound of a young bird. *(For a moment his eyes meet Kakuju's. Then he turns away.)* And if the young bird cries, its parent too will cry. Such is the way of all living things.
NARRATOR: He shrouds his sorrow
    In a veiled poem.
SUGAWARA: Because it calls, just so,
        The cock quickens our farewell.
        In country hamlets
        Where no cockcrow is heard,
        How lovely is the break of day.[24]

(As he speaks, Kakuju writes the poem on a narrow slip of paper, then puts it inside the basket.)
SUGAWARA: With many farewells left unsaid, I now must take my leave. *(They exchange bows.)*
NARRATOR: And since the time of this poem
        This village has known
        No heralds of the dawn,
        Has heard no beating of their wings.
        As from beneath the basket
        Are heard her sobs,
        Kariya, disconsolate in her longing,
        Is like a creature of the air
        Bereft of plummage and of flight.

---

[24] The story of Michizane's visit to Dōmyōji on his way into exile and his writing this poem are noted in the 1679 work *Kawachi no Kuni Meisho Kagami* (*kan* 4), quoted in both Yuda, *Bunraku Jōruri Shū*, p. 373, n. 20, and in Yokoyama, *Jōruri Shū*, p. 561, n. 23. The authenticity of the poem, however, is questioned.

(Sugawara looks down at the basket. Perceiving his feelings, Ka-kuju lifts an edge of the robe for Sugawara to glimpse Kariya, but he closes his eyes and raises up his sleeve to block the view.)

> Her father too,
> Encircled by his captors,
> Seems a caged bird
> That dreams of long ago
> When he soared in freedom,
> A minister in His Majesty's service.
> Such is the grief at his exile
> That, though the night dawns bright,
> His heart is yet in darkness,
> On a path lighted only
> By the Buddha's mercy.
> And thus the name of the temple
> Dōmyōji—
> Temple of the Enlightened Way.
> And this has been the story
> Of the wooden image of Sugawara,
> Lifelike and divine,
> That yet remains there to this day.
> Inexhaustible, past all restraint
> Are Sugawara's tears of grief
> That spill out jewel-like
> As he fingers his rosary, over and . . .
> Over and again sounds forth
> The lament of Kariya.

(With great dignity, Sugawara descends the stair. Kakuju can bear it no longer. She throws back the robe from the basket, revealing Kariya holding the paper bearing Sugawara's poem)

> He turns to face her one last time.
> Not knowing if it is to be

In this present world
Their last farewell,
He takes his leave.

(Overcome, Sugawara tries to approach Kariya, but Terukuni, mindful of his duty, steps between them. Saddened, Sugawara turns away toward SR and moves away, leaving behind the grieving Kariya, supported by Kakuju. All pose as the clappers accompany the closing of the curtain.)

Act III

Scene 1. Tearing the Carriage Apart

(As the scene opens, the stage is covered by a thin light blue curtain. Against this backdrop Sakuramaru and Umeōmaru meet,
Sakuramaru entering from SR, Umeōmaru from SL. Each is
dressed in a knee-length kimono having a bold pattern of broad
horizontal and vertical stripes. Headgear for each is a large and
deep basketlike hat of woven straw, the fiber ends gathered in a
tuft at the top, the brim an unwoven fringe. At the point marked
"Set Change" in the text below, the blue curtain drops and stage
assistants pull it off to SL. The setting revealed is outside the
Yoshida Shrine. At SL is the large bright red gateway into the
shrine. Stretching from the gateway to far SR is a red picket fence
atop a low stone wall. Pink and white blossoms adorn small trees
behind the fence. Further back is the wall of the shrine itself, its
lower portion planked, the upper part a green latticework frame
in black and red. In this scene separate narrators appear as the
voices of Sakuramaru, Umeōmaru, Sugiōmaru, Matsuōmaru, and
Shihei.)

NARRATOR: A young bird out of the nest,
        A fish that has climbed onto land—
        To such is the masterless servant likened.
        After Lord Sugawara's exile,
        His groomsman Umeōmaru
        Has settled his affairs in the Capital

And set out in search
Of Lady Sugawara.

(To drum and flute music, Umeōmaru enters from SL.)
He is heavily disguised
In his deep hat of woven sedge,
As he heads for the rows of trees,
Deep green along the riverbank.
Toward him, from afar
Comes another, dressed alike,
Wearing the same deep hat of sedge.

(Drum and flute accompany Sakuramaru's entrance from SR.)
A recognition,
As one calls out.

SAKURAMARU: Is it Umeōmaru?

UMEŌMARU: Well, well, Sakuramaru! I've been hoping to come across you. I've things to tell and things to ask of you.

NARRATOR: In the shadows of the trees
They doff their woven hats.

UMEŌMARU: Well now, first a question. I heard from your wife Yae that a while back you left the Kamo riverbank searching for the Prince and Lady Kariya. Did you manage to find them?

SAKURAMARU: Oh yes, I caught up with them on the road. Then after we learned of Lord Sugawara's banishment, they hoped they might be allowed to speak with him, and I accompanied them to Yasui on the coast. But they were not allowed to meet him. Terukuni advised them that remaining together would jeopardize petitions that Lord Sugawara be allowed to return to the Capital. So they severed their relationship, Lady Kariya going to the home of Lord Sugawara's aunt in Haji Village, Prince Tokiyo going to stay at the palace of the Retired Emperor. While it seemed that things had been settled, it is all my fault that they are not. It was a kindness greater than I deserve that the Prince permitted me to be groomsman to his carriage, and I totally forgot about that. Lowly though I am, I played go-between in his love affair, and I have thus done him great injury. When I think it was I who caused the slander and the charges of conspiracy leveled against the Prince, and that it was my doing that brought on the banishment of Lord Sugawara to whom I owe so much, I am sick at heart. Today I will commit suicide, I think, or tomorrow I will throw away my life. But there is father living in Sata Village,[1] and this year he will be celebrating his seventieth birthday. He has been overjoyed since this spring at the prospect of seeing all of his three sons and their wives at the celebration, and if I alone am absent it will mean that to my crime of disloyalty I would add unfilial conduct. This worthless life will last at best only until the celebration is over. Umeō, please understand my shame in having gone on living this long.

NARRATOR: As Umeō watches his brother
    Clench his fists
    And gnash his teeth in remorse,
    He too is deeply moved,
    And for a while can find no words . . .

UMEŌMARU: Yes I know what you mean. With my master sent into exile, I had no reason to remain in the Capital. However, since the fall of my lord's house I have not been able to find out where Lady Sugawara has gone. I've been uncertain whether first to seek my lady's whereabouts or go to my master's place of exile in Tsukushi. But, as you say, this month is the celebration of our father's seventieth birthday,

[1] In modern Moriguchi city in the northeastern quarter of the larger metropolitan area of Osaka, a short distance east of the Yodo River.

and this too has been on my mind, so I must have uncon-
sciously put off other matters. We both have much to oc-
cupy our thoughts. Yet, it seems there is nothing one can
do.

NARRATOR: As the brothers face each other,
    Eyes heavy with tears,
    A vanguard officer arrives,
    Gripping a staff of iron.

*(Officer enters from SL, followed by two attendants. He is Su-
giōmaru. Drum and flute herald their entrance.)*

SUGIŌMARU: Out of the way! Over to the side!

NARRATOR: The lesser official shouts
    In a voice of great authority.
    Umeō approaches.

UMEŌMARU: Who is coming?

SUGIŌMARU: His eminence the Minister of the Left, Lord Shihei,
    is making a pilgrimage to the Yoshida Shrine.[2] Interfere and
    you'll get a knock with this iron staff!

NARRATOR: He spits out the words,
    And passes quickly on.

(Drum and flute as he exits with attendants at SR.)

UMEŌMARU: What! Sakuramaru, did you hear that? It's the min-
    ister Shihei, who's caused all the trouble for Prince Tokiyo
    and Lord Sugawara. We couldn't have asked for anything
    better, could we?

*(As he speaks, Umeō removes his sandals and flings them to his
rear. Sakuramaru follows suit. Both brothers then strike poses,
Sakuramaru holding his straw hat at his left side with his left leg
thrust forward, Umeō holding his hat like a corona behind and
above his head with his right leg thrust forward, eyes crossed.*

[2]Now located in the central part of the city of Kyoto, the Yoshida Shrine en-
shrined the patron deity of the Fujiwara family, hence Shihei's visit.

Clappers accent the pose. Then the two throw their hats aside.)
SAKURAMARU: Right you are. What luck to have met here!
(Both brothers hitch up the hems of their robes and tuck them into their sashes.)
NARRATOR: The brothers range themselves
          Left and right along the road,
          Hike up their robes for action,
          And lie in wait expectantly.
(They exit hurriedly at SR.)
          Moments later comes
          The rumble of a carriage.
          As merchants and travelers
          Clear the road, the procession
          Of minister Shihei approaches
(Set change. See beginning of this scene.)
          In panoply and splendor
          Quite like an emperor's progress,
          Guards and household men
          Ranged in file before and to the rear,
          The road so narrow,
          The carriage creaks and groans.
          Out leap the brothers
          From the shadows of the trees,
          And block the way.
(They leap out from SR, clappers heightening the excitement. Each has now pulled down the upper part of his costume, revealing beneath a bright red robe. That of Sakuramaru bears large white cherry blossoms; Umeō's robe is decorated with white plum blossoms.)
UMEŌMARU AND SAKURAMARU: No passage! Stop the carriage!
SUGIŌMARU: What insolent creatures commit this outrage?
NARRATOR: Then he sees their faces:

Umeōmaru and Sakuramaru,
Brothers of Matsuōmaru.

SUGIŌMARU: Ah, I've heard of you. No master, no stipend. Are you out of your minds to be so insolent? But then, did you stop this carriage knowing it contained Lord Shihei? Or were you unaware? Depending on your answer, you may get no pardon, even if you are Matsuōmaru's brothers. *(Puts down his iron staff, poses with his arms spread wide as clappers accent the pose.)*

NARRATOR: He rolls his full white sleeve
Up about his arm,
And grips it with a lusty vigor.
Umeōmaru laughs derisively.

UMEŌMARU *(a low, deep-throated, sneering laugh, gradually gathering in tempo)*: Hm hm hm hm. Ha ha ha ha ha! Be quiet, you! We're neither crazy nor did we mistake this carriage. You, great minister Shihei . . .

SAKURAMARU: . . . by your slander, Prince Tokiyo and Lord Sugawara have been ruined. *(He breaks down and weeps. Umeō taps him on the back, and he collects himself, posing strongly to the clap of the clappers.)* Their resentment runs deep. This very day we both had determined would be our last, but now I, Sakuramaru . . .

UMEŌMARU: . . . and Umeōmaru here, we know how to use the cattle driver's bamboo whip, and we will never rest if we do not *(with strong emotion)* b-b-*beat* the ass of Shihei, so fat and boastful of his rank, twice! *(Slaps his right knee.)*

SAKURAMARU: . . . Thrice! . . .

UMEŌMARU: . . . Five, six hundred times. You make faces like you are backing up your worthless master.

UMEŌMARU AND SAKURAMARU: Don't get yourself hurt by standing in our way!

SUGIŌMARU: You go beyond your station, insolent rogues! Strike them down, men! Tie them up!

NARRATOR: Shouting to one another,
His men run out, around the pair,
In front and back,
To the left, the right.
Though they try to take them,
The brothers maintain their calm
And fling their foes aside.

(Clappers accompany the action.)
Shihei's men try to seize the two
But are battered and hurled about,
Till none dare approach.

MATSUŌMARU *(offstage):* Wait! Wait! WAIT, I say!

(Drums, clappers in increasing tempo, then final sharp strikes of the clappers. While the narrator for Matsuō enters and assumes his seat, a short samisen interlude. Matsuō enters forthrightly from the area of the shrine gateway at SL. The upper part of his robe is decorated with pine boughs. He carries a long-handled traveling parasol wrapped in a blue cover. Before continuing, he puts down the parasol.)

MATSUŌMARU: Yaaai! Reckless roughnecks! Men, leave them alone. This is a time for me to discharge my duties before my lord. I'll show you a loyalty different from that between kin. *(To the brothers):* If you think you can stop this carriage I accompany, then go ahead and try!

NARRATOR: He takes the ox's halter
And leads the carriage forth.

SAKURAMARU: Ohoo, Sakuramaru here . . .

UMEŌMARU: . . . and I Umeōmaru—if we weren't here, I don't know what would happen. But now that we are, . . .

SAKURAMARU and UMEŌMARU: . . . let's see you proceed an inch!

NARRATOR: They seize the carriage shafts.
(Clappers.)
SAKURAMARU and UMEŌMARU: Heave! Heave!
NARRATOR: They push the carriage back,
        And the ox, its legs unable
        To withstand the thrust,
        Trundles backward, backward.
        To the rear of the cart
        Moves Matsuōmaru,
        And throws out both his arms,
        Puts power in his legs.
        Such is the struggle
        Over the progress of the cart,
        A clash between blood triplets
        (And rare they are in this world!),
        No one less ardent than another
        In loyalty to his lord,
        As they press forward, push back,
        Each with all his life,
        With all his vibrant might.
        The ground is rutted out,
        Deep cut by the carriage wheels.
UMEŌMARU: Damn beast! You're in the way!
NARRATOR: He loosens the ox from the yoke,
        And at full tilt
        The creature dashes away.
        The inside of the carriage
        Seems to shake and sway,
        And he who now emerges,
        Crushing under foot
        The blinds and ornaments—
        None other than Great Minister Shihei.

Wearing upon his head
A golden coronet of state,
His attire no different
From imperial garb.
As he speaks,
His countenance fairly shines.

SHIHEI *(slowly, with gathering anger):* Yaaa! Eaters of cowherd's food! Miserable blowflies! Men, if they seize the shafts of this carriage or get rowdy, run them down and kill them!

SAKURAMARU and UMEŌMARU: Yaaa! Let's run down and kill the great minister who says so!

NARRATOR: And by themselves
They lift the carriage up
And try to topple it.
Matsuō grapples with them,
A push to the right,
Another to the left;
Up the carriage is lifted,
Then lowered down again,
Twice, thrice,
Four times, then five,
And with the outcome
Hanging in the balance,
The jostling of the carriage
Is like that of a portable shrine,
Shoulder-borne at noisy festivals.
Standing in the coach,
Shihei seems a pillar of power,
And fearful the echoing sound
As he stamps his feet.
Both carriage and its axle
Reduced to mangled splinters,

Sakuramaru and Umeō
Each takes up a wagon tongue,
Waves it in the air
To strike at Shihei.

(The brothers pose with the black lacquered carriage tongues held above their heads. Matsuō and Sugiōmaru are seated on stools at SL.)

SHIHEI: What insolent conduct against me! *(Rolls his left sleeve around his arm and looks menacingly at the brothers.)*

NARRATOR: Sharp flashes of light in his eyes,
As he glares at his assailants,
Like the radiance
Of a thousand suns and moons
In a thousand Buddha worlds.

(The brothers try to strike Shihei, falter under his glare.)

Valiant though they are,
Umeō and Sakuramaru
Unwittingly stagger back,

(Clappers as they retreat.)

Shrunken in body,
Immobile in their chagrin.

MATSUŌMARU: Aha! There, did you see the power of my lord? Raise a hand against him again, and here in his very presence I'll cut you down with a single blow!

NARRATOR: He places his hand
Upon the hilt of his sword.

(Matsuō is still seated on a stool.)

SHIHEI: Wait Matsuo, wait.[3]

---

[3] In Yokoyama, *Jōruri Shū*, p. 567, the narrator's line "He leaps down from the carriage" follows Shihei's words. The line is also in Tadami Keizō, *Kaion, Hanji, Izumo, Sōsuke Kessaku Shū* p. 57, part of the *Yūhōdō Bunko* series; and doubtless it occurs in other complete texts. The line is not in Yūda, *Bunraku Jōruri Shū*, which follows current production practice. And, it was excised in the May

MATSUŌMARU: Yes, my lord.

SHIHEI: I wear the golden coronet of state, therefore I am the same as the Emperor. I have become Chancellor, exercising control over affairs of state. Spill blood before me and it would be a defilement of my pilgrimage to the shrine. I find it difficult to pardon you mischiefmakers, but out of consideration for the fidelity of Matsuō, whose actions place him above such rabble, I shall spare you. Be thankful for your lives, insects! Ha ha ha ha ha . . .

(Shihei's laugh, lasting over two minutes, begins as a growling, sneering utterance, gradually rising to a full-throated roar that boasts his power and prestige and derides his attackers. He holds out his wide sleeves.)

NARRATOR: He looks about him with a scowl,

　　　And proceeds toward the shrine.

(Exits through the gateway at SL, followed by Sugiōmaru and attendants.)

　　　Matsuōmaru turns to his kin.

MATSUŌMARU: You're lucky to have such a fine brother as me. You barely escaped with your lives. Show some gratitude and respect! *(He moves from SL position to stand between his two brothers, Sakuramaru on his right, Umeō on his left.)*

NARRATOR: At his words, suddenly

　　　The pair are filled with wrath.

SAKURAMARU: We have some things to say to you, but it can wait until after the celebration of father's seventieth birthday. Right, Umeō?

(Matsuō picks up the long-handled parasol.)

UMEŌMARU *(punning on Matsuō's name which contains the word*

1972 production in Tokyo, in which Shihei remained standing on the demolished carriage. In keeping with the general practice in performance, therefore, I have deleted it here.

"matsu," *"pine tree")*: What's more, we'll break every pine branch, sever your roots, and make all your needles shrivel up!

MATSUŌMARU *(returning the pun, he plays on the other brothers' names:* "ume," *"plum" and* "sakura," *"cherry)*: Ah, well then, after we celebrate father's birthday, I, Matsuō, will take both the plum . . .

UMEŌMARU: Eh?

MATSUŌMARU: . . . and the cherry . . .

SAKURAMARU: What?

MATSUŌMARU *(loudly and forcefully)*: . . . and chop them up so all their flowers fall! Now, before it's too late for you, get away from here quickly, get away!

UMEŌMARU and SAKURAMARU: Such insolence! Think we must be told by you when to leave?

NARRATOR: The two sides edge forward,
    Press upon each other.

(With the parasol, Matsuō lightly taps Umeō on the head, forcing him back to SL. He then taps Sakuramaru lightly on the head. The latter flinches back.)

    Then by common understanding
    They hoard their vengeful passions
    Until a later time,
    And with rancorous glances
    Go their separate ways.

(To drum and flute, all pose in a tableau as the curtain closes across the stage.)

Scene 2. Sata Village

(*Beginning at SL and occupying most of the stage is the thatched-roof country farmhouse of Shirokuro, father of the triplets Matsuō-maru, Umeōmaru, and Sakuramaru. Typical of traditional Japanese houses, this one is raised two or three feet off the ground. The interior is a large room in which most of the action occurs. At center is a doorway leading to the inner part of the house. It is hung with a dark blue curtain divided into four vertical panels, each panel decorated with a group of three fiddlehead ferns in white. SR of the doorway is a high shelf on which are several black lacquered bowls. To SL is a painted-on set of two wooden panels representing the doors to a closet. At extreme SL is another room closed off by shōji panels. The main room is bare of furnishings except for a small altar to the gods attached high on the SL post of the center doorway. The forestage in front of the house is the courtyard. Here, at extreme SL and enclosed by a low bamboo fence, are three medium-size trees just outside the shōji-enclosed room: cherry, pine, and plum, in that order going toward SL. The cherry and plum are in bloom. Outside the low fence in front of the trees are three straw rice bales piled in pyramid fashion. Left of center stage, in the courtyard, is a wooden well curb. Apart from props introduced in the course of the acton, this set remains unchanged throughout the remainder of Act 3. As the narrator's lines open the scene, Shirokuro is seen with a broom sweeping the courtyard. As the narration proceeds, he approaches the three trees,*) *pauses before them, bows and then continues his sweeping, moving toward SR. Presently he leans the broom against the house at SR and, removing his sandals, enters the house.)*

NARRATOR: The very early spring[4]
    Means leisure for the farmers.
    In village after village
    Even plow and hoe can take their ease.
    Ever inclined to merriment
    Is Shirokurō of Sata Village,
    Well known for his long years of life
    And for his upright honesty.
    On the domain of Lord Sugawara,
    Here in this village of Sata,
    Is a simple country villa.
    Old Shirokurō has been charged
    With the cleaning of its garden,
    And with the care
    Of his lord's beloved trees—
    The pine, the plum, and cherry—
    To break the soil about their roots
    And give them water.
    In the beginning a farmer,
    A wielder of the hoe,
    Shirokurō does not feel his age.
    Far more joy to him
    Than tilling of the fields
    Are his gardening tasks
    Of nourishing his master's trees.
    From the gateway,

[4] According to the lunar calendar, the first three months of the new year constituted spring. The "very early spring" here might be around February under the Gregorian calendar of the West, hence a time of inactivity for farmers.

His hoe upon his shoulder,
Old Jūsaku of the riverbank
Calls out.

(Jūsaku enters from SR. A small light blue towel is tied over his head bandana-fashion. Hanging from his waist is a tobacco pouch and a short tube containing the typical long-stem, thimble-bowl Japanese pipe. Over his shoulder he carries a hoe. As he speaks he pulls the towel from his head so it rests like a scarf about his neck.)

JŪSAKU: Shirokurō, are you in?

NARRATOR: Shirokurō notices him enter.

SHIROKURŌ: Ah, Jūsaku. Headed for the fields?

JŪSAKU: No, the work is finished now, but as I was returning home I recalled the wife saying that you were having some sort of happy celebration here. We received a great big tiered box with seven tiny little rice cakes in it, hardly enough to go with one's morning tea. *(Makes small round motions with his right hand over the palm of his left.)* But, they're more welcome than nothing at all. I wanted to come over and thank you for them. Well now, just what sort of celebration is it?

(As Shirokurō speaks, Jūsaku takes out his pipe, stuffs it with a small wad of tobacco, and lights it from the smoking tray before Shirokurō. He smokes as Shirokurō talks.)

SHIROKURŌ: Well, there has been Lord Sugawara's sudden exile, and I suppose those of us who live on his domain shouldn't actually be observing any festivities. But since I must, I will. I am embarrassed that everyone might hear of this, so I distributed small rice cakes—like the tiny ones offered to the Buddha—because I, Shirokurō, am exactly seventy years old. When I went to pay my respects to Lord Sugawara at the beginning of this year, he inquired about my age, and when I told him that I was seventy, he said that was indeed a rare longevity, and that moreover I was the father of a remarkable set of triplets. He noted that I receive a stipend from the Imperial Court, and that my sons have become grooms. "You are lucky, very lucky," he told me. "In the same month, on the same day, and at the same hour that all your sons were born," he said, "you should celebrate this very special seventieth brithday." And he said that from this day I should change my name. Listen to this: he gave me the name Shiradayū, after the name of some famous priest or someone at the Ise Shrine. Now, today is my birthday, and I've thrown that old name of mine on the trash heap. (*He mimes throwing something away.*) From today I'm to be known as Shiradayū. Please remember that.

JŪSAKU: You're very lucky. Now, let me ask you something. Did Lord Sugawara tell you why you were given a stipend at the birth of the triplets?

SHIRADAYŪ: Oh yes. At the time my late wife gave birth, we thought it was a terrible thing (*presses his right hand to his forehead*) and we feared for our reputation in the neighborhood. But it turned out to be an unlooked for stroke of fortune, because the father of the triplets was granted three parcels of land to be tax free during his lifetime. I understand the event was noted not only in Japan but all the way to China. If the children were boys they would be made grooms, and if girls they were to serve as maids or something in the palace. That decree was a real blessing. My master has been exiled, but I haven't been driven from my home, and my lands are just as they always were. (*Then, jokingly.*) Your wife is still young; if she gives birth, you have her do just as we did!

(*Both men are smoking with long-stemmed pipes. As Shiradayū concludes the above speech he looks at Jūsaku, who looks away*

shyly and begins to scratch his head with his pipestem in an embarrassed manner. Shiradayū too becomes rather embarrassed at his outspokenness, and he too scratches his head with his pipe.)
NARRATOR: They talk on together,
    As down the road,
    Picking her way along,
    Comes Yae,
    Wife of Sakuramaru.
(She enters from SR, a parasol in her right hand, a small parcel wrapped in lavender cloth in her left. Yae wears a pale green kimono with very deep sleeves, each sleeve decorated with cherry blossoms.)
    Since today is the birthday
    Of her husband's father,
    She carries in her hand a parcel
    Wrapped in a bit of cloth.
YAE: Ah, good, here it is.
NARRATOR: She removes her woven hat.[5]
(Yae bows a greeting to Jūsaku.)
SHIRADAYŪ: Oh, Sakuramaru's wife Yae is it? *(Puts away the smoking tray.)* You're early. Did the other wives come with you? Here, come in and take off your traveling sash.
YAE: Thank you. *(Enters house, disposes of the parasol.)* The others haven't come yet? I was afraid I would be late, and I hopped on the boat along the bank of the Yodo River. The boat moved quickly, so I'm not tired. It's good I got here early.
JŪSAKU: Shirokurō, you seem to have a guest, so I'll be getting along. *(He adjusts his sandals, but makes no move to leave.)*
SHIRADAYŪ: Eh? Jūsaku, you've got a bad memory, calling me Shirokurō. Have you so quickly forgotten Shiradayū?
JŪSAKU *(shakes his head)*: Oh no, I haven't forgotten. Besides the

[5] Production practice, however, is to use a parasol, which at this point she closes.

rice cakes, if I don't drink some wine to celebrate your change
of name, it's going to keep right on being Shirokurō.

SHIRADAYŪ: Oho, you say you haven't drunk a full cup of sake.
Or is it that you just haven't drunk your fill?

JŪSAKU: Heh, heh. You fibbing old rascal. When did you ever
really fill my cup with sake?

SHIRADAYŪ: Why, I gave you some just a little while ago. Since
a sake barrel or a sake cup would have been a little con-
spicuous, I used a bamboo tea whisk and sprinkled some
sake on the rice cakes. *(Mimes the action by pretending to
sprinkle sake from his right hand into his left palm.)* So that's
celebrating my birthday and my change of name all at the
same time, isn't it?

JŪSAKU: Ah, now I see. The wife said that the rice cakes smelled
of sake. You can be a bit more cautious with others, but
you and I are good friends. I'll come over in the evening
and you can treat me to a nightcap. Well, madam, make
yourself comfortable. *(Picks up his hoe and exits at SR.)*

SHIRADAYŪ: Did you hear that, daughter? People nowadays are
sly ones. He saw through my little economy trick. Come
over in the evening for a nightcap, he says. Ha ha ha ha
ha. Ah, there's a bit of craft in that man's good nature.

YAE: Oh, you're too much. Sake from a tea whisk. *(She mimes
the action as Shiradayū had done earlier.)* I never heard of
such a thing. Ho ho ho ho ho.[6]

SHIRADAYŪ: Ha ha ha ha ha.

(They trade the laughter back and forth several times.)

NARRATOR: Warm this affection between
            Daughter and father-in-law.

[6]A convention of the puppet theater, women laugh "ho ho ho," while men laugh
"ha ha ha." It seems worthwhile to point this out, since in the West the "ho ho
ho" laugh is associated with such rotund masculine figures as Santa Claus.

(Shiradayū points to his shoulders. Yae nods, goes behind him, and starts massaging his shoulders.)

> The wives of the brothers
> Umeō and Matsuō now appear,
> Having lingered along the road
> To gather into hats of woven reeds
> The wayside dandelions,
> Leaves of starwort.
> They make their way to the boxthorn hedge.

(Enter from SR. Chiyo and Haru pause to pick greens from the roadside. They wear the same pale green kimono as Yae, decorated similarly but with different motifs: on Chiyo's sleeves are pine boughs, while on Haru's are depicted stylized plum blossoms.)

CHIYO: Ah, here we are. You go in first, Haru.

HARU: No no, after you, Chiyo.

NARRATOR: Watching the wives of his sons
> Bowing to each other at the gate
> Shiradayū is amused.

SHIRADAYŪ *(calls to them)*: How can wives of triplets all born at the same time bother about who goes first or last? Yae has already been waiting here some time now. Stop worrying which of you is to be first, and come in, come in. *(He waves to them with affectionate gruffness.)*

HARU: Oh, Yae, you really got here quickly. I live along the road you would take, so I thought you'd drop by my house and pick me up, but the more I waited, the later it became. Then, as I was hurrying along I met Chiyo, and we dawdled on the way. *(To Shiradayū)*: But we picked some starwort and dandelions to make pickled greens for your birthday.

YAE: It was good you kept track of the time, Haru. What with the day's advance and the bustle to hurry here, I forgot all about my promise to drop by for you. I'm glad you met Chiyo on the way.

CHIYO: Meeting Haru was fortunate: I had a lively traveling companion. Well now, father, has dinner been prepared?

SHIRADAYŪ: No, it hasn't. I intended to leave it to you all. You don't have to make anything fancy that takes a lot of time. Make some soup with the rice I pounded this morning. You can put some salt seaweed on it. I've already boiled it so it won't take you any time. And, there are radishes and potatoes over there. But, you probably don't know what they look like, so . . . ah . . . oh . . . uh . . . *(Puts his hand to his back.)*

NARRATOR: With a groan, he stands up.

(The wives all stop him.)

HARU: No, wait. We're to celebrate your birthday today, so until the cooking is done you needn't concern yourself with a thing. Why don't you take a little nap.

NARRATOR: Though unfamiliar with kitchen matters,

When three get together,

Something will be whipped up.

SHIRADAYŪ: As you say. But now that I'm up, I'll get some things off the shelf for you. Here, look at this. These are some lacquered Negoro bowls handed down from my grandfather. And here are ten lacquered plates. I'm healthy and strong, and these bowls and plates are strong too, because they were made with good materials. I say strong, girls, but they're not harsh to the touch. Now, why are those sons of mine so late? I guess I'll just catch a few winks until they come.

NARRATOR: He lies down on his side,

Head on a hard pillow stand;

But tough as his pillow,

This robust old man.

(Shiradayū lies down, then gets up, looks out at the three trees and bows, then lies down again.)

HARU: Listen, you two. No matter what father says, it won't do to have soup alone. We'll have to boil some rice, and even if we make nothing else there will be a bonito and vegetable salad. The greens we picked along the road should be good for a broth. Yae, Chiyo, give me some help. I'll start the rice.

(All three exit through the center curtained doorway. When they return by the same door, each now wears a white kerchief arranged bonnetlike on the head.)

NARRATOR: One by one they take

> The carving block and grating bowl,
> And measure rice
> Into the washing pail—
> Three wives working together.
> Taking the chopping knife,
> One chops and chops and chops
> With a practiced hand.
> The house is busy
> With the sound of grinding bean paste.

(Haru goes to the well outside at SR where she draws water and washes the rice. Inside the house, Yae starts grating the bean paste in a bowl which refuses to stay still under her clumsy efforts. Chiyo takes over from her, turning over to Yae the chopping of the radishes. But again Yae is awkward, nicking her finger with the knife. The scene is a mixture of comedy and a display of virtuoso puppet manipulation.)

> Shiradayū wakes up.

SHIRADAYŪ: Haven't my sons come yet? They've known since the beginning of the year that it's my birthday. There's no reason for them to have forgotten about it. But, just the other day I heard from somebody . . . Oh yes, it was Jūsaku who just left. He asked if I'd heard that the three boys had a big argument in front of Shihei's carriage. Chiyo, you're married to Matsuō, and he's in Shihei's service. Come over here and tell me what happened.

NARRATOR: Being thus singled out,
        Chiyo shows a troubled face.

CHIYO: The three of them were agreed that it would be best not to let you hear of it until the birthday celebration was over. But since you've been given some trivial tale by someone else, it can't be kept quiet, so I'll tell you. Against Umeō and Sakuramaru there was my husband Matsuō, who, as usual, was short-tempered. As his language grew more and more violent, they had a brotherly quarrel. But you needn't worry. The three of them suffered no injuries, and everything ended right there. But they're still grumbling about it. *(Looks down, rubs her knee in some anxiety.)* Haru, Yae, that's the way it was, wasn't it? But, I'm worried about my husband's ill-humor.

YAE: Yes, yes, it was just as Chiyo has said. We had hoped to reconcile them, using your birthday as a pretext. But Father, if you don't speak to them, then . . . well . . . I'm afraid . . .

NARRATOR: Concerned about her husband,
        Her plea is indirect.

SHIRADAYŪ: Eh? I thought I might learn from you all if I asked. You know the reason for the quarrel, but you won't tell me? My sons, all born of the same parents and at the same hour, yet their hearts are so different. They say that persons who closely resemble each other are twins, but look-alike faces don't necessarily mean they are twins. There are boy and girl twins, and there are twins whose faces are not at all alike.

As a rule, if they look like each other, so will their hearts be alike, and they'll get along well with each other. No matter who looks at my sons, he would never believe they were even born of the same parents: the almost too mild expression of Sakuramaru, Umeō's features that make him seem so reasonable, and *(pensively and a bit distastefully)* that somehow perverse countenance of Matsuō. Ah, but I speak too rashly here in front of Chiyo. Please, take no notice of me. *(Laughs good-naturedly.)* Well, so there were no injuries. That's happy news. Now, no injuries to them. *(Speaking to Chiyo.)* And my grandhcild is healthy? Too bad you didn't bring him so I could see him. Here, I'm rambling on. It must be about four o'clock now. You know, I was born at four in the afternoon. I suppose dinner is just about done now. Girls, aren't you going to bring out the trays?

HARU: All right, coming. Why haven't our husbands arrived? It's way past the time they should be here. Chiyo, Yae, shouldn't we go out to the road and look? Come on, let's all go and look for them. It's better than waiting here.

SHIRADAYŪ: What are you talking about. They're right here.

HARU *(excitedly)*: They're here? Where? Where?

SHIRADAYŪ: You dull-witted women. Don't you know they're right there? Look, those three trees over there are my children: *ume* the plum, *matsu* the pine, and *sakura* the cherry, all of them together. *(He indicates the three trees outside the house at SL.)* Lord Sugawara most graciously and quite specifically told me that it is improper not to observe the right time on one's birthday. And for the celebration, it is customary to set a place even for one who is not present. Quickly now, trays for them.

NARRATOR: Shiradayū has spoken,

> And there can be no delay.
> Quickly the young girls serve the food,
> Put chopsticks on the trays.
> On little saucers opposite the bowls
> They place small dried sardines.

YAE: Now first, father, you take your place.

NARRATOR: Yae, though untrained in
> The etiquette of serving,
> Has learned by watching and listening,
> And now her graceful movements
> Are in the best manner of the palace.

SHIRADAYŪ: No wait, I'll go over there. *(Starts to go to the trees.)*

HARU: No, you'll get a chill from the ground. You'll stay right here.

NARRATOR: She makes him remain at his place.
> Now each wife takes up her husband's tray
> And steps into the garden.

(Each in turn goes before the appropriate tree, places her tray before it, and bows.)

HARU: This plum tree is Umōmaru. How straight and strong the branches, so like my Umeō's nature.

YAE: Just like the manly husband I have married, this tree is Sakuramaru, handsome in its contours like the cherry trees of Yoshino.

CHIYO: And this pine, strong and graceful and with a handsome sheen on its young green needles, is a symbol that we are bound forever as man and wife. This pine is my husband Matsuōmaru. *(As she returns to the house):* All of our husbands are here, so . . . *(The three wives kneel in a row before Shiradayū and bow deeply.)*

ALL THREE WOMEN: Happy birthday, father. Now, for your meal.

SHIRADAYŪ: Oh yes, let's eat by all means, let's eat. My seat is raised up, as befits a father, but first I must go and pay my respects to my children there.

HARU: You needn't do that just yet. Eat before your food gets cold.

SHIRADAYŪ; No no, Haru, that won't do. There's the proper etiquette to be observed, whether one is a parent or a child.

NARRATOR: Into the garden he descends,

And with single-hearted devotion

Bows before the trees.

SHIRADAYŪ *(speaking to the trees)*: My children, the fare is meager, but please partake. I have come down here especially to bow to you. Though you cannot bow in return, I understand. Here here, young ladies . . . Ha ha ha ha ha! Bring out the rice cakes.

NARRATOR: Back upon his buttocks

He totters in joyous laughter.

Returning to his tray,

He gives himself to his meal.

SHIRADAYŪ: Oh, yum yum! The flavor is delicious, delicious. Well, you three, I suppose I must eat three portions so I won't seem partial to any one of you. Oh-ho, aha, a ha ha ha ha. Well now, who brought this new tray and little clay cups?

HARU: Oh, they're from Yae.

SHIRADAYŪ; How thoughtful of you, Yae. Thank you. Haru, do you have something for me?

HARU: Oh, I had forgotten all about it.

NARRATOR: From her sleeve

She produces her gift:

Three folding fans.

HARU: The pictures on them are the plum tree, the pine, and the cherry, to celebrate your three sons. May they prosper well as these fans spread wide. Happy birthday, father. *(Bows to him.)*

SHIRADAYŪ; This makes me very happy. My thanks, Haru. I understood what you had in mind when I saw the pictures on the fans. There was no need for an explanation. I accept them with thanks. *(Bows to Haru.)*

NARRATOR: Now Chiyo, in good spirits,

Draws something from her sleeve.

CHIYO: Here is a cap for you to wear. It's a clumsy affair that I sewed myself from some scraps at hand. If it doesn't fit, I can sew it over again. Here, put it on.

SHIRADAYŪ *(puts on cap)*: Oh, you've all done well by me! Gifts that suit me well from each of you. Well now, we've finished our toasts. You can take the cup from my tray. Look, my sons' trays haven't been touched, and now the food must be cold. Here, you all eat theirs and give them another serving.

HARU: No no, let's wait a bit and celebrate after our husbands have come.

SHIRADAYŪ: Very well. Oh, then I think I'll go down and offer my thanks at the village shrine.

CHIYO: That will be fine.

SHIRADAYŪ: Ha ha ha ha. Well, I'm off. Oh, there's a packet of coins for an offering right there. Give them to me, will you. And I'll take along these three fans. I can show them to my friends, and I'll pray that the prosperity of my sons may grow just as these fans spread wide. Yae, you probably haven't been to the shrine yet. This is a good opportunity for you. Come along with me. Come on, let's go.

(Haru gives him his light cloak which he throws across one shoulder. Chiyo gives Yae the parasol. Shiradayū and Yae exit at SR.)

NARRATOR: And in high spirits

They head for the gate
And leave.

(The following scene, in the same set, is usually treated separately as the scene of "The Quarrel," and there is a change of narrator and accompanist.)

HARU: What a good memory father has for his age, Chiyo. You and I have already been to the village shrine, but this is the first time for Yae.

(Chiyo takes a pipe from the tobacco tray, lights it, passes it to Haru, who takes a few puffs and returns it.)

CHIYO: That's true, now that you mention it. But, unlike their father and his good memory, his sons are terribly forgetful. Why is Matsuō so late?

HARU: And why hasn't my husband come?

CHIYO: Or might it be that they have no intention of coming?

HARU: How could they fail to come on this of all days? But look! Here comes Matsuō!

(Matsuō enters from SR.)

CHIYO: Well, you've kept me waiting and waiting. Don't you know it's past the promised time?

(Matsuo enters the house, speaking gruffly to his wife Chiyo as he passes her.)

MATSUŌMARU: Don't annoy me with your chatter, woman. *(Holding his long sword in his left hand, he sits at SR, facing toward the audience.)* I had some business to take care of for Lord Shihei, and I couldn't get away until it was finished. Did you forget that I told you to go on ahead and explain that? Looks like Umeōmaru and Sakuramaru haven't come yet either. Is father inside?

CHIYO: No, he went out with Yae just a little while ago to offer prayers at the village shrine. Your brothers haven't come yet.

MATSUŌMARU: There, you see. You tell me I'm late, but I have a master to serve. Both Umeō and Sakuramaru are unemployed and without a master. When such rascals as that are late, that's really being late. Isn't that right, Haru. *(He fills and then smokes his pipe as Haru fidgets in her embarrassment.)*

NARRATOR: The bitter grudge he bears

Still lingers in his words.

Umeō now comes in,

(Umeō enters from SR.)

Anxious at the flight of time,

A quarrelsome cast in his demeanor.

He averts his face from Matsuō's gaze.

(Umeō sits at SL facing Chiyo and Haru.)

UMEŌMARU: Sorry to have kept you waiting, Chiyo. Father and Sakuramaru, and Yae too—Haru, why aren't *they* here?

HARU: Matsuō was just asking that too. Sakuramaru isn't here yet, and the other two have gone to the shrine.

UMEŌMARU: Hmmm. *(A pensive pause.)* I wonder why Sakuramaru hasn't come. The one you've waited to see doesn't come, but the ugly and disgusting face is always there.

NARRATOR: Stung by Umeō's words,

Matsuōmaru,

Headstrong and quick-tempered,

Responds in kind.

(Matsuō raps his pipe angrily against the edge of the tobacco tray.)

MATSUŌMARU: Hold on there, Umeō. If you've got any insulting remarks to make, say them to my face.

UMEŌMARU: For some reason you put me off. Every time I see your face *(slowly and intensely)* I just get sick . . . to . . . my . . . stomach.

MATSUŌMARU: Eh! Ah . . . ha ha ha ha ha! Listen to him go on! I can hardly keep from splitting. Ah, but Matsuō here is by nature sentimental. Unpaid and masterless samurai such as Sakuramaru and you are pretty skinny jowled. When I think how hungry you must be, I really pity you—but only because you're my brothers.

UMEŌMARU: What's this? Unpaid? Huh, you laugh at me for having no stipend, but do you think yours is such a proper one? You think it's proper!? It was the great god Hachiman who said that no honorable samurai, even if starving, would accept food from a blackguard. But you're happy enough to take your pay from that dirty Shihei. You're nothing but a stinking swine!!

MATSUŌMARU: You wag a long tongue, Umeō, calling me a swine. Just try that one more time!

UMEŌMARU: Oh, if that's what you want, more than happy to oblige. (*Rises belligerently, goes to where Matsuō is seated, shouts at him.*) Swine! Swine! Filthy swine!!

MATSUŌMARU: That does it! I've taken all I'm going to from you! (*Jumps up, grabbing his sword.*)

NARRATOR: As Matsuōmaru reaches for his sword,
            Umeō, too, readies his blade for battle.
            As they advance upon each other,
            Their wives cry out.

CHIYO: What is this, Matsuō. Have you lost your mind?

NARRATOR: Chiyo clasps her arms
            About her angry husband.

HARU: Here, you've come for father's seventieth birthday celebration, and you haven't even seen him yet. What do you mean, going for your sword like this? How can you draw your sword, Umeō, on such a day of celebration?

NARRATOR: She clutches at his sword hilt,
            But Umeō thrusts his wife aside.

UMEŌMARU: I don't care if it is father's birthday, or if there's a

celebration. I've no more patience with him. Don't get
yourself hurt trying to stop us. *(To Matsuō):* Lost your
courage, eh. Big talk, little do. Lucky for you my wife stopped
me.

MATSUŌMARU: What do you mean, lucky for me your wife stopped
you! Examine your own heart, Umeō, and see if you're not
the frightened one before you go throwing your lousy in-
sults at me. It wasn't your wife who stopped you but rather
her reminder that we haven't seen father yet. I've put up
with your insolence as long as I can, but I've had enough!
(Shaking with rage.) We'll settle this matter once and for
all after we see father. In the meantime, as some consola-
tion, I've just got to dump you into the dirt. I'll leave these
with Chiyo.

*(Matsuō and Umeō both remove the upper parts of their outer
kimonos, revealing their under robes: Umeō wears a bright red kimono printed with plum blossoms in gold and light green; Matsuō's is light blue with a pattern of stylized pine boughs in pale
lavender, dark green, and gold.)*

NARRATOR: Matsuō removes his swords, both long and short,
        And flings them to the side.
        Hitching up his garment's hem
        He readies himself for battle.

*(Angrily Matsuō gives the swords to Chiyo, then thrusts his arms
behind him and tightens his sash.)*

UMEŌMARU: Oho, the swine's got a good idea. Until Sakuramaru
        comes, I leave Matsuō's life in his own hands.

NARRATOR: And like his brother
        He casts his blades aside.

(Umeō gives them to Haru, moves toward Matsuō at center stage.)

MATSUŌMARU: No swords, no blood. Women, don't interfere.

NARRATOR: Suddenly Umeō moves upon him.

(He kicks Matsuō's feet from under him.)

And from the porchway
Matsuō stumbles into the yard.
Yet even as he does so,
The nimble Matsuō
Sweeps Umeō's feet from under him,
And head over heels
He falls atop his brother.
They wrestle with one another,
Throw each other down,
Grapple, disentangle,
Then seize each other again.
Each wrenches his partner about,
Drags the other down,
Kicking, trampling.
(Matsuō leans forward and drives his head into Umeō's stomach.
Umeō pummels Matsuō's buttocks, then grabs him about the waist
and tries to lift him up, but to no avail.)
But equal the ages
And equal the strength
Of these full-blooded youths,
As they fight out
A contest of endurance.
Chiyo and Haru, half fearful
The swords they hold
Be taken by their husbands,
Will not go near,
But wait impatiently,
Beside themselves with fear.
(Chiyo at SR, Haru at SL, both clasp their husbands' swords to
their breasts, nervously watching the fray.)
CHIYO: Neither of you will win or lose. You've fought your fill
now, haven't you?
HARU: That's enough, Umeō!

CHIYO: You too, Matsuō, stop it!
HARU and CHIYO: Stop it! Stop it!
NARRATOR: The men will pay no heed.
MATSUŌMARU: If no one wins, it's a wasted effort. I'm going to
flatten you.
NARRATOR: He presses his attack with strength,
But Umeō unflinchingly strikes back.
He twists his shoulder about,
Making his assailant's charge
Glance off.
As Matsuō grabs him from the side,
His grip is strong as the pine.
And like the plum tree's power,
Umeō's elbow is fully a match.
Arms entwined, they twist
And push against each other.
(Matsuō picks up a rice bale from the pile in front of the trees at
SL, throws it at Umeō. The latter catches it as Matsuō grabs an-
other, and the two push and shove the bales against each other.
They throw the bales aside and try to grab their swords from the
wives.)
At that moment,
Both fall down and lean
By chance upon the cherry tree.
A scant few inches from the ground,
The sapling breaks and topples,
As the wives look on in shock.
Their wrestling contest ended,
With no decision gained,
The battlers shake themselves apart
And look in fear at what they've done.
They pause, and all too quickly

> Return Shiradayū and Yae
> From their visit to the shrine.

CHIYO: Oh! Father's back!

HARU: Its Shiradayū!

NARRATOR: At their words, the two men
> Put arms back in their sleeves,
> Lower their garments' hems,
> And hardly has each thrust
> His swords into his sash,
> Than their father enters the house.

(The scene known as "The Quarrel" ends at this point. Typically there is a change of narrator and samisen accompanist to start the next scene, "Sakuramaru's Suicide." There is sometimes a division between the next action sequence, known as "The Petitions," and the scene of Sakuramaru's suicide, which would then begin with his entrance on stage.)

> However burdened by his years,
> A parent inspires a dreaded respect.
> His sons rise not, but stay
> Doglike on all fours
> In deep obeisance.

(Matsuō and Chiyo are in the garden at SR, Umeō and Haru at SL.)

MATSUŌMARU and UMEŌMARU: Congratulations, father, on this felicitous day.

NARRATOR: Though they speak the happy greeting,
> Their faces are flushed crimson,
> And they remain in nervous discomposure.
> Their father chuckles happily,
> His face a picture of cheer.

SHIRADAYŪ: The girls came early and celebrated my seventieth birthday, so we've finished the day's festivities. Though you already knew about the time, I thought perhaps something must have kept you from coming. Well, Umeō, Matsuō, I'm very glad you came. Girls, I suppose it's overdone by now, but did you have them eat some soup to celebrate the occasion?

NARRATOR: He observes the broken cherry.

(He looks at the tree for an instant is taken aback, then regains his composure.)

But to whoever did the deed
He offers no reproach.
No rebuke where scolding there should be,
But in his heart a plan appears to form.

(Turning away from the tree, Shiradayū nods slightly as though decided on a course of action.)

Umeōmaru takes from his breast
A letter he has prepared.

(As Umeō draws out the document, Matsuō produces a similar one.)

UMEŌMARU *(very formal)*: The felicitations having ended, I should like to present this letter which contains my considered and most heartfelt request. *(Places the letter directly before the still-standing Shiradayū and returns to his place in the garden.)*

NARRATOR: From Matsuō, another missive.

(Matsuō too places his letter before his father and returns to his place.)

MATSUŌMARU: This is a very personal request.

NARRATOR: As though by prearrangement,
They place the letters in the same spot
Neatly before their father.
Shiradayū laughs aloud.

SHIRADAYŪ: Between parent and child, brothers and husbands, and wives, things should be friendly and relaxed. Gathered together as we are, if someone has a request he should just speak out. But instead, here are these formal letters. Well, in that case, I'll be ceremonious about it too, and pass judgment with all the formalities of a magistrate's proceedings. *(He squares his shoulders, arranges a cushion slightly in front of him. Chuckling lightly, he sits, removes his cloak and cap. From his sleeve he produces a pair of spectacles which he puts on.)*

NARRATOR: He takes up the petitions
    And reads them carefully to himself.
(First reading Umeō's.)
    Though of such appeals
    Haru and Chiyo know nothing,
    One would think these wives
    Would know their husbands' hearts.
    Completely in the dark, alone,
    Is the apprehensive Yae.

YAE: Chiyo, Haru, we agreed to ask father today to heal the rift among his sons, so what is going on here? After all, my husband isn't here, and I hadn't counted on any of this. I wonder if Sakuramaru got sick on the way here.

NARRATOR: Already beside herself
    Because her husband has not come,
(Yae rises and goes to the doorway where, leaning on the frame, she looks off into the distance.)
    These two petitions
    But cause her greater anguish.
    In worry, her head droops to the side.
    The father completes
    His reading of the letters.

SHIRADAYŪ: Now Umeō, your request begs leave to travel. Hmmm. That can mean only one thing: you're going to Lord Sugawara's place of exile?

UMEŌMARU: Yes, precisely that. Unlike his fine mansion in the Capital, his dwelling now is but a humble cottage. He has no one to handle his affairs, so I, Umeō, wish to go and serve him. I beg your leave to go.

SHIRADAYŪ: I see . . . There's a saying, you know, "Face of a man, heart of a beast" for persons who have no sense of gratitude to those who have helped them. The face may be a man's, but the heart is that of a beast. Your wish to go to Lord Sugawara's place of exile and serve him shows that your heart is hardly that of an ungrateful beast. I gather that Lady Sugawara and the young lord are safe, and that you're setting out on your journey knowing where they are.

UMEŌMARU: No, I have not seen Lady Sugawara since my lord went into exile. I don't know where she is. However, she is only a woman; the young lord Kan Shūsai is different. As for him, he is for certain . . .

NARRATOR: He is about to speak
But flashes with just his eyes
A glance at Matsuō.

(Umeō thrusts out a knee and leans forward intently, as though to impart a confidence. Shiradayū jerks his head toward Umeō and regards him fixedly. A pause, as Umeō and Matsuō look penetratingly at each other, each trying to peer into the other's heart.)

UMEŌMARU: . . . for certain . . . ah . . . his whereabouts is unknown to me. But he is safe . . . so go the rumors.

SHIRADAYŪ (shouting): What! You idiot! You've only heard that our precious Kan Shūsai is safe, not seen him, don't know where he is! You call that performing in a loyal manner?

And your lord's wife, whom you refer to as just a woman; why, she's as much your master as he is, isn't she? It's true, Lord Sugawara is in uncomfortable surroundings in exile, but going there and tending to his needs, that's service even a cripple could perform—a suitable task for me to undertake! *(Strikes his breast for emphasis.)* Here you are in the prime of youth, a time when you're most fit to serve your lord. Yet, amid the machinations of his slanderers, who are searching high and low to destroy him—against whom we must never be off our guard, must watch with the eyes of a hawk—*(he holds out his right sleeve to hide a quick gesture with his left hand indicating Matsuō at SR)* in such a time of danger you've no thought of serving him without considering yourself.

(Matsuō strokes his chin, apparently feeling awkward.)

SHIRADAYŪ *(continues):* Asking for a job fit for a cripple, do you hold your life so dear? Are you afraid of the enemy? I cannot grant your request! I cannot! I reject your petition!

NARRATOR: He flings the letter,
> Striking Umeō in the face.
> Such is the burden of logic
> In the old man's glaring rage,
> Umeō and his wife can only
> Show abject apology.

SHIRADAYŪ: Now Matsuō. I see in your petition that you wish to be disowned from this house. Oho ho, aha ha ha ha ha. This is the most remarkable request since the founding of the country! Aha ha ha ha ha. Ah, if there was ever an unfilial rascal, none can compare with you. A most remarkable request, but I grant it. *(Puts Matsuō's letter into the fold of his kimono.)*

MATSUŌMARU: Ah, my humble thanks.

NARRATOR: His spirits high,
     The happy Matsuō stands.
MATSUŌMARU: Since you permit me, without interrogation, to sever
     my family ties, it must mean that you have guessed I am
     doing this out of loyalty to my master Shihei. *(Bows to his
     father.)*
SHIRADAYŪ: Ha ha ha ha ha. Talk is so convenient. Ha ha ha ha
     ha ha. Listening to *you* speak of loyalty to a master, why
     it's the most ridiculous thing I've ever heard. Loyalty, that
     depends on how you define it. Swinging off to the side of
     the true path, that's called crab loyalty! *(Strikes the floor in
     angry emphasis.)* A crab digs its hole to suit its shell; people
     pursue their own ways according to their characters. You
     think now that you've got yourself disowned and cut all ties
     with your brothers you can kill anyone who defies Lord
     Shihei, is that it? All right, go ahead and be loyal to your
     master without considering the good and the bad. Disobe-
     dience to one's parent is disobedience to the way of heaven!
     You've gotten what you wanted, wretch. Hurry up and go!
     Dawdle around, and for a parting gesture I'll thrash you with
     this broom! *(Picks up a bamboo broom and shakes it at
     Matsuō.)*
NARRATOR: So furious his voice, that veins stand out
     Upon his forehead.
     Matsuō, having had his way . . .
MATSUŌMARU: Come on, wife.
NARRATOR: He leads his wife away.
     Sad, the separation
     Of parent and brothers,
     But for poor Chiyo more sorrowful
     The farewells to the other wives.
*(Chiyo comes back to center stage. Shiradayū angrily throws at
her the cap she gave him. Matsuō comes back, picks up the cap.*

At this point Shiradayū flings the broom, hitting Matsuō on the shoulder.)

> She tries to see their faces,
> But such is the flood of tears
> Her eyes are dim.
> As they leave,
> She wrings her tear-soaked sleeve.

(Matsuō makes an apparently unconscious bow to his father, quickly catches himself, and marches stolidly off at SR, followed by the weeping Chiyo.)

SHIRADAYŪ: Well, happily that takes care of the troublemaker. *(To Umeō):* And you, you idiot! Aren't you going out to find Lady Sugawara and her son? Get off with you!

NARRATOR: Again he gives his son

> A strong rebuke.

UMEŌMARU: Then who's to go to Lord Sugawara?

SHIRADAYŪ What! I'm the one who's gong there, that's who! Now, be off! Go! *(He throws his cushion at Umeō.)*

NARRATOR: Haru cowers at the command.

HARU: Yae, please make apologies to him for us later.

NARRATOR: Thus her parting words,

> As husband and wife move to the gate,
> And Shiradayū, strained and taut,
> Enters the inner room.

(Shiradayū glances sadly at Yae standing at the gate watching Umeō and Haru depart, then leaves through the center stage curtained doorway, concealing under his arm as he goes the small tray stand Yae had earlier given him for his birthday. At the gate, Umeō whispers to Haru, and the two leave upstage right and hide offstage outside the house.

If the production involves a finer subdivision of scenes, "Sakuramaru's suicide" would begin at this point, with a change of narrator and accompanist.)

Now separated
From brothers and their wives,
Yae is left behind,
Not knowing what to do.
Sunk in meditation,
She stands at the doorway
Thinking of her husband.

(She stands, both hands on the post of the doorway, looking longingly out toward the road.)

Then unexpectedly,
From the inner room
Sakuramaru appears,
Sword in hand,
Smiling quietly.

(Sakuramaru is dressed in a formal black kimono edged in white at sleeve openings and hem. On each sleeve is a small white cherry blossom. He enters through the parted curtains, pauses tranquilly, both hands resting on the top of his sword as though it were a cane before him.)

SAKURAMARU: Dear wife, you've waited a long time.

NARRATOR: Startled by the voice,

Yae runs to him.

(Yae runs into the room from the gateway.)

YAE: What! You've been here all along and said nothing? This is no way to treat your wife. I've been worried to death about you. Father was in a rage at the other brothers, and you didn't even come out. Why did you stay inside? Eh? Tell me why, tell me.

(Sakuramu has by now moved slowly into the room where he sits at center, holding his black lacquered sword vertically in his left hand. Yae kneels at his right.)

NARRATOR: How natural her wifely concern.

A moment later Shiradayū enters,
Bearing on a plain wood standing tray
A short dagger.

(Shiradayū enters from the inner room. The upper part of his brown kimono has been pulled down, revealing beneath it one of saffron edged in dark green at the neck and hem. The light blue towel formerly tucked into the folds of his robe is now tied around his head.)

Heavy, heavy of heart,
He falters on his aged legs.

(He totters, catches himself, proceeds slowly.)

Before the groomsman Sakuramaru
He places his burden.

(Withdraws slightly, depsondent.)

SHIRADAYŪ: If you are prepared, then do it quickly, do it quickly.

NARRATOR: For the young wife, his words
Bring yet a further jolt.

YAE: Father! What is all this? Sakuramaru, what is going on? *(Breaks into sobs.)* Why are you going to die, why kill yourself? If there is some good reason, tell me. I can be brave. If you won't speak, then father, just a word of explanation. Put my fears to rest, oh please. Have mercy on me, have mercy!

NARRATOR: Nothing can she do
But join her hands in prayer,
And weep away her heart.

SAKURAMARU: Is there need to trouble father? You and I have had a warm and happy life together until now. I will tell you all that is in my mind. My master—and I speak his name with deep respect—is Prince Tokiyo. Though I was but the son of a farmer, Lord Sugawara treated me most kindly; he gave my father a stipend to live on, and he named my brothers and me after his favorite trees: the pine, the plum, and the cherry—Matsuō, Umeō, Sakuramaru. I am deeply indebted to him. *(Places his two swords to his right.*

(The following passage is by and large in poetic meter and is delivered by the narrator in song.)

> Far more than is my due,
> His kindness to me.
> When we came of age,
> He was our godfather;
> And were this not enough,
> He did take us all
> Into courtly service.
> Of the brothers three,
> I, Sakuramaru,
> Was most favored:
> My service was to
> The royal house itself,
> Its members not of mortals born.
> I, of basest birth,
> A lowly carriage groom,
> I would serve in close attendance
> Upon a royal Prince.
> In his love affair
> With the daughter of Lord Sugawara—
> The Lady Kariya—
> I was the bearer of his missives,
> And this has spelled his downfall.
> By the tongues of slanderers were spread
> Rumors of this romance.
> Till finally a charge of treason
> Was brought against Lord Sugawara,
> And thus the ruin of his noble house.

Ah, it wrenches my very heart!
Nothing remained for me
But to ensure safe haven
For the Prince and his lady,
And through my own death
Prove my heart was faithful.

I came here early this morning and explained matters to father. He gave me his blessing to end this life I can no longer
bear to live. See, my wife, I have received from my father's
hand the knife that will end my life. (*Looks fixedly at the
knife on the stand, then looks at Yae.*) Thank him for me,
and after I am gone, look after him. I beg you.

NARRATOR: At her husband's words
Of steadfast loyalty,
His wife bursts into tears.

YAE: If you would kill yourself because your handling of that love
affair brought on the evil rumors about the Prince and the
banishment of Lord Sugawara, then Yae too cannot remain
alive. You tell me to live on and care for father. How can
you say such a cruel thing? (*She stands, moves toward Sakuramaru.*) Even more heartless, you ask me to thank him
for letting you die! How could I give thanks for such a thing
as that? Don't be so unreasonable! (*Kneels beside Sakuramaru, places her hand on his knee imploringly.*) Listen to
me, tell me, please tell me that I may die with you. (*Runs
over to Shiradayū's left, pulls at his sleeve.*) Father, can't
you help us? (*Moves to a place between Shiradayū and Sakuramaru, pulls at Shiradayū's sleeve.*) Here . . . here, don't
just sit there with your head cast down. Give us your wis-
dom. My husband's life hangs on your words. Have you no
feelings of grief? With your own hand you bring in this tray
. . . this sword of death! How can you do this? (*Strikes the

stand before Sakuramaru, then finally dissolves in tears. Returns to her original position at SR, weeping piteously.)

NARRATOR: Now lamenting, now pleading,

> Down she flings herself in anguish;
> Such is her torment
> She seems as one possessed.
> Shiradayū lifts his face.

SHIRADAYŪ *(weeping as he speaks):* What I am going to say may not serve as an excuse to prevent you from thinking me a cruel-hearted father who would give his son a sword and say "Die," but hear me out. *(Wipes his tears with the blue towel.)* Since it was my birthday I arose this morning earlier than usual, and when I opened the gate, there was Sakuramaru. "Oh, you're early," I said. "You must have walked all night if you came on foot. Or did you come by boat?[7] Never mind, come in, come in." I told him. When I asked how things were, his story was as you have just heard it. *(Sobs.)* For the son of such a humble person as myself, his courage truly astonishes me. I tried to reason with him, but he wouldn't listen. I refused to let him see you until the celebration was over, but made him hide in the inner room until I told him to come out. *(More weeping.)* I tried to put it off for a little while. Should I stop him, or shouldn't I? I couldn't make up my mind. *(Weeps as he picks up the fans he received from Haru.)* I decided I would leave it to the gods to decide. Fortunately, on these three fans I received for my birthday are pictures of the plum, the pine, and the cherry. Pretending that I was going off to pray for the future of my children, I

---

[7] Two daily passenger boats plied the Yodo River between Kyoto and Osaka, a day boat and one at night. The one Sakuramaru might have taken in order to reach Sata Village around dawn would have been the night boat that left Fushimi in the southern part of Kyoto, arriving the next morning at Hakkenya not far from Sata.

went and presented the fans at the village shrine, praying
with all my heart that Sakuramaru might be spared. *(Clasps
his hands and bows as in fevent prayer.)* I placed them on
the altar so I couldn't see the pictures, and I prayed: "Please,
oh god," I said, "please send your spirit into these fans and
let me pick from them first the *sakura*, the cherry tree." I
took up a fan *(raises a fan, opens it revealing the plum blossom)* and when I opened it, it was the plum. *(Drops his head
in sorrow, slowly lowers the fan.)* Oh no! I thought in de-
spair. Was this a sign that my prayer was not to be answered? I shouldn't try again, since that would be to doubt
divine will. But, so strong was my desire to save my son,
that I picked up another fan. This time . . . *(racking sobs)*
. . . this time . . . again it was different—*(takes up another fan, opens it)* it was the pine. *(Sobs.)* There was nothing more I could ask for, my strength was gone. *(Picks up
in his right hand the plum fan, holds it above his head and
gazes at it; does the same in his other hand with the pine
fan. Then, slowly he lowers them. Midway down they limply
drop from his hands and flutter down.)* When I returned
home, I saw that broken cherry tree. *(Points at tree.)* I resigned myself to the will of fate. Thus am I a father who
gives a sword of death to his son. I've made up my mind; I
won't weep. *(Controlling himself with difficulty.)* You too,
Yae, don't weep . . . *(stifling sobs)* . . . you hear?

YAE *(struggling with tears)*: A-a-all right.

SHIRADAYŪ: N-n-no crying.

YAE: Y-y-es.

SHIRADAYŪ: D-d-d-don't weep.

YAE: Y-y-y-yes.

SHIRADAYŪ: D-d-d-don't you weep.

YAE: Y-y-yes, y-yes.

SHIRADAYŪ: T-t-there'll be n-n-no weeping!

(Throughout this interchange, each becomes progressively less controlled, until both finally break down into convulsive lamentation.) [8]

SAKURAMARU: You heard him, my dear wife? So precious to this old man is my life that he endures such anxiety. To precede you in death, without repaying all your kindness—oh, father, forgive your unfilial son! *(Turns to Shiradayū and bows deeply.)* I may be of low birth, but I have a sense of honor, and in death will I prove my loyalty.

NARRATOR: Reverently, in his hands
    He takes the plain wood tray.

YAE: Then . . . this is our farewell?

NARRATOR: So firm her husband's resolve,
    So deep her grief,
    That though she tries to weep,
    The tears refuse to flow.
    Shiradayū blinks back his tears.

SHIRADAYŪ: At the death of his brave son, the father must assist as second. [9] And for my sword, look here.

NARRATOR: From the folds of his robe
    He draws forth a Buddhist handbell
    And its little mallet,
    And with these he will
    Pray out his heart.

SHIRADAYŪ: When I stand as your second with this as my sword, you will in the future life gain the power divine nevermore

---

[8] Though not specifically indicated in the text, this dramatic scene of grief is regularly performed in this manner.

[9] In the act of ritual suicide through disembowelment as practiced by warriors, a second *(kaishaku)* stood by to assist the dying man, beheading him at the proper instant.

to stray from the true path. The very name of the Buddha,
like the sharp sword that cleaves through all things, will dissolve away all delusion.

NARRATOR: He raises the mallet,
　　　　Strikes at the bell,
　　　　Which rings in wild confusion.

SHIRADAYŪ: Namu Amida, Namu Amida, Namu Amida . . .
Namu Amida . . . Namu Amida. *(With each invocation,
he strikes the bell, he himself becoming increasingly overcome with tears.)*

NARRATOR: As his father's voice
　　　　Intones the litany,
　　　　Sakuramaru makes loose
　　　　The robe about his neck.

*(Sakuramaru pulls down the upper part of his black garment, re-
vealing the white silk robes of death beneath. He takes the dagger
from the stand with his right hand, lifts the stand with his left
hand, bows to it, then places it behind himself.)*
　　　　He takes the nine-inch sword,
　　　　And into his left side
　　　　He stabs the blade,
　　　　As Yae's weeping voice
　　　　And the tinkling of the bell
　　　　Set up a wild pulsation.

*(Yae clings to his right arm, but he holds her against his knee and
stabs himself. Outside the house at SR, Umeō and Haru emerge
from concealment and move toward the gate.)*

SHIRADAYŪ *(rapidly, almost in desperation, strikes the bell with
each invocation)*: Namu Amida, Namu Amida, Namu
Amida, Namu Amida!

NARRATOR: On his right, beneath the ribs,
　　　　Sakuramaru turns the blade.

SAKURAMARU *(painfully holding out his left hand to Shiradayū):*
    May it please you . . . the final stroke . . .
SHIRADAYŪ: Oh, the final stroke . . .
NARRATOR: Behind his son he moves,
        Waves the hammer on high.
SHIRADAYŪ *(holds the bell near Sakuramaru's ear; his emotion-
    charged voice speaks the syllables slowly and with strong ca-
    dences):* Namu . . . Amida . . . Butsu. *(His legs falter, he
    collapses in front on his son.)*
NARRATOR: He pounds the bell
        And chants the liturgy,
        For souls departing this world.
        Sakuramaru grips the blade anew,
        Slashes through his throat,
        And quickly as the final breath is gone,
        Forward he falls in death.
        Resolute, Yae too
        Would follow her husband in death,
        And takes up the bloody dirk.
        From the shadows of the hedge of quince,
        In rush Umeō and his wife.
UMEŌMARU: No, don't!
NARRATOR: He wrenches away the dagger,
        Casts it aside,
        Then bows before his father.
(Yae clings to Haru, weeping.)
UMEŌMARU: A little while ago when you ordered us to leave, we
    went out the front of the house, but I thought it strange that
    Sakuramaru hadn't come; and then you didn't even inquire
    about Lord Sugawara's precious cherry tree being broken.
    With first one thing and then another, I became suspicious,
    so we secretly returned from the back. We've heard every-

thing. Sakuramaru's life has withered away along with that tree, and there was nothing we could do. Watching from outside the passing of my brother, we both silently joined our prayers to your tolling of the bell. *(Takes Sakuramaru's body in his arms.)* That so young a man should kill himself, ah such a loss!

NARRATOR: The mourning Umeō and wife,

       The listening parent, and Yae

       Telling over and again her plaint

       That she too could not die,

       All are gripped by helpless tears,

       As one last time the old man sounds the bell,

       Droning a final prayer.

(Shiradayū places the bell on the altar at the curtained center doorway. Then, leaning on Haru's arm, he enters the inner room. Presently they return, Shiradayū now dressed in more formal attire for his journey. In one hand he holds a long bamboo cane, in the other a shallow, wide sun hat of woven straw.)

       The mallet is laid aside

       As Shiradayū takes up in its place

       His cane and traveling hat.

       Not a moment will he wait

       But follow now Lord Sugawara

       And travel to his place of banishment—

       For Shiradayū, the beginning

       Of a journey in this present life;

       For the soul of Sakuramaru,

       A voyage to an unknown future world.

SHIRADAYŪ: Umeō, Haru, please see to my son's body.

NARRATOR: His parting gift

       To those he leaves behind:

       This last appeal

And words for Yae's care.

His gift to a son,

Gone to the land of no return:

Only a Buddhist prayer.

ALL FOUR: Namu Amida Butsu, Namu Amida Butsu, Namu
Amida Butsu.

NARRATOR: To the last intoning,

Shiradayū dons his woven hat.

He to the western provinces;

To the western realm of paradise

The spirit of his now departed son.

And those who send him forth:

Umeō, the living loyalty,

Sakuramaru, the loyal heart now still.

One tree has withered—

The evanescent cherry.

And two remain—

Matsuō, the pine,

Umeō, the plum.

That in this place did dwell

This father of three sons,

And that his story may be known

To ages yet unborn,

At Sata Shrine yet lingers

The traces of a holy place

To Shiradayū consecrated.

All this the blessing of that god—

Sugawara no Michizane.

*(Shiradayū starts to leave, turns back to the three trees in the
garden, bows low. Standing up, he pauses, then at the words "And
two remain," he strikes the pine with his cane. Again he starts to
leave but looks back. Umeō and Haru raise Sakuramaru's body*

for Shiradayū to see his face. It is too much for the old man. He drops his cane and hat, stumbles back to embrace Sakuramaru a last time. He retrieves his cane and hat, and joins his hands in prayer as the curtain is drawn across the stage.)

Act IV

Scene 1. Mount Tenpai

(*It is the middle of the second month of the year 903; approximately a year has passed since the action in Act 3. The scene is the countryside near Dazaifu in Kyushu, Lord Sugawara's place of exile. Between clumps of pines at extreme SL and SR is a distant landscape of yellow rice fields dotted with small clusters of farm houses amid groves; several mountains rise in the far distance against a blue sky. Holding a thick red-and-white braided rope, Shiradayū leads a black ox on whose back sits Lord Sugawara. To emphasize the hardship and melancholy of his exile, the puppet head for Sugawara is now different. In earlier scenes the rather rotund Kōmei head with its gentle, noble features has been used. The Shōjō head used in this scene is leaner and more angular around the jaw, the eyes larger and more deeply set and brushed with red veining. In contrast to the Kōmei head with its narrow painted eyebrows and relatively slight accenting lines about the eyes and nose, Shōjō has bushy movable eyebrows, a long moustache, a full and less carefully coifed shock of black hair tied at the back, striking brownish red accent lines about the eyes and nostrils. The general countenance is a mixture of grief and anger. At his first appearance, and until noted later in the scene, the lower part of the Shōjō face is covered by a mask which presents a calm countenance and hides the more dramatic features of the face until they are revealed at the end of the scene.*)

NARRATOR: When I think upon my love,
                    With a *yo-ya hoi ho*,
              Ah bitter do I feel.
              For as the knot won't come undone,
              Her heart to me won't yield.
                    Ah *ha-ri-na*,
                    Oh yes, 'tis bitter.[1]
              . . . And bitter too this exile here in Tsukushi,
              Where march away the months and years.
              He passes his days in a humble dwelling;
              The years have gone as though
              All was only yesterday,
              And now today so swifty come—
              Mid-second month of Engi three.[2]
              To this field and mountain landscape
              With its springlike sky, comes Lord Sugawara
              Astride an ox released to paddock.

(Ox led in from SL by Shiradayū.)

SHIRADAYŪ: Ah, I love those country songs.
                    When I think upon my love,
                          With a *yo-ya hoi ho* . . .

Ha ha ha ha haaa. How refreshing they are. And what fun
the cowherds too, singing away till their voices are hoarse.
Eh, and the more I look at this ox the finer seems its fur.
The turn of its horns, the set of its eyes, the shape of its
head and neck, the frame, muscles—the whole of this pitch
black ox. More handsome in color and lustre by far he is
than the satins brought from China. Horns pointed to
heaven, eyes to the earth. Just look at him: fired-black and
bushy, brow straight 'n direct, two small quartered ears, teeth

---

[1] Probably a rural song once popular, though the source is not now known.

[2] The third year of the Engi era corresponds to 903 by the western calendar.

offset—he's an excellent beast indeed. Oh yes indeed, yes indeed.

NARRATOR: At these unfamiliar terms of praise
Lord Sugawara marvels.

SUGAWARA: Ah, Shiradayū. *(Shiradayū bows.)* In spring you have it till the ground, in fall you have it carry the harvested grain. You *should* know the fine points of the ox that helps you in your farming. When you say "horns pointed to heaven, eyes to the earth," I can tell you're talking about the horns and the eyes of the animal. But when you say "five slack bushels, allow eight pecks, two tall quarts clear," might this refer to an estimate of an ox's purchase value measured out in rice?[3] Tell me more; I listen.

SHIRADAYŪ *(bowing)*: Well, that beats all! *(Slaps his knee.)* Lord Sugawara who knows everything about everything under the sun, doesn't know a thing about cattle. That you entrust me with your question, however, shows that being born a farmer does have its virtues. Your pardon, then, and hear . . . heh heh heh . . . my lecture on cattle. The term "fired-black and bushy" hasn't a thing to do with the measurement of grain in bales. When one examines the color of an ox's fur, black is most prized, so we say "fired-black and bushy." Next, that phrase "brow straight 'n direct" refers to the things to look for in the animal's pate. "Pate," that means "head." Looking straight ahead without turning to right or left is what one wants, so we say "brow straight 'n direct." And it's not "two tall quarts clear"; it's "two small quartered ears." What you want is that the ears be very small. Now, "teeth offset."

---

[3] I have taken some small liberties in this passage in an effort to preserve the humor in Sugawara's misunderstanding of Shiradayū's practiced appraisal of an ox. Shiradayū's enumeration of the desirable qualities in an ox are homophonous with the listing "one *koku*, six *tō*, two *shō*, eight *gō*," all of which are various volumetric amounts used in measuring quantities of rice.

It's bad for the upper and lower teeth of the beast to meet
as it chews its cud. For the teeth to grow out so they don't
meet—that is, offset—is a point to look for. Now, noting
these off in order, we say "fired-black and bushy, brow straight
'n direct, two small quartered ears, teeth offset." Lo-o-o-o
(spoken like the lowing of an ox), thus concludes my lecture
on cattle.

SUGAWARA: Ah, truly each man is wise according to the specialty
he follows. Listening to Shiradayū here has been a lesson
for me.

NARRATOR: At his words, Shiradayū
    Dances a little jig.

SHIRADAYŪ: My my, what's this you say? Since the time of my
parents I've been a farmer on your land, and you've ex-
tended your favor even to my three children. I'm so thankful for one kindness on top of another. Ah, those three sons
of mine—so different from their father, who even when
asleep cannot forget his gratitude. One . . . has died. The
other two are not of like mind. Having gotten rid of the
trouble-maker among them, I've come here to Dazaifu. That
was, let's see . . . the third month of last year. And your
dwelling here, so lonely and uncomfortable. A year has
passed, and yet you've not gone out to view the moon or
see the blossoms. Now today—though I can't guess your
thoughts—today comes your order to lead forth the ox, so
I've straightened out my wrinkles and stretched . . . aaah.
*(He stretches as though to get the kinks out, then, looks out
across the fields.)* Ah, how peaceful the spring fields. I suppose you are going to the Anraku Temple to pray for your
return to the Capital.[4]

---

[4] Anrakuji, formerly a Buddhist temple dedicated to Sugawara and located on the
grounds of the Tenman Shrine at Dazaifu. With the enforced separation of

SUGAWARA: No, that is not it. I am without blame, so I have no
intention of troubling the Buddha with prayers for my benefit. If His Majesty knew of the slander laid against me, the
world would learn that I have committed no crime, and an
imperial command would surely be issued for my return to
the Capital. Until then, I, Sugawara, will view neither the
moon nor the flowers. And even though the Emperor remains unaware of my unselfishness, there is no doubt that
the gods of heaven see the truth. I go to the Anraku Temple
because of a manifestation in a strange dream I had early
this morning. As I thought of my home in the Capital and
of how my beloved plum tree must in this second month
be at the height of its blossoms, I drew to me the inkstone
kept at my pillow. Letting my brush move as it might, I
wrote this poem:

> When blows the eastern wind,
> Send to me your fragrance,
> Oh flower of the plum.
> Though absent from your master,
> Forget not the season of spring.[5]

Thus did I speak my heart. And as I drowsed, a mysterious
heavenly child stood at my pillow and spoke to me. "Moved
by your deep compassion for others," it said, "and your service as a loyal minister who observes humanity and justice,
even plants that have no feelings yearn after the master who
has shown them love. Blossoms cannot speak, but as proof
of what I say, go to the Anraku Temple and see." It is because of this divine message that I go.

Buddhist and Shinto institutions in the Meiji era, the temple was disestablished
in 1868.

[5] The poem is in the *Shūi Shū* (997), third of the series of imperially sponsored
anthologies of Japanese poetry.

NARRATOR: As he speaks,

> A priest of Anraku Temple
> Approaches on aged feet,
> Leaning on a staff.

(Priest enters from SL. He wears a saffron robe and a bag of black and gold brocade across his left shoulder. He carries a long T-shaped staff.)

> Spying Lord Sugawara,
> He bows and draws near.
> From his saddle
> Lord Sugawara descends.

(Shiradayū assists him.)

SUGAWARA: Where might your reverence be going? I was just on my way to your temple. How happy I am to meet you here.

PRIEST *(bows)*: Ah, I am only an ignorant priest, but there is a reason why I wanted to come and see you. In a most strange dream I had last night I was told to show to its master in exile his dearly beloved plum tree. Then, true to this divine message, I found that mysteriously and in the space of but a single night a plum tree had taken root to the left of the Kannon Hall.

NARRATOR: For both teller and listener

> It is like a matching up of tallies,
> As proof the dream is true.
> "The temple is this way," speaks the priest
> And accompanies them on foot.

(The priest leads Sugawara and Shiradayū off SR. The backdrop portraying the rice fields and trees lifts into the flies, revealing the grounds of Anraku Temple. Across the rear a bricked wall extends the breadth of the stage, a small temple building set before it at center stage. In front of the temple stands a small plum tree with

*white blossoms. Sugawara, Shiradayū, and the priest enter from
SL.)*

> As they enter the temple grounds
> The fragrance of the plum,
> So clearly recognized,
> Summons up the feeling
> Of incense burned and
> Wafted into sleeves.

PRIEST *(to Sugawara):* Rest here a bit and look upon this marvel.

NARRATOR: At his direction,

> A seat is placed,
> A cloth is laid upon it.

(A wooden bench covered with a red cloth is brought out.)

> Sweet cakes and wine
> Poured from a bamboo flask
> Complete the priest's diversions.
> Slowly and on faltering legs
> Shiradayū inspects
> The ground about the plum.

SHIRADAYŪ: This is strange. Indeed, a thing rare in this world.
First Lord Sugawara back along the road, then our honored
priest's talk about his dream. Well, I chuckled to myself and
had my doubts as to the plausibility, on the face of it, of
what he said. After all was said and done, I wondered, how
could such a thing truly be? But, having seen the tree, I'm
quite at a loss. This tree—the shape of its branches, the fragrance of its blossoms—the tree I had in my care at your
villa in Sata, this is it! It is that very plum! There's no dis-
puting these holy revelations. Since I came here there has
likely been no one to give it water; yet from the healthy color
of the tree, the way the buds are quickly growing forth, the

many clusters of flowers, I'd say for certain ten to twelve gallons of plums will form by pickling time.[6] (*Musing.*) Let's see, a gallon and a half will go for land rent, and I'll give some to the temple here. The rest of the takings will be mine. Ah, but first now, a little "takings" for our stomachs; let's have a drink of wine. Here let me pour. (*At Sugawara's right, he pours wine from the bamboo flask and hands it to Sugawara.*) My cup, as ever, this one of black *temmoku* glaze. Oh, drinking while standing reminds me of funerals,[7] so . . .

NARRATOR: . . . near the bench he stoops.

(*Shiradayū pours for himself and drinks.*)

> Just as his thoughts are formed
> They issue from his mouth;
> A man no less upright than he seems.
> Just as Lord Sugawara is warming
> To the view of his precious plum,
> Shouts come from without.

VOICES: Look, a fight! Oh, they've drawn their swords! Here they come, slashing at each other! Don't let them into the temple! Close the gate!

NARRATOR: Yet, even as the shouts are heard,

> Into the temple grounds they rush,
> Two samurai locked in combat.

(*Umeō and Heima enter fighting from upstage right. Rapid drums accompany their entrance.*)

[6] Young plums are often pickled in salt, dried, and used as garnishing to rice and other foods. Much loved by the Japanese, these *umeboshi* are salty in the extreme to Western taste.

[7] Sake is most commonly drunk while seated, and it was thought to be unlucky to drink while standing as a funeral procession set out. Shiradayū is thinking of the recent death of Sakuramaru. For another reference to this superstition, see Chikamatsu's play *The Woman Killer and the Hell of Oil*, in Donald Keene, *Major Plays of Chikamatsu*, p. 453.

The priest is thunderstruck;
Shiradayū hovers about his lord.

SHIRADAYŪ: Oh, look there, both are dressed in traveling clothes. Quarrels start without warning, they say, but we mustn't let them settle it here. Leave! Get out!

NARRATOR: They pay no heed, but then he sees
That one man in the fray
Is his own son Umeō.

SHIRADAYŪ: What's this? What are you doing? Oh, look out! Don't get hurt!

NARRATOR: So frets the anxious parent's heart.

(Drum beats continue to underscore the action.)
At these encouraging words,
Umeō strikes away his rival's sword,
Gives his foe no passage for escape,
But leaps upon him,
Grabs him with a single hand,
Flips him in a somersault,
And pins him beneath his knee
In a show of manly valor.

SHIRADAYŪ *(comes toward Umeō at SR)*: Well done! You've given a good account of yourself, a good account! Ha, a fight well fought! But what started this quarrel? And what brings you here to Tsukushi? As luck would have it, Lord Sugawara, who's been worrying about affairs in the Capital, is right here. Now, give us the details.

UMEŌMARU *(his captive still pinned beneath his left knee)*: Yes sir. And may I say most respectfully that for me, Umeō, to have my prayers answered and see my esteemed lord in good health has been my most cherished desire. Since my lord's lady and son who were in the Capital are now in hiding, I have been unable to keep them together. The young master

I have left in the care of Takebe Genzō. My wife Haru and Sakuramaru's wife Yae are looking out for Lady Sugawara. It is at her command that I have left her and come to see how things are with you in your place of exile. Fortunately, I was able to arrange for passage by ship. Thanks be to heaven, I was favored with good weather, and I have covered a thousand leagues as though in a single bound, arriving here by the Tsukushi boat last night. Among the vessel's passengers was a follower of Shihei, this Washizuka Heima. This fool *(strikes Heima)*, he didn't recognize me, and by a stratagem I was able to deceive him and find out what he was up to. By his own admission, he has come here to kill Lord Sugawara, an act of rashness that now hastens his own death. He was well aware that my lord would be at this temple, and he had the audacity to come here directly to carry out his evil mission. Here, he is my present to you.

NARRATOR: He throws a rope about his captive
        And cinches it securely.
        How cheerful his demeanor
        As he binds his prisoner to a post.
        Great is Lord Sugawara's joy:
        This flower of fidelity,
        Bringing tidings from his beloved Capital,
        Here, this warm and feeling Umeō;
        The flower that has flown to him
        As an oracle of the gods,
        The plum that lacks a human heart.
        Yet showing no distinction,
        The feeling and insensate,
        Both attend their lord.
        As words of praise to both,
        A poem:

> The plum has flown to my side,
> The cherry has withered away.
> Why in this indifferent world
> Yet stands so heartless the pine?[8]
> . . . yet stands so heartless Matsuō,
> The groomsman of Shihei.
> Now withered and gone, Sakura the cherry
> Was groomsman for the Prince.
> For Lord Sugawara, Umeō is the groom.
> And yet remaining manifest today
> Is the glory of the plum,
> Famed as the plum that flew
> And inexplicably took root
> At the Temple Anraku.

SHIRADAYŪ: Ah Umeō, how grateful we are for our lord's poem. He praises you, likening you to this plum here. In the line, "The cherry has withered away," he mourns my dead son Sakuramaru. "Yet stands so heartless . . ." for that evil Matsuō surely speaks to his fawning on Shihei.

UEMŌMARU: Just as you say, father. It disgusts me even to call him brother. But, enough of Matsuō, the bastard. The enemy on the spot right now is this Washizuka. Well, Heima, tell us of Shihei's plot. Refuse, and your requiem will be this sword. How about it! Out with it!

NARRATOR: Umeō stands up, ready to strike.

HEIMA: Oh, wait, don't be hasty! Loyalty through and through between master and retainer, that's the ancient way. Re-

---

[8] Surely one of the most famous of the Japanese poems attributed to Michizane, it has appeared in numerous collections, several of them noted in Yokoyama, *Jōruri Shū*, p. 598, n. 1, and Fujino, *Sugawara Denju Tenarai Kagami Hyōkai*, p. 227, n. 135. Chikamatsu alluded to the poem in his 1721 play *The Love Suicides at Amijima*. See Keene, *Major Plays of Chikamatsu*, p. 419. Nonetheless, it was probably not actually written by Michizane.

vealing nothing, even at the risk of one's life, that too is the ancient way. But killing one after getting him to talk is also the ancient way. I'll use a *new* way to save myself and I'll tell you everything. My Lord Shihei has his eyes upon the throne, and he ordered me to take the head of the troublesome Lord Sugawara and return with it to the Capital. With Lord Sugawara as his scapegoat, he is going to make his move. He'll engineer an incident for his great ambitions, dispose of the Emperor, the Prince, and the Retired Sovereign one after the other and seize power in a single swoop. And for me *(brightening somewhat)*, there's to be the joy of becoming a fine lord. *(Gloomily.)* Now my flight of happiness has gone off course, and I find myself most shamefully trussed up. *(Whimperingly.)* Please . . . untie me quickly.

NARRATOR: As the treacheries of Shihei
> Fall one by one upon his ears,
> Lord Sugawara's countenance
> Alters suddenly.
> He stares with bloodshot eyes,
> His eyebrows rise in rage!
> Toward the Capital he directs a withering glare,
> And rises up as one gone mad!
> Shiradayū looks on amazed.

SHIRADAYŪ *(to Sugawara)*: Why, you've known about that conspiracy of Shihei's all along. And yet, as though somehow or other you've just heard about it, your face is more furious than I have ever seen it. You may glare from here, but it won't reach to the Capital. If that tightness in your chest should recur . . . Oh *(almost weeping)* that would be most lamentable.

(During this speech, Sugawara folds down the upper part of his robe, revealing the white silk undergarment beneath.)

NARRATOR: The old man frets
And shows an anxious face.

SUGAWARA: Umeō, Shiradayū! Hear me, both of you! So dire is
Lord Shihei's treasonous plot it cannot go unchallenged. I
have received no pardon, so I cannot return to the Capital.
Yet the Emperor is in danger, unaware of the traitor who
aspires to the throne. My loyalty to his majesty rots away
uselessly here in exile. My mortal self has been falsely ac-
cused of a crime, but after I am dead I will be free to do as
I must! My spirit will return to the imperial Capital and serve
as protector of the Emperor. Now, before your very eyes, as
a token of this my prayer that I swear to heaven . . .

NARRATOR: And from the white blossomed plum
That stands before their very eyes
He snaps a young bough.

SUGAWARA: As a first step in exterminating these fawning villains
in league with the imperial traitor, see this!

NARRATOR: With the branch he strikes,
And Heima's head goes flying,
Flung away as are the blossoms
From the branch of the flying plum,
Blossoms showering in waves
Like the tempering ripple
On the edge of a well forged sword—
Yet in Michizane's hand a sword of plum,
Renowned far more than genuine blade.
Shiradayū and his son
Can only cringe in fear.

SUGAWARA: Yaaa! Hear me, both of you! You have heard of this
terrible danger. Now go without a moment's delay to the
Capital and report to the Emperor about Shihei's evil de-
signs. I will go to the summit of this Mount Tenpai to which

I raise my eyes,[9] and there for three days and three nights will I bend my mind to the most austere of disciplines. I swear an oath to Bonten, to Taishakuten, and King Emma,[10] and my ghost will become chief of the one hundred sixty-eight thousand rumbling thunders that reverberate through the heavens.

(*A white mask that has hitherto inconspicuously covered the lower part of Sugawara's face is pulled away, revealing a face with more dramatic eyes, deeper color lines around the eyes, nose, and mouth, a grey hue on the cheeks—a generally more forceful countenance, now also enhanced by the loosening of previously tied-back shocks of hair.*)

SUGAWARA: I will gather my stalwarts, move upon the Capital, and smash the traitorous wretches! This is our final meeting in the present life. Now, go!

(*Throughout this speech, Sugawara moves about with angry gestures, tossing about his long hair.*)

NARRATOR: Together with his voice
>   A raging wind blows up, blows up,
>   Smashing roof tiles of the main hall.
>   From the priests' quarters and the abbot's cell
>   Blinds and doors fly off
>   Like so many leaves.
>   Great trees and the flying plum,
>   Flowers and sand in the courtyard
>   Blow violently about.

(*Rapid drums as the theater lights grow ominously dim.*)

[9] Located about two miles southwest of the town of Futsukaichi in northern Kyushu, there is a shrine dedicated to Sugawara atop Mount Tenpai.

[10] Bonten is Brahma, the supreme creator in Brahmanism, often appearing in Buddhist legend along with Taishakuten, the Japanese name for the Vedic and Brahmanic deity Indra. Emma is the Plutonic lord of the nether world of the dead.

Shiradayū, Umeō, the priest,
All gaze on dumbfounded.

SHIRADAYŪ and UMEŌMARU: Even if your prayers to the gods are
answered, how much grief it will bring to Lady Sugawara
and the young master for you to throw away your precious
life before its time. Put such thoughts from your mind, we
beg you!

NARRATOR: Shiradayū and Umeō seize his sleeve,
But left and right he sends them flying.

*(The vigorous action of the remainder of the scene is accompanied
by drums, gongs, and clappers.)*

SUGAWARA: You, priest. I pray you make no great effort to stop
me! Now, by the grace of the gods, I will show you the miracle of changing my very form to that of the thunder god!

NARRATOR: Taking the scattered flowers
And placing them in his mouth,
He faces toward the heavens
And spews them out—
White blossoms of the plum!
The whirling petals turn to flames
As far off to the sky he goes,
His flight into an unknown realm
Both strange and fearsome.

*(At "whirling petals," Sugawara flails his way to SL as the set
transforms from the temple to swirling gray and black clouds in
the sky. Mounting a platform behind the clouds, Sugawara strikes
a fierce pose as the curtain is drawn closed to the ringing smack
of wooden clappers.)*

Scene 2. North Saga Village

(*The time is a short while later in the second month of 903; the place, North Saga Village, located on the northwest outskirts of modern Kyoto. The major part of the stage is occupied by a rustic open building extending from SL past center stage. At extreme SL is a room enclosed by shōji panels. Hanging against the depiction of four other sliding doors at the SR portion of the house is a long halberd having a black shaft and a blade encased in a red and gold brocade cover. The foreground represents an outside courtyard. Boughs of red leaves hang in from extreme SL, and a small red-leafed tree stands outside the house at SR. Behind the latter tree is a distant landscape of other green trees and beige-colored undulating fields. In front of the small tree, at a right angle to the audience, is a wooden gateway, but no gate itself.*

First to come on stage is a mountain priest, who remains an obscure figure throughout the scene: we learn his identity in scene 3. Around his neck a rosary can be seen, and the black hilts of two swords protrude from the robes at his left side. On his head, and quite concealing his face, is a broad and deep wicker hat. Also slung about his neck is a conch-shell trumpet which he blows periodically. He enters from SR and prowls about observing the house.)

NARRATOR: Shattering sleeping dreams,
            An ascetic mountain priest

Blows incessantly
On his conch-shell trumpet
(Sound of the conch, which continues at intervals.)
As he walks about
The countryside and mountain huts
Of North Saga Village, off the beaten track,
Where careful watch is kept.
Following in the footsteps
Of the founder of his sect,
En the Hermit of long ago,[11]
Each morning, every night,
Skillfully he cajoles his meals
With begging bowl and tray—
Ascetic practice for the stomach,
Some would say.

(Haru comes out of the room enclosed by shōji, goes to the house's entrance at SR. There is the continuing sound of the conch.)

HARU: What an annoyance. Mister priest, please don't blow your conch shell so. The master's not feeling well and he can't sleep at night. He's just dozed off. Ah! There it goes again! He won't listen to me. Outrageous priest, won't you ever stop? And on top of it all you're impudent. Entering the house without removing your hat, snooping around—what are you looking for? If you think there are only women in here, you're going to be most sadly disappointed. Well, won't he leave? Why won't he go away?

NARRATOR: Roundly scolded,

---

[11] Born in 634, En the Hermit (En no Gyōja) was the founder of an ascetic Buddhist sect known as Shugendō. Because of his habit of living on mountains and often climbing them to dedicate their peaks to Buddha, his followers are known as *yamabushi*, or mountain priests.

The priest departs the gate,

Goes his way, but casts behind him

Glances of regret.

(Priest exits the way he came.)

HARU *(goes to the sliding shōji doors of the SL room)*: Some stupid lout came around. How is our lady feeling?

NARRATOR: She bows before the shōji.

(The shōji open, revealing Yae and Lady Sugawara, the latter still in her bed.)

HARU: That unexpected blowing of the conch must have wakened her. How is she, Yae? Hasn't her stomach trouble let up any?

YAE: That's just it. Lady Sugawara had just gotten to sleep when the sound of that conch seems to have startled her. She's covered with a cold sweat. That hateful mountain priest!

HARU: Makes me angry too. I didn't give him anything for his begging.

NARRATOR: As the two are talking,

Lady Sugawara rises.

LADY SUGAWARA: No, it wasn't the priest. I had a terrible dream. I'm still shaking from it. Haru, Yae, both of you listen while I tell you my dream. The place was the Anraku Temple in Dazaifu. My husband was rejoicing that his precious plum tree had flown to him in Tsukushi, and at the same time Umeōmaru had come. Right away he composed this poem:

The plum has flown to my side,

The cherry has withered away.

Why in this indifferent world

Yet stands so heartless the pine?

That I can recall this poem verbatim must mean that my dream was true and was a message that something had happened. But there was more: a plot in which Shihei's men were to kill Lord Sugawara. This was discovered, but when my husband heard his would-be assassin's confession about events in the Capital and of the plotting by his enemies to seize the throne, he flew into a rage. Having received no pardon, return to the Capital was impossible, and yet there was danger to the Emperor. He prayed to the Buddhist deity Taishakuten, and he then became the god of thunder. So great was his rage that he set out to destroy Shihei and all in allegiance to him. It was all so violent and frightening that I cannot believe it was just a dream.

YAE: It's only natural that such a dream should cause you anxiety. On the other hand, it may be a false dream, one that tells the reverse of what is true. Then, on the contrary, it is news for rejoicing. Isn't that right, Haru?

HARU: Yes, indeed it is. I'm sure it means that Lord Sugawara will soon return to the Capital. But that awful mountain priest who was just here—nosing around, his face covered by that wicker hat, then leaving without saying a word. I'm really worried about him. It was my husband Umeō's plan that Lady Sugawara come secretly here to North Saga. Might not that priest be an enemy spy come here to smell out her hiding place? Shiradayū and Umeō have both gone off to Tsukushi, and we're here all by ourselves. We cannot stay here any longer. Fortunately, I heard recently that his holiness the priest Hosshōbō has come to Lower Saga Village. He was Lord Sugawara's teacher in the faith, so we should tell him of our difficulties and ask him to help Lady Sugawara. I want to find another hiding place this very day. I'll just run over to where he is and come back. Yae, keep your eyes open for anything. Don't let down your guard.

YAE: Good idea, Haru. That's a lot of trouble for you, but by all means go. Don't worry about us.

NARRATOR: Quite like a gallant man she speaks,
　　　　And Lady Sugawara is most pleased.
LADY SUGAWARA: And Haru, when you see his holiness, please tell him about my dream and find out if it portends good or ill.
HARU: Yes, yes, I understand everything. Well, I must hurry.
NARRATOR: She fumbles with her sash,
　　　　Grabs her wicker hat.
HARU: I'm sure I'll bring back good news.
NARRATOR: In a flurry of excitement
　　　　Off she goes.
(Haru goes out at SR as Yae sees her off from outside the house.)
　　　　Hardly has she gone
　　　　When Hoshizaka Gengo,
　　　　Minion of Shihei,
　　　　Comes upon the scene.
(To a roll of drums, Hoshizaka enters from SR with two armed men.)
HOSHIZAKA: That's Lord Sugawara's wife, for certain.
NARRATOR: With his men he dashes toward the house.
　　　　Swiftly from the lintel
　　　　Yae takes down the halberd;
　　　　A signal from her eyes
　　　　Sends Lady Sugawara
　　　　To the inner room.
(Yae takes the halberd from its hooks on the lintel, whips the brocade cover from its blade. Lady Sugawara enters the SL room and the shōji close about her.)
YAE: Whoever you are, try to force your way in and you'll pay dearly for it!
NARRATOR: She brandishes the halberd.

HOSHIZAKA: Yaaa, impertinent woman! We're here on orders of
    Lord Shihei to take Lady Sugawara. Men, if she tries to stop
    us, cut her down!

NARRATOR: Responding to his orders,
    His men thrust forward,
    Spear tips flashing silver
    Like miscanthus flowers,
    But Yae slashes, cuts them back,
    And scatters them away.

*(The fight, inside then outside the house, is a choreographed se-
quence accompanied by a rhythmical samisen tempo while there
is a pause in the narration. Yae fights off the intruders, chasing
them off at SR.)*

    But too great the numbers
    Against a lone contender,
    And Yae struggles back,
    Ravaged by many a wound,
    Her halberd now a walking staff.

*(She stumbles back from SR, leaning heavily on the halberd, the
upper part of her green robe pulled down, revealing the bright red
one beneath. She enters the house and collapses before Lady Sugawara.)*

YAE: Oh, Lady Sugawara, I couldn't overcome them. Hurry, make
    your . . . escape. Haru hasn't returned? *(Bitter sobs.)* How
    bitter it is to fail you! How wretched to have been of so little
    help!

(Yae falls, and Lady Sugawara takes her in her arms.)

NARRATOR: Thus she speaks and dies.
    At the sight of Yae's tragic death,
    Lady Sugawara clings
    To her lifeless body

And wails her deep lament,
Heedless of all about her.
Hoshizaka runs up quickly

(Hoshizaka enters from SR.)

And is about to drag her off,
When, striding with a slow and measured gait,
In comes the mountain priest
Who was here before.

(No longer wearing his wicker hat, the priest enters from the SR wing.)

PRIEST *(towering above Hoshizaka)*: Here now, for my alms I'll take Lady Sugawara.

NARRATOR: He springs on Hoshizaka,
Seizes him by the neck,
And lifts him higher than the eye.

(Clappers and drums accent the action.)

PRIEST: Off with you to the land of darkness!

NARRATOR: And he smashes him
Into the muddy ground.
Quickly into his arms
He lifts Lady Sugawara.
Then heedless of the rocky fields,
Of roadways strewn with sand,
He runs off as though flying.

Scene 3. The Village School

(About two-thirds of the stage, from the center area extending into the SL wings, is the interior of Takebe Genzō's village school. At center in the room is a curtained doorway to the inner part of the house. The curtain is a medium blue, unadorned. SL of the doorway, students' desks are seen stacked three high against the wall; SR of the doorway is a Buddhist altar, a simple alcove with two potted plants, a plain wooden tray stand, and a hanging scroll displaying Chinese characters. At extreme SL and slanted so that it faces partly toward the audience is a set of four shoji panels. At SR, outside the house, are some bushy shrubs, behind which is a landscape of fields, a farmhouse, and green hills. The forestage is a courtyard in front of the schoolhouse. As the curtain is drawn aside, the stage is uninhabited, but shortly a number of young schoolboys emerge from the inner part of the house, bringing with them their writing desks which they place at SR where they set about writing practice. Another child, Sugawara's son Kan Shūsai, whom Genzō is hiding under the pretext he is his own child, places his desk at SL apart from the other students. The children, including Kan Shūsai, are all dressed in simple padded kimonos with striped patterns of black, green, brown, and rust, varying from child to child.)

NARRATOR: One character learned
    Is a thousand pieces of gold,
    Two thousand pieces of gold—

In all the wide three thousand worlds,
A treasure beyond compare.
Such are the teachings of the brush
Passed on by Takebe Genzō
To the children of his school,
Among whom mingles
The son of Lord Sugawara,
Kan Shūsai,
Cared for and cherished
By Genzō and his wife,
Given out to the world
As a child of their own union.
Genzō has moved his dwelling
To a house in Seryō Village,
Remote within the mountains.
There he gathers about him
The local children
And teaches reading, writing
To apt and awkward alike,
To urchins who smear their faces with ink,
Scribble on their hands,
Draw pictures of their teacher,
And sheepishly scratch their heads
When caught at their roguery.
The teacher, it seems,
Knows all the mischief-makers.
Oldest among the boys
Is the son of farmer Gosaku.

(In the middle of the group of children at SR.)

NOODLEHEAD: Hey everyone, look here. What a big waste to practice calligraphy while the teacher's away. See, I've drawn a picture of a bald-headed man. *(Holds up a caricature face to show the class.)*

NARRATOR: Displaying his drawing

> Is the class clown, Noodlehead,
> A full fifteen years of age.
> Young Kan Shūsai is well behaved.

KAN SHŪSAI *(speaks in a high-pitched voice with rather flat intonation)*: Study one character each day and you will know three hundred sixty in a year, goes the saying. We shouldn't be drawing that sort of thing; it's better to write one's characters properly.

NARRATOR: To be chided by a child

> Only eight years old,
> Piques the oafish Noodlehead.

NOODLEHEAD: Listen to the smarty, listen to him!

NARRATOR: Pointing with his finger,

> He mocks his classmate,
> But into the fray
> Leap the other lads.

ONE OF THE CHILDREN: Noodlehead has too big a mouth. Let's give him a drubbing.

NARRATOR: One following another,

> They brandish their paper weights,
> Spontaneously rising
> To Kan Shūsai's defense—
> Drawn to his side perhaps
> By the virtue and the power
> Of his father's calligraphic art.

(A general melee ensues as the boys pile on Noodlehead at center stage, while Kan Shūsai remains out of the disorder at SL.)

> From within comes Genzō's wife Tonami.

TONAMI: What's this! Fighting again as usual! You really try one's patience. Just today my husband Genzō has been invited out, and I don't know when he'll return. Whenever he is gone, you all are such rascals that I can't wait for him to come back. And especially today, when a new child is supposed to enter school. I'll let you off at noon, so work hard, work hard.

CHILDREN: Yippee! A holiday!

NARRATOR: Down go the brushes,
　　　　Up go the voices
　　　　Reading off their lessons.

1st CHILD: "I, RO, HA, NI . . ."

2D CHILD: "Yours, honored sir, of a recent date received . . ."

3D CHILD: "Respectfully taking brush in hand, I your humble . . ."[12]

NARRATOR: . . . servant in accompaniment,
　　　　On his shoulder a balance pole
　　　　Hung with both a tiered container
　　　　And a desk and chest for school,
　　　　Enters an alert young wife,
　　　　Leading by the hand a child
　　　　Of but seven years.

(From SR enters Chiyo, wife of Matsuōmaru. Chiyo and her son Kotarō are followed by a servant, Sansuke, carrying a balance pole loaded with the school chest and desk and a tiered lacquer box.)

CHIYO: Is anyone at home?

NARRATOR: At her greeting,
　　　　She is quickly answered from within.

[12] The first child recites the Japanese syllabary, much as an English-speaking child reels off the ABCs. The second and third children parrot typical opening phrases used in formal correspondence. Through a pun, the end of the third child's speech leads into the narrator's lines.

(Tonami comes to the doorway.)

TONAMI: Please, do come in.

CHIYO: Oh, thank you.

(Chiyo enters the house with her son. The two women bow to each other.)

NARRATOR: This cordial exchange—
>   Each woman drawn
>   By love for a son—
>   Betrays their common bond.
>   With a smile,
>   The visitor continues.

CHIYO: I live in a modest fashion some distance from your village. When I came to inquire if I might place this child in your school, the master was gracious enough to accept him. Taking advantage of his kindness, I have presumed to bring the boy over right away. I'm afraid you will find him terribly spoiled. I understand that you too have a child in the school. Which one might he be?

TONAMI *(indicating Kan Shūsai)*: Yes, this is Genzō's son.

(Her half-opened gold-and-silver-colored fan at her chin, Chiyo looks at him carefully, comparing him with her own son.)

CHIYO: My my, what a fine young man. It must be quite a burden for you with all the other children.

TONAMI: Oh, you're most kind. Well now, this child is to be the new pupil? What is his name?

CHIYO: We call him Kotarō. I'm afraid he's a very naughty boy.

TONAMI: Oh no. He's a very noble, a fine lad. Unfortunately, my husband Genzō has been invited out today.

CHIYO: Oh, he isn't at home?

TONAMI: If you wish to see him right away, I'll be happy to go and call him.

(She starts to get up, but Chiyo stops her.)

CHIYO: Oh no, it happens that there is somewhere I must go. In the meantime, I'm sure he will be back when I return. Sansuke, bring the things you've brought over to this lady.

(Sansuke, the servant, has been dozing off outside. At Chiyo's words, he awakes with a start.)

SANSUKE: Uh? . . . Oh, yes madam.

NARRATOR: Both tiered box
>   And package on a tray
>   He places near Tonami.

TONAMI: Oh, you shouldn't have gone to such trouble.

CHIYO *(bowing):* I'm embarrassed it is so modest, just a memento of this visit. This box is a present for the children. Please pass it among them.

NARRATOR: Buns of bean jam,
>   Steamed cakes of fish and greens—
>   Though its contents go unspoken,
>   This gift to one entrusted
>   With the young boy's care
>   Betokens a mother's adoring love
>   For her cherished child.

(The two bow to each other. While they do so, Noodlehead sneaks his hand into the box of cakes and steals one, dashing off. Miming her actions, Tonami scolds him mildly. The two women look at each other and laugh at the incident.)

TONAMI: My, you've been so thoughtful in everything. I must show all this to my husband when he returns.

CHIYO: Oh no, it's merely a token. Permit me to leave the boy in your care. Kotarō, I'm going to the next village for a while. Behave yourself and wait for me here. Don't get into any mischief. Well, madam, I'll be going now.

NARRATOR: As she moves to the gate: . . .

KOTARŌ: Mother, I want to go too.

NARRATOR: He clings to her,
  But she brushes him aside.
(Her hand on Kotarō's shoulder, Chiyo fights back the tears, then regains her composure.)
CHIYO: Oh, come now, son. A big boy like you, you're going to tag after mother? *(To Tonami, laughing):* You see, he's such a baby.
TONAMI: That's only natural. *(To Kotarō):* Look, auntie has something nice for you. Please hurry back, madam.
NARRATOR: A glance from Tonami
  Hurries her on.
CHIYO: Yes, well, I'll be on my way.
NARRATOR: Drawn back by the child
  Who would follow her,
  Backwards she casts
  Many a parting glance.
  Then, taking her servant along,
  She hurries on her way.
(Looking back at Kotarō, she bumps into the dozing Sansuke, scolds him, then quickly recovers, snapping her fan open to hide her tearful face. The fan still at her face, she exits downstage right, followed by Sansuke carrying his now unburdened shoulder pole. Tonami leads Kotarō into the inner room through the center stage curtained doorway, leaving Kan Shūsai and the other children on stage.
  This marks the end of the scene known as "Entering the School." Normally there is a change of narrator and accompanist. Tonami returns from the inner room with Kotarō and takes him to where Kan Shūsai is sitting.)
TONAMI *(to Kotarō):* Here, come along and get acquainted with this boy.
NARRATOR: To the young lord's side

She brings Kotarō,
And as she tries to lead his mind
From thoughts of loneliness . . .
Her husband Genzō returns,
An unwonted pallor in his face,
Sunk in brooding
As he enters his home
And looks about at the children.

(Genzō enters from SR, his arms folded across his chest, head bowed and deep in throught. He enters the house and looks disapprovingly at his students working at their desks.)

GENZŌ: Hmmm, just as the saying goes, "Upbringing surpasses pedigree." So unlike those from houses of the noble and the wealthy, every one of these children bears the marks of a peasant. Nothing has come of the trouble I've taken with them. They'll not serve my purpose. *(Sits at center stage.)*

NARRATOR: So troubled of mind he seems,
His wife moves to his side,
Misgiving in her heart.

TONAMI: I've never seen you so pale. You must have had a bit too much to drink at your party. Of course these are peasant children, but it does your reputation no good to speak ill of them. Especially today, when the new pupil has come. It would be an unfortunate thing for him to think of you as being ill-natured. Brighten up and meet him.

NARRATOR: She brings Kotarō to him,
But Genzō remains with lowered head,
Deep in thought.
With childish charm
Kotarō bows to his teacher.

KOTARŌ: Master teacher, please accept me henceforth as your obedient pupil.

NARRATOR: At his words,
　　　　　Unthinking,
　　　　　Genzō lifts his face
　　　　　And looks intently at the child.
(Genzō unfolds his arms, looks fixedly at Kotarō. Then quietly glances at Kan Shūsai, back again at Kotarō. He raises his eyebrows with interest.)
　　　　　He pauses for a moment,
　　　　　Staring at the boy.
　　　　　Then suddenly
　　　　　His expression softens.
(Genzō's general demeanor is now more cordial.)
GENZŌ: Well well, look here. What a handsome, what an excellent lad. One wouldn't hesitate to say he was from a princely or a noble family. Indeed, what a fine boy you are. *(Laughs.)*
NARRATOR: Though puzzled
　　　　　At this sudden turn of humor,
　　　　　Tonami joins in the praise.
TONAMI: Yes, he'll make a fine disciple, won't he.
GENZŌ: Excellent indeed, superb. Where is the mother who brought him here?
TONAMI: Since you were out, she said she would just go to the next village for a while and then come back.
GENZŌ: Oh, that's good, that's splendid! Well, run along now inside and play nicely with the other children.
TONAMI: That will be all, children. Here, take Kotarō along with you inside.
NARRATOR: She beckons to them all,
　　　　　Including Kan Shūsai.
(The children leave through the center curtained doorway, clumsy Noodlehead leading Kotarō by the hand. Genzō removes his cloak and divided skirt, sits facing Tonami.)

Then, glancing around,
She turns toward her husband.

TONAMI: I was puzzled when you seemed so troubled just a while ago. And now, having seen that new child, you've changed completely, you're in fine spirits. I'm all the more perplexed. There must be something wrong. Don't be upset. Tell me what's the matter.

GENZŌ (*straightens up, puts both hands on knees*): And well I should be upset! Being invited out to a party turned out to be a trick. I was summoned to the village headman's house, and there was Shihei's retainer Shundō Genba along with another person—Matsuōmaru, that blackguard who serves Shihei even though he owes everything to Lord Sugawara. He was weak from an illness, but even so it appeared he was to be in charge of an investigation. I was quickly surrounded by several hundred of his men, and he said to me: "We know from an informant that you're hiding Lord Sugawara's son Kan Shūsai in your house, pretending he's your own child. You are to cut off his head at once. Or, shall we break in ourselves and take him into custody? What's your answer?" I was in an impossible position with nowhere to turn. There was nothing for me to do but agree to deliver his head.

(*Tonami cries out in a mixture of astonishment and dismay.*)

GENZO (*continues*): I was thinking that among all the children in the school, one of them might do for a substitute. I counted them off on my fingers (*mimes the action*) all the way home, but there is simply no way a child of noble birth can resemble one brought up in a rough country hut. As I was coming back, I felt how pitiful, how wretched it all was; had our luck finally run out? I felt like an animal being led to the slaughterhouse. Perhaps it's the power of providence, but when I saw that new pupil with such noble features, it was like seeing a white heron among black crows! Once we've deceived Matsuōmaru by substituting that boy for Kan Shūsai, we'll escape from here and take the young lord directly to Lord Sugawara's aunt in Kawachi. But, for a while the situation is going to be touch and go.

TONAMI: But wait! That scoundrel Matsuō is the evil one among the three brothers, and he surely remembers the young lord's face.

GENZŌ: Well, that's a chance we must take. There's a difference between a living face and a dead one. Kotarō looks rather like Kan Shūsai, so it's just possible Matsuō won't think the head's a fake. If by chance, however, he should see through the scheme, I'll cut the villain in two and fight it out with the rest of his men. If that fails, then I'm determined we'll die with the young lord and be his escort in the other world. But there's still one problem. When Kotarō's mother comes back for him, what are we going to do? I don't know, and right now that's our main problem.

TONAMI: Don't worry about that. We women know how to have our way with people. I'll see if I can work some deception on her.

GENZŌ: No, that's not likely to work. Important affairs are ruined by a small carelessness. Depending on how things go, the mother too may have to be . . .

(Both are still seated. At the words "Depending on . . . ," Genzō speaks slowly, thoughtfully; with ". . . the mother too . . ." he is speaking with tense emotion. He picks up his sword with his left hand, places his right hand on the hilt.)

TONAMI: Oh no! *(Sinks to the floor, drained of strength.)*

GENZŌ: Stop it! We cannot exchange Kan Shūsai's life for anyone's. You know it's for our lord's sake!

NARRATOR: At his words

Tonami braces herself.

TONAMI *(controlling herself with effort)*: Yes, you're right. If we are weak of will, we may fail. We must have no compassion.

NARRATOR: Husband and wife stand up,

Exchanging heartfelt glances.

(They rise, facing each other, tense, Genzō with his right hand on the hilt of his sword.)

GENZŌ: My pupils are the same as my own children.

TONAMI: Can all this be due to the child's own misdeeds from a previous life, or is it retribution upon his mother that he has come to our school on this of all days?

GENZŌ: And we must be the ones to carry out the punishment of this retribution. *(Brings his right sleeve up to wipe the tears from his face. Looks down dejectedly.)*

TONAMI: Soon we too will surely be visited with our own retribution. *(Sinks to the floor in tears; holding to Genzō's waist, she looks up at him.)*

NARRATOR: As his wife weeps piteously,

Genzō too wipes his tearful eyes.

GENZŌ: None suffer such hurt and sadness as those lowly ones who serve noble masters at the court.

NARRATOR: Both are dissolved in tears.

At this very moment,

Upon the scene arrives

Shundō Genba,

Followed in a palanquin

By the sickly Matsuōmaru,

His duty to identify

The severed head.

(Genba enters from downstage right; he clutches in his right hand a fan and a cylindrical wooden container for the head. Genba is

followed by a palanquin borne by two porters. Inside the house, Tonami looks toward the gate, then slips quietly out through the center curtained doorway. In her place Genzō goes and stands at the doorway to the house.)

> At the gate
> The palanquin is set down,
> And in its wake arrives
> A crowd of villagers.

(Four peasants enter from SR, approach Genba, bow very low. Each wears a plain padded kimono, a white towel tied about the head.)

1ST PEASANT: Sir.

2D PEASANT: Sir.

3D PEASANT: Sir.

4TH PEASANT: Sir.

ALL TOGETHER: Sir, please sir, oh sir.

1ST PEASANT *(bowing frequently):* Please sir, all of us have children who have come here to learn their writing. If there is some mistake and one has his head chopped off, that's something that can't be undone.

2ND PEASANT: Please sir, return them to us.

NARRATOR: To their entreaties
> Genba replies with scorn.

GENBA: Don't annoy me, you sniveling maggots! Don't you think
> I know who are your brats? Take them and get out of here.

NARRATOR: Upon this tongue-lashing
> Matsuōmaru intrudes.

MATSUŌMARU: Hold on! Wait a moment, Genba.

NARRATOR: He emerges from the palanquin,
> Using his sword for a cane.

(Matsuo's ill condition is indicated by two things: a lavender band about his head, and a bushy black wig known as a hyaku-nichi,

or "hundred days" wig, implying that his illness has made it im-
possible for some time to have his hair cut and dressed. Two large
flat-folded sections of stiff white paper rise in a V from the back
of his head.)

MATSUŌMARU: Your pardon for breaking in, but we cannot be too
    careful about these people. I am ill, yet the task of identi-
    fication falls upon me, since there are no others who would
    recognize Kan Shūsai. I have requested of my master Lord
    Shihei that, because of illness, I be given leave once today's
    duty has been carried out. Grateful for his permission, I shall
    give full attention to my charge. Since a relative of Lord
    Sugawara has been placed in this village, these farmers may
    conspire to aid Kan Shūsai by taking him away on the pre-
    tense that he's one of their sons. *(To the peasants):* Shut up
    and listen, you miserable clod-turners. Call out your brats
    one by one. After we've examined the face of each one, you
    can take him home.

NARRATOR: The farmers stand rooted to the spot,
        As though nailed down,
        Clamped in place
        By Matsuō's fierce words—
        Words that find response
        Inside the house,
        As Genzō and his wife,
        Though prepared to meet the worst,
        Feel their hearts pound with the fear
        Their efforts have come to naught.

(Genzō, using his sheathed sword, urges Tonami out through the
curtained door. He then exits into the room at SL. Genba seats
himself outside the doorway to the house to await the children.
Matsuō sits on his right.)

        Outside the house,
        Unaware of the dread within,

> A white-haired father
> Calls loudly from the gate.

1ST PEASANT: Chōmatsu, hey Chōmatsu!

NARRATOR: An answering response to his call,
> And out comes a child,
> His mischievous face
> Besmeared with writing ink—
> No more like Kan Shūsai
> Than charcoal is to snow.

(Genba holds out his fan to stop the child, looks at Matsuō.)
> "Not him," says Matsuō,
> And lets him go.

2D PEASANT: Iwamatsu, you in there?

CHILD: What is it, grandpa?

NARRATOR: In answer to his call,
> A small boy races out,

(Child skips out playfully.)
> His innocent rotund face
> Like an eggplant wrenched from the vine.

MATSUŌMARU: No need to examine him! Let him go.

NARRATOR: . . . and Matsuō glares . . .

2D PEASANT: Oh, oh, oh dear, how frightful! Here, this grandchild of mine—so precious I don't even trust his own mother
with him. I feel as though I've plucked my little eggplant
from the very jaws of death!

NARRATOR: Holding the child in his arms,
> Away he runs. Next to emerge
> Is fifteen-year-old Noodlehead,
> Who comes to his father's beckoning.

3D PEASANT: Bo - - - y! Oh, my boy!

NOODLEHEAD: Papa, give me a ride home.

NARRATOR: Rotten spoiled, the face of a horse,
> His voice like a cricket's chirp.

(Noodlehead runs out, pauses outside the doorway for inspection. Genba raps him on the head with his fan. Noodlehead bawls as he goes to his father, who makes him blow his nose.)

3D PEASANT: Oh, don't you cry now. I'll carry you.

(He hoists Noodlehead onto his back but collapses under the weight. Noodlehead then reverses the procedure, carrying his father off through the SR curtain. Much of this stage business has been adapted by the puppets from kabuki.)

NARRATOR: Purring like a cat

       Carrying off a salmon,

       The father pampers his child

       As off they go.

4TH PEASANT: My son's a handsome one, he is. Please don't go and mistake him for the one you're looking for.

NARRATOR: The father makes his pleas,

       And the son he summons forth

       Is truly white of skin and oval-faced.

MATSUŌMARU: This one's suspicious.

(Matsuō holds out his sheathed sword to stop the child. Genba straightens up and regards the boy sharply.)

NARRATOR: He stops the child and looks:

       So grimy black his neck

       One cannot tell if it be

       Writing ink or birthmark.

       "Not this one," Matsuō growls

       And pushes the lad on.

       One and all, the rest are summoned out—

       Children from mountain hamlets

       And from rustic villages,

       But among them none, of course,

       Resembles him they seek.

       All are sons of the earth—

Like so many little potatoes
Sold in fields by the pound—
And by his parent each is carried off.

*(The foregoing action involving the school children is performed
in a generally light-hearted vein as a contrast to the tense preceding scene and the tragic one that follows.)*

Knowing that the time has come,
Genzō and Tonami steel themselves.
Hardly a moment have they waited,
When in come their two visitors.

*(Genzō emerges from the SL room, Tonami from the curtained
doorway. Both prostrate themselves near the entrance of the house.
Genba enters first, striding arrogantly across the room and seating himself at far left. Matsuō follows more slowly, leaning on
his sword. He sits in the center, holding his long sword vertically
on the floor with his left hand. One of Genba's followers comes
to downstage center and places the head casket in the room near
Matsuō.)*

GENBA: Well, Genzō, you agreed to behead Kan Shūsai before
my very eyes. I've come for his head. Quickly, hand it over.

NARRATOR: He presses his demand,

But Genzō displays no fear.

GENZŌ: I cannot just unceremoniously behead the young son of
the exalted Minister of the Right. I beg you for a little time.

NARRATOR: As he rises, Matsuō speaks.

MATSUŌMARU: That ruse won't work—trying to gain time in order to prepare for an escape. I've stationed several hundred
men on the back roads. There's not even room for an ant
to crawl through. And if you're thinking a live face and a
dead one look different . . . *(sneering laugh)* heh, heh . . .
using a substitute won't work either. Don't try old tricks you'll
regret.

NARRATOR: Genzō's anger bursts forth.

GENZŌ: Stupid precautions that serve no purpose! Your eyes, clouded by illness, must have done a back flip on you, so that everything you see appears upside down. But I will show you the unmistakable head of Kan Shūsai!

MATSUŌMARU: Enough talking. Behead the boy!

GENBA: Be quick about it!

NARRATOR: Arrogantly,

> Genba flaunts his power.
> Genzō takes a deep breath,
> And making up his mind,
> He leaves the room.

(He quickly picks up the head casket and moves slightly toward Matsuō, looks intently at both Matsuō and Genba, trying to read each man's heart. Genba shoots a sharp glance at Genzō. At Genba's glance, Genzō quickly alters his mood and walks rapidly from the room, exiting through the center curtained doorway.)

> Tonami, listening nearby,
> Is absorbed with the thought
> That now is the moment of truth.
> With their eyes, the two officials
> Search every nook of the room.
> Matsuōmaru counts
> The desks and writing chests.

MATSUŌMARU: What's this? There's something odd here. Eight children left just now, but there's one extra desk. Where is that child?

NARRATOR: At Matsuō's challenge

> Tonami catches her breath.

TONAMI: Ah . . . that one . . . ah, today a child entered the scho— . . . I mean, paid a visit to the temple.

MATSUŌMARU *(shouting sharply)*: What! That's nonsense!

TONAMI: Oh, I mean . . . that is to say . . . that is Kan Shū-sai's desk and writing box.

NARRATOR: Just as paint conceals
　　　　　The wooden desk's fine grain,
　　　　　She tries to evade the answer.

MATSUŌMARU: Well, whatever, he's taking too long. Something's amiss.

NARRATOR: Genba and Matsuō
　　　　　Rise impatiently.

(Genba stands up abruptly, Matsuō rising more slowly as he leans heavily on his sword.)

　　　　　In this room they stand
　　　　　On the threshold
　　　　　Between life and death.
　　　　　From within is heard
　　　　　The sickening sound
　　　　　Of the beheading.

(A sound from offstage.)

　　　　　Tonami clasps her breast,
　　　　　Stands petrified on the spot.

(At the sound of clappers, Matsuō drops his sword, seems to reel. He then picks up the sword, rests it on his left shoulder, his right hand raised to hide the distress on his face. Genba stops in mid-step, both hands on his sword hilt. Tonami crumples to the floor.)

　　　　　Takebe Genzō . . . slowly enters,
　　　　　Bearing on a white wood tray
　　　　　The casket with the severed head.
　　　　　He places it before the two men's eyes.

GENZŌ: Though far beyond my wish, . . . *(then, slowly and with emotion)* . . . I have beheaded Kan Shūsai. It is . . . a most precious head. Compose yourself, Matsuō, and . . . *(pause)* . . . examine it with care.

(Genzō watches Matsuō carefully. Matsuō lays down his sword. As he reaches for the head casket, Genzō leans forward aggressively, placing his right hand on the casket. Matsuō withdraws slightly, and the two men's eyes meet in mutually searching scrutiny. Genba, seated on a stool at SL, braces himself, leans forward, hand on sword hilt, watching intently.)

NARRATOR: Stealthily, from its scabbard
> Genzō loosens the hilt of his sword.
> "Call it false, I'll kill him;
> Pronounce it genuine,
> I will spare his life," thinks Genzō
> As he waits in breathless tension.

(During this time, Matsuō sits before the casket, motionless but for his eyes which roll first toward Genzō, then to Genba.)

MATSUŌMARU *(a growling laugh)*: Ha ha ha ha ha. For such a thing as this, I should compose myself, you say? *(Sneering)*: Ha ha ha ha. I am that mirror of the seat of judgment that reflects a dead man's life. This is the moment when we know whether he goes to hell, his name inscribed on iron, or travels with a golden badge to paradise.[13] Guards! Watch these two.

GUARDS: At once, sir.

(Two guards stand behind Genzō and Tonami, their truncheons raised above their heads.)

NARRATOR: The guards stand near them,
> Waving their truncheons.
> Tonami steels herself;
> Her husband is intent and poised.

---

[13]Reference to the belief that there was in the underworld a mirror that reflected the good and bad deeds of the dead. Sinners had their names placed on iron tablets and were sent to hell; the good received nameplates of gold and were sent to paradise.

GENZŌ *(leaning forward, both hands on his knees):* Now, Matsuō, the examination. Commence your inspection!
NARRATOR: His very life hangs on the words.
Behind them the guards;
Before them, villainous Matsuō;
And Genba keeps a ceaseless vigil.
Now is the desperate moment.
Quickly Matsuō draws the casket to him.
He opens it, and within—
The head of Kotarō.
Genzō loosens his blade,
Prepared for that single slash
Should Matsuō pronounce it fake.
Fervently Tonami prays for pity
To all the gods and Buddhas
Of heaven and of earth.
(Matsuō takes folded paper from his breast, gently wipes the head. Adjusting his seat, he leans forward toward the head.)
Matsuō—wary, searching—
With rapt attention
Regards the severed head.
MATSUŌMARU: Ah! That he has beheaded Kan Shūsai . . . *(deliberately and with great emotion)* . . . there can be no doubt, no question. *(Replaces the casket cover. As he pronounces his judgment, Matsuō looks first at Genzō, then searchingly at Genba.)*
NARRATOR: Jolted with amazement
At what they hear,
Genzō and Tonami stare
At each other in disbelief.
Genba accepts as proof
Matsuō's pronouncement.

(Genba picks up the head casket and starts from the room.)

GENBA: Excellent, excellent. You've done well, Genzō. As a reward, you are forgiven for hiding Kan Shūsai. Come on, Matsuō. Let's report immediately to Lord Shihei.

MATSUŌMARU: To be sure. He will not wish us to waste time. However, I would now like to take my leave and recuperate from my illness.

GENBA: Your task is completed. Do as you please.

NARRATOR: Off to his lord's mansion
        Genba takes the casket.

(Exits at SR.)

        Weakly, Matsuō
        Enters his palanquin,
        And leaves.

(Leaning heavily on his sword, Matsuō sadly watches Genba depart. He recovers his composure and gets into the palanquin outside the house at SR and is carried off.)

        The couple hurriedly bar the gate.
        Incapable of speech,
        They are breathless, drained,
        Can only sigh with relief.
        Regaining his composure,
        Genzō gives prayerful thanks
        Up to the gods of heaven,
        Down to the gods of earth.

GENZŌ: Thanks be to heaven! The gods be praised! The virtue of our master has manifest itself. It was a divine miracle that clouded Matsuō's eyes so he mistook the head for that of the young lord. Now will the young master live ten thousand years! Rejoice, my wife!

TONAMI: No ordinary happiness, this. Was it Lord Sugawara who was in that Matsuō's eyes? Or did a shining golden Buddha stand in place of that head as he watched? That child may have vaguely resembled the young lord, but they were as different as a roof tile is from gold. Ah, so happy am I that the golden flower of our young lord's destiny has opened with such promise, tears overcome me. How thankful I am, what a precious thing his life.

NARRATOR: Yet, in the midst of their joy
    Kotarō's mother runs in,
    Breathless, to meet her son.
    She knocks upon the gate.

(Chiyo runs in from the SR curtain, casting glances behind her.)

CHIYO: I am the mother of the new child. I've just returned.

(Tonami is surprised, runs to Genzō at center stage.)

TONAMI: Just through one crisis, now another! Oh, what shall we do?

NARRATOR: Though Tonami is in a ferment,
    Her husband remains calm.

(Genzō picks up his sword.)

GENZŌ: Quiet! This is just the problem we spoke of before. We must save the young lord's life at all costs. Don't be so nervous. Get hold of yourself!

(Using his sheathed sword, Genzō urges Tonami out the curtained doorway. Holding his sword behind his back, he goes to the gate.)

NARRATOR: He pulls Tonami aside.
    With a jerk, he opens the gate.
    The woman bows.

CHIYO: Oh! Is it Master Genzō? I've come for that mischievous child of mine. Where might he be? I'm sure he must have been a bother for you.

(She bows, peers beyond Genzō into the room.)

NARRATOR: Genzō uses her words to advantage.

GENZŌ: Oh no. He's inside playing with the other children. You
   may take him home if you wish.

NARRATOR: His face is solemn.

CHIYO (*slowly, as though searching Genzō's heart*): Oh . . . then
   in that case, I will take him home.

*(She bows again and moves toward SL, never dropping her guard.
As she advances into the room, Genzō gradually moves in behind
her.)*

NARRATOR: Genzō watches her pass,
            Then, from behind—
            Just one blow, he thinks,
            And tries to cut her down.
            Though but a woman,
            The resourceful Chiyo dodges,
            But Genzō allows no escape.
            With her child's school chest,
            Desperately she fends off
            His sharp-bladed attack.

*(The struggle is a closely choreographed sequence, with the two
exchanging sides of the stage. As Genzō brings his sword down a
second time, Chiyo—now on SR—holds aloft the school chest,
blocking the blow.)*

CHIYO: Wait! Please wait! What are you doing?

NARRATOR: Relentless the keen-edged sword,
            As again it strikes,
            Splitting the box in two.
            Scattering from within it
            Fall sheets of scriptures,
            A burial robe for a child,
            And a banner of white cloth
            Imprinted with a Buddhist prayer.

(Genzō hesitates in his attack.)

GENZŌ: What . . . what is this?
(Poised, sword raised.)
NARRATOR: In his consternation
        The barb of his attack is dulled,
        It seems he cannot press on.
(As Genzō looks on perplexedly, Matsuō enters quickly from SR and waits tensely outside the gate. He is now dressed all in black. A dark cowl conceals his face.)
        The mother of Kotarō
        Speaks through her tears.
CHIYO: Did my son serve well as a substitute for Kan Shūsai? Or did he not? I must know!
NARRATOR: Genzō is dumbfounded.
GENZŌ: But . . . then . . . you *sent* him for that purpose? *(He lowers the sword, stares intently at Chiyo.)*
CHIYO: That's right, I sent him. If not, why these burial robes?
GENZŌ: Then . . . whose wife are you?
NARRATOR: As he questions her,
        From the gate comes a voice.
MATSUŌMARU *(enters the house as he removes the cowl and recites the following poem):*
        The plum has flown to my side,
        The cherry has withered away.
        Why in this indifferent world
        Yet stands so heartless the pine?
        Rejoice wife! Our son has been of service.
NARRATOR: Scarcely has she heard the words
        Than Chiyo gives way to convulsive tears.
MATSUŌMARU: Don't quarrel with your lot, wife.
NARRATOR: Matsuō enters the room,
        Passing by Genzō and his wife.
(At the sight of Matsuō, Genzō is about to attack him, but Mat-

suō holds out a restraining hand, then throws down both his swords before Genzō, a sign that he is defenseless and wishes no contest.)

> They stand amazed yet a second time
> At the scene before them.
> Is it but a dream?
> Or can it be reality?
> This is Matsuō's wife?
> Staggered by the thought,
> The two stand speechless.
> Takebe Genzō straightens himself.

GENZŌ: Let's dispense with courtesies. I cannot understand at all this sudden change, Matsuō. Until now we thought you our enemy.

MATSUŌMARU *(much softer in tone):* Oh, quite natural for you to be suspicious. As you know, Genzō, we three brothers went our separate ways into official employment, and through a wretched fate I, Matsuō, entered the service of Lord Shihei. I cut off all ties with my father and brothers, and I became an enemy of Lord Sugawara, to whom I owe so very much. Though done at my master's command, everything has been for me a terrible disaster. I wanted to end my service with Shihei, but when I pretended to be ill and begged leave to retire, he told me he would grant the request if I identified Kan Shūsai's head—hence my role in today's events. I knew you could not possibly kill the young lord, but without a child to use as a substitute I didn't know what to do. Now indeed, I thought *(slaps his knee decisively)*, now was the time to repay my debt of gratitude to Lord Sugawara. I discussed the matter with my wife Chiyo, and we decided to send our only son ahead. He became the substitute. My counting the children's desks was to make sure he had come. Lord Sugawara knew what was truly in my heart. "Why stands so heartless the pine?" he wrote. Thus others have come to read the poem as meaning *(slowly, with great emotion)* Matsuō is without a heart, indifferent, and I have had to bear the shame. Have compassion for me, Genzō. *(Matsuō clasps his hands in supplication to Genzō.)* To those who would say "he who is without a son remains but a beast," I would answer, "most precious to a man is a son!"

NARRATOR: At his words, his wife
    Is choked again with tears.

CHIYO: If from the shadows of the grave, Kotarō could hear you, how happy he would be. *(Weeps.)* "Most precious to a man is a son"—how fitting an offering to our child. How it saddens me to think that the last time we parted, I scolded him . . . scolded him when, so unlike his usual self, he wanted to come with me. *(Weeps.)* Did he already have some premonition that entering the village school was but the beginning of his journey to death? I said I was going to the next village, but halfway there I came back. And yet, having sent my child to his death, how could I expect him to be able . . . to be able to come home? *(More weeping, at first fought back, then becoming full-throated sobs.)* I wanted once more at least to see his face, even in death, and for this my husband laughs and chides me for my frailty. *(Her lines now become more song and poetry.)*

    The coins I wrapped and brought
    As a token for his teacher
    Have become a funerary offering.
    I even had him bring as gifts
    Sweet buns, and these are now
    Oblations for the dead.
    Can there be in all the world
    Such sadness as is here?

Had his birth, his care,
Been rustic and humble,
No thought there would have been to kill him.

(Chiyo picks up the prayer banner, holds it for Matsuō to see, then clasps it to her breast.)

"How fair the child died young,"
The proverb goes.
Born so fair, my son,
How cruel has been your misfortune.
What is the nature of a fate
That thusfar in grave illness
Has spared him, only
To let this come to pass?

NARRATOR: Now choked with tears,
She flings herself down
And weeps anew.
Grieving with her,
Tonami comes to her side.

TONAMI: A little while ago, when my husband thought of using the boy as a substitute, Kotarō went to his side and said, "Master teacher, please accept me henceforth as your obedient pupil." When I think back on that scene, stranger though I am, yet it breaks my heart. How much more the heart of a parent.

NARRATOR: She joins in common tears.

MATSUŌMARU: No, do not cry, Tonami. And you, wife, why are you bawling? We made up our minds on the substitution. Didn't you cry enough at home? Control yourself in front of others. *(Though a rebuke, the foregoing is not harsh, but is essentially a scolding for the sake of form in front of another person. Now, more gently, to Genzō.)* Now, Genzō, I was careful to tell the boy what to do before sending him to you. Doubtless he was . . . was . . . unmanly in his death.

(Matsuō leans eagerly toward Genzō, nervously opening and closing his fan. Chiyo too now pays close attention to Genzō.)

GENZŌ: Oh no. When I instructed him that he was to be the substitute for the young lord Kan Shūsai, he . . . he bravely thrust out his neck.

MATSUŌMARU: He didn't try to . . . to run or hide?

GENZŌ *(choking with emotion):* He just . . . smiled. *(Holds his hands before his face to hide the sorrow and the tears.)*

MATSUŌMARU: Oh! He smiled! *(Laughs.)* Ha ha ha ha . . . ha . . . *(chokes up, begins to weep, using his fan to hide his face from Genzō)* . . . aha aha ahaa ahaa *(checks himself, again laughs)* . . . ha ha ha ha . . . *(again melts into racking sobs)* . . . ahaha ahaha ahaaahaa . . . *(the laugh is now shorter, more forced)* ha ha ha *(again the sobbing)* . . . uhuh uhuh . . . uhuuuuh . . . .

(This alternation between weeping, choking, and increasingly painful laughter continues as Matsuō expresses pride at his son's courage and grief at his death. Matsuō finally draws a fold of tissues from his breast, covers his face and succumbs to unrestrained sobbing. One of the emotional peaks of this scene, the nakiwarai, *or laughing through tears, lasts nearly a minute and a half before Matsuō regains his poise.)*

MATSUŌMARU: He did well. Sharp-minded lad, splendid lad . . . brave . . . lad!

(Again the narration becomes song.)

> At the tender age of eight or nine,[14]
> He repays for his parents
> Their debt of gratitude.
> When I think how well he took his part—

[14] There is an inconsistency here: Kotarō, as he enters the village school, is said to be "but seven years." The playwright wished to alliterate further the sounds *yatsu* ("lad" in the preceding line, "eight" in this one), but surely no member of the audience, caught up in the emotions of the scene, would have noticed or been concerned with chronology.

As faithful son, as stalwart hero—
To mind comes Sakuramaru.
Debt unrequited, he was first to die,
Now even from the shadows of the grave,
How he must envy this moment.
(Weeps.)
In thinking on my son,
I remember,
I remember Sakuramaru.

NARRATOR: Like his brother
From the same womb sprung,
Small wonder he cannot forget,
And tears of grief consume him.

CHIYO: Oh, Kotarō will meet his uncle Sakuramaru in the after-
world. *(Goes over to the grieving Matsuō.)*

NARRATOR: She clings fast to her husband
And sinks down in tears.
Kan Shūsai hears her grieving voice
And comes out from the inner room.

*(Kan Shūsai emerges from the SL room, now richly dressed as be-
fits his rank. Matsuō and Chiyo notice him, draw back and bow.)*

KAN SHŪSAI: Had I known he was serving as substitute for me, I
would never have let it be done. The poor child.

NARRATOR: He soaks his sleeve with tears,
As Matsuō and Chiyo
Join in tears of thanks.

MATSUŌMARU: Oh, and now I have a gift for our young lord.

NARRATOR: Matsuō leaps up.

(Matsuō leaves the room, goes out the gate and to downstage SR.)

MATSUŌMARU *(calling out)*: Quickly, quickly bring in the palanquin I ordered.

NARRATOR: His men respond to the call,

And place the palanquin
Before the young master.

(Two bearers bring in the palanquin from SR.)

MATSUŌMARU: Come in, come in. *(He goes to the palanquin, opens its sliding panel and leads out Lady Sugawara.)*

NARRATOR: He opens the door, and from it emerges
The wife of Lord Sugawara.

KAN SHŪSAI: Mother?

LADY SUGAWARA: My child!

(They embrace.)

NARRATOR: At the unexpected meeting,
Genzō and his wife
Clap their hands for joy.

GENZŌ: We've asked about you everywhere. Where have you been?

MATSUŌ: Let me tell you. Shihei's men found out about the secret house she was in at North Saga Village, and I learned that they were going there to capture her. I disguised myself as a mountain priest and saved her from the danger. I then quickly escorted her to Kawachi Province where she met Lady Kariya. *(Pause.)* Now wife, let us place Kotarō's body in that palanquin and see that he is laid to rest.

CHIYO *(choked with tears)*: Yes.

NARRATOR: But before she can act,
Tonami, reading their hearts,
Brings in the body of Kotarō.

(Tonami enters from the SL room bearing Kotarō's body wrapped in white cloth. She places it in the palanquin at downstage right.)

Into the palanquin,
Laced with bamboo,
She places the still form.
As Matsuō and Chiyo
Remove their outer garments,

There emerges the painful proof
Of their earlier resolution:
Beneath the outer dress
Are funeral weeds
For those who mourn the dead.

(Both are dressed entirely in white, the color worn at funerals. On Chiyo's head is a large cowl of white. Each carries a Buddhist rosary of crystal beads.)

Genzō and Tonami
Have solace in their hearts.

GENZŌ: It is not right that parents should lay to rest their child. Let us perform that service for you. *(Starts to rise.)*

MATSUŌMARU: No, no. This is no longer our child. We accompany the body of Kan Shūsai. Let the funeral fires be burned at the gate.

(Chiyo leaves the house, goes to the palanquin and opens its door. There she kneels with clasped hands to pray for Kotarō. From the upstage center doorway, Genzō brings in a small bundle of straw. Tonami brings a small candle, and together they light the fire at the gate.)

NARRATOR: He calls for gate fires for the dead.

Lady Sugawara and her youthful son
Dissolve in tears together.
Entry into the village school
Has been but the beginning
Of a journey to the land of death,
His teachers there to be
The Buddha Sākyamuni
And the Buddha Amida.
There will he be a disciple
Of Jizō, who guards the young;
And there his copybook the shifting sands

Washed by the river of no return.
Children who learn their letters—[15]
Ah, how helpless we stand
As their youthful lives are strewn away.
On the morrow,
Who in that far off realm of death
Will suckle and comfort their child?
Passing all that one may bear,
This grief that tears the heart
Of parents bereft of child.
Today will the departed lad
Stumble 'cross that nether peak
Sown thick with swords,
The mountain known as Shide,
Slope of torment.
All, all,
So like an unreal dream.

[15] This concluding passage is known as the *i-ro-ha okuri*, a name suggesting the escorting of Kotarō's body to the grave, mixing into the wording the old formula children used to learn the simple Japanese phonetic script. Using the Japanese standard poetic meter of alternating lines of five and seven syllables, each phonetic character occurred once, the whole constituting a syntactically comprehensible poem on a Buddhist theme. Kotarō being a pupil in a school where this would be a cardinal part of his education, the use of the poem is appropriate; its artistic interweaving with the rest of the context of this final passage heightens the drama and pathos of this, the most famous, scene of the play. A translation of the sense of the poem may enhance a reading of the passage.

> Though the color of the flowers be fragrant,
> Soon they are strewn away.
> Who in this world forever lasts?
> Today we cross beyond
> The remote mountain
> Of life's unending change.
> No more the dreams
> Of shallow unreality we see,
> No more the intoxication
> With life's transient illusions.

Behind them burn the gateside funeral fires,
Melting away life's transient illusions.
Back to the Capital,
Where Kotarō was born,
Back to Toribeno's smoky graves[16]
They make this final journey with their son.

[16] An area in the hills along the eastern part of Kyoto where a cemetery and a crematorium used to be located.

Act V

Scene 1. Tumult in the Palace

(The scene is a large room inside the imperial palace. Across the top of the stage hangs the upper paneling of the room, divided into six sections enclosed in black lacquered frames, the panels decorated with white cloud patterns against a gold ground. Directly below, at floor level, a black lacquer and gold balustrade runs across the stage, broken at center stage by a black stairway of three steps. The forestage represents the palace garden. Sliding panels across the back of the room bear the same white clouds on gold design, except for the two in the center which are painted with a large stylized pine tree. These two panels have been drawn apart, revealing a gold and white wall beyond. In front of the open panels stands a Buddhist altar of black lacquer ornamented with gold fittings. On the altar at each side are gold vases holding golden lotuses. In the middle of the altar is a black and gold lectern, behind which sits the Buddhist priest Hosshōbō, clad in flowing red robes. In his hands is a long, flat black baton.)

NARRATOR: Time shifts,
        And already it is late
        In the sixth, the rainless, month
        In the imperial palace,
        Tranquil beneath clear skies.
        Yet regularly every day
        Lightning sweeps the heavens

(Rolling drums.)
> And violent thunder rolls.
> Unwonted these endless
> Convulsions of the firmament.
> Responding to envoys
> Thrice sent with imperial commands,
> The high priest Hosshōbō
> Has appeared at the palace

(More rolling drums.)
> That he might offer prayers
> To ensure the Emperor's safety
> And turn away the thunder's roar.
> Within the palace itself
> An altar has been raised,
> Ringed with sacred hangings,
> The dais set with cryptic devices
> Of the mysterious rites,
> And there prays Hosshōbō.
> Surely divine safeguard
> Will come of all these litanies.
> As emissary of the former Emperor Uda—
> Retired and priestly sovereign—
> Hangandai Terukuni makes his entry,
> Accompanied by Prince Tokiyo,
> The Lady Kariya, and young Kan Shūsai.
> At the south stairway of the palace
> They present themselves.

(Prince Tokiyo, Lady Kariya, and Kan Shūsai enter from SL.)
> From his altar, Hosshōbō
> Descends and offers greetings.

HOSSHŌBŌ: Ah, most fortunate you have come.

NARRATOR: As he takes the Prince's hand

And leads him to the honored seat,
Terukuni bows in reverence.

TERUKUNI: His holiness the Retired Emperor has commanded me to come and inquire if your reverence has, on an occasion of the Emperor's good spirits, reported to him the matter discussed earlier of Kan Shūsai's succession to the head of the Sugawara house.

NARRATOR: As he speaks, Prince Tokiyo too
Turns to Hosshōbō.

TOKIYO: These natural calamities of late, as I think about them, must surely be the work of the ghost of Lord Sugawara, aggrieved over the baseless charges brought against him. If this spirit is to be quieted, then as the Retired Emperor has said, Kan Shūsai should be pardoned of any transgressions against the Emperor and the house of Sugawara should be reinstated. If done, this would dispel the spirit's bitterness and would be most conducive to the happiness of the country and the people. We beg your reverence most earnestly to convey this to His Majesty. And, I would appreciate your offering my apologies to His Majesty for the displeasure caused him by the groundless rumors about myself.

NARRATOR: He speaks with great deference.

HOSSHŌBŌ: Just as you say, these unseasonal happenings are surely due to the lingering rancor of Lord Sugawara. For some time, his lordship was my disciple in the faith. I will most gladly recommend to the Emperor that Kan Shūsai's succession to the Sugawara house will pacify the spirit's wrath. Let this be conveyed by Terukuni to the palace of the Retired Emperor. The rest of you please come with me.

NARRATOR: They accompany the priest inside.
Terukuni is overjoyed.

(All but Terukuni exit SL.)

TERUKUNI: I must go at once to the Retired Emperor and report to him that his reverence has promised to sponsor our request.

NARRATOR: In high spirits
He returns the way he came.

(Terukuni exits downstage left. Shihei enters from SR, accompanied by Genba, Mareyo, and Kiyotsura.)
Now, Minister Shihei
Is staggered to learn,
Through Shundō Genba's news,
That into the palace secretly have come
Prince Tokiyo and the Sugawara children.

SHIHEI *(shouting):* Mareyo! Kiyotsura! Follow them quickly! I can see beyond into the Emperor's chambers; it is just as Genba says. They are Shihei's mortal enemies. Cut them down one and all! I shall exile the Emperor and the Retired Sovereign, and I myself will ascend the imperial throne! After them Kiyotsura, Mareyo!

NARRATOR: His fierce eyes search everywhere.
Now, unaware his enemy lies in wait,
In comes Kan Shūsai.

(Kan Shūsai enters from SL.)

KAN SHŪSAI: Has Terukuni returned?

SHIHEI: There he is!

NARRATOR: At Shihei's bellow,
Abruptly Mareyo runs forward,
Grabs Kan Shūsai by the arm,
And twists him to the floor.
Shihei roars with evil laughter.

SHIHEI: You're little more than a fly right now, but if I spare you, you will later become my adversary. I thought I'd cut off your head, but you've had the impudence to deceive me. It's that rascal Matsuō's plotting that has left you alive until today. *(To Genba):* You stupid lout! Deceived by a false head!

NARRATOR: He seizes Genba by the shoulder.

SHIHEI: For disloyalty through your negligence, here's your reward.

NARRATOR: He rips off his head
        And flings it away.

SHIHEI *(to Kiyotsura and Mareyo):* Here, you two. Leave the imp Kan Shūsai to me. Bring Prince Tokiyo and Lady Kariya here!

NARRATOR: Kiyotsura and Mareyo
        Acknowledge the command,

(They begin to move toward SL.)
        But as they are about to enter
        The palace's inner precincts
        Suddenly the limpid sky
        Swarms with turbulent clouds,

(Gongs, rolling and tapping drums.)
        Wind and rain descend,
        And bolts of lightning
        Blaze across the firmament,
        While claps of monstrous thunder
        Rend heaven and earth—
        Crack! Bang! Rumble! BOOM!!
        Kiyotsura, Mareyo quaver with terror,
        Panic racks their bodies,
        They pale with fright
        And seek escape this way and that.
        Great Minister Shihei stands
        Unflinching in the tumult.

SHIHEI: Agh! You sniveling cowards! Let the thunder roll, let the
    lightning fall! I'll trample beneath my feet and snuff out both
    thunder god and lightning fire!
NARRATOR: Beneath his arm he grips Kan Shūsai,
        And standing upright glares back at the sky.
(Shihei holds Kan Shūsai about the neck with his left arm.)
        The thunder echoes on and snarls,
        And in the lightning flash and tremors of the earth
        Mareyo feels more dead than of the living.
        As he leans over the bottom of the stairs,
        Above his head a wheel of fire
        Appears to descend, and Mareyo's body
        Is enveloped in the searing flames.
(Mareyo falls down.)
        This chastening of heaven before one's very eyes
        Is vengeance exacted by Lord Sugawara.
        Indeed, for Mareyo an end so well deserved.
        Yet this too fails to daunt
        The sturdy spirit of Shihei.
SHIHEI: Miyoshi no Kiyotsura! Where are you? No god of thun-
    der can defy me! Come here if you are afraid.
NARRATOR: His voice gives Kiyotsura heart;
        He approaches his master's side.
        In a twinkling, Kiyotsura too
        Is struck down by a lightning shaft,
(Pounding drums, gongs.)
        And on the spot the breath is severed from him.
        At the deaths of his two minions,
        Bold though he may be, yet now
        Shihei shrinks back, knees atremble.
        The captive Kan Shūsai

Slips from his grasp and flees
Into concealment.
(Kan Shūsai exits off to SL.)
SHIHEI: Now, I can only rely on the Law of Buddha.
NARRATOR: He dashes up to the altar, and
Covering his face with both hands,
Cowers down before it.
As from each of his ears appear
Small snakes but one foot long,
(Snakes held on long poles by stage assistants.)
He writhes and falls upon his back.
Backward pitches his head,
And the two snakes slide away,
Entering it seems the sacred hangings
That adorn the altar.
But then from the altar appear the forms
Of Sakuramaru and his wife,
Shades no longer of this world.
Like shadows they rise
Abruptly from the sacred place.
(Rapid beating of drums. The lights dim, leaving the two white-clad ghosts bathed in a greenish glow.)
SAKURAMARU *(the drums continue as he speaks slowly)*: Oooh, the anger . . . the rancor! Because of you, Lord Sugawara was most foully slandered, and of a tormented heart did he die in Tsukushi. Unable to dispel the bitterness, he became the flames of the thunder god that booms through the murky skies. *(Speaking louder, more impassioned.)* As the red blooming cherry, the *sakura*, scatters its blossoms, I Sakuramaru will tear you apart! Here, come here!
NARRATOR: He grips Shihei's head

And seeks to drag him off.
Startled by the sounds,
Into the palace runs Hosshōbō.
He sees the ghosts before him,
Vividly, as the night blooming cherry.
To drive the spirits away, he prays,
Rubbing his rosary, endlessly reciting
A spell recondite to the goddess Kannon,
Deity of a thousand arms.
Shihei stands dazed, not knowing
If the scene be dream or substance.
But clouds and mist stand between him
And the phantoms' malevolent obsession.
Their forms are visible,
But hands can touch them not.
Shihei tries to escape, but quickly
There before him, blocking flight,
Stand Yae and Sakuramaru.

(Rapid drums.)

YAE: Cut down by the sword, I departed this world, whence my body has by the tormenting flames of hell been seared red as the carmine cherry. This old man may pray as he will, yet will my loathing pursue you ever. You cannot get away. You will not escape![1]

NARRATOR: Like the hounds of passion,
        Though driven off,
        Yet they return again.

HOSSHŌBŌ: See how I will make these spirits of the dead depart.

NARRATOR: He rubs his rosary,

[1] There are in this speech several puns involving the names of different varieties of cherry blossoms. To include them in the translation would be awkward; to unravel them would be tedious.

Rubs away, and chants his prayers,
But the wraiths speak back.
SAKURAMARU: No no no! Invoke your litanies as you will, we shall
    make him suffer with us the agonies of the damned!
NARRATOR: They advance;
        The priest prays.
        And as he casts his spells,
        Their forms shift in and out of view.
        Slowly, as the petals fall
        From the late blooming cherry,
        Slowly the spirits disperse.
        Before the chafing beads
        They seem to dread approach—
        Most eerie the powers of his prayers.
        If the priest is in the main palace,
        The forms of the ghostly pair
        Are in the Empress's apartments.
        Should Hosshōbō shift there,
        The specters appear
        In the Emperor's quarters.
        If to these quarters moves the priest,
        Then to the Pear Chamber, the Plum Room,
        The Bedchamber, the daytime lodgings—
        Now losing one another,
        Now coming together.
        Hosshōbō recites his prayers;
        The angry wraiths refuse to leave,
        As they struggle against their exorcist.
        At length, brought to his knees by prayer,
        Sakuramaru shouts out.
SAKURAMARU: Enough! Wait, reverend priest! I cannot fathom your
    protection of Shihei, who unjustly accused Lord Sugawara

of crimes and who plots to usurp the throne. Do you lend
your might to an imperial foe?

NARRATOR: At these words, Hosshōbō
  Stands astonished.

HOSSHŌBŌ: What! I did not know that he was such a rebel against
the crown. What sacrilege to have profaned my rosary for
him!

NARRATOR: He leaves his place of prayer
  And goes within.

(Hosshōbō exits SL.)
  Now Shihei, fearful of the apparitions,
  Tries to flee to the waiting chamber,
  Only to be stopped by the ghosts,
  Who seize his topknot
  And drag him back.

SAKURAMARU: Now shall we do with you as we wish! You will
accompany us on the pitch-black road to death!

(Drums roll.)

NARRATOR: Waving aloft their whips
  Made of cherry branches,
  They drive Shihei before them,
  Drive and pursue him.
  Lashed and lashed without mercy,
  Shihei falls senseless,
  Like an empty cicada husk,

(Intermittent drums.)
  Bereft of life.

SAKURAMARU: Now, the rancor has been dispelled.

NARRATOR: The phantoms kick Shihei's corpse
  Into the palace garden.
  Then joyously their forms

Dissolve away,
Waning as a flower fades,
Till they are seen no more.
Now is laid to rest
The spirit of Lord Sugawara.
The heavens clear,
(Lights come up again.)
And the great wheel of the sun
Shines forth in all its brilliance.
Watching the spectacle,
Kan Shūsai and Lady Kariya
Quickly run to the garden.
(Kan Shūsai and Lady Kariya enter from SL.)
KARIYA: No escape for you, enemy of my father!
NARRATOR: From her breast she draws
A dagger saved for this occasion.
KARIYA: Know you, this is the sword of my hatred!
NARRATOR: Through and through
She stabs him again and again.
Now indeed is the time
For her rejoicing!
Now, anxious for the safety
Of the Prince and Lady Kariya
And young Kan Shūsai,
Matsuōmaru appears at the palace,
Joined by Terukuni.
(Matsuō and Terukumi enter from SL.)
Returned from Dazaifu,
Shiradayū and Umeōmaru too
Present themselves in attendance.
At the stairway's foot.

(Shiradayū and Umeō enter from SL.)
>   As they hear in full
>   The tale of how the wrathful ghosts
>   Of Sakuramaru and Yae
>   Brought to light the evil of Shihei,
>   The hearts of all soar up in joy.
>   Rejoicing with them, Hosshōbō comes forth,
>   Leading in the Prince.

(Hosshōbō and Prince Tokiyo enter from SL.)

HOSSHŌBŌ: In accordance with all your desires, there has been an imperial proclamation that Kan Shūsai be permitted to succeed as head of the house of Sugawara. On Lord Sugawara is conferred the Senior First Court Rank. A shrine is to be erected in his honor at the equestrian grounds of the palace guards of the Right, and he is to be worshiped as the All Honored Heaven-Filling Deva King, divine protector of the imperial palace.

NARRATOR: He speaks the words
>   And all join in the jubilation.
>   Hearing the echoes of that happy time,
>   One thinks upon that grove
>   Of a thousand pines at Kitano,[2]
>   The noble shrine, glorious forever:
>   A palace lasting full a thousand,
>   Nay, ten thousand years—
>   Its curtains of brocade,
>   Finest crystal pillars,
>   Crossbeams wrought in agate,

[2] Though most (and more reliable) versions of this story date the pine grove from 947 when the Kitano Shrine was established, legend has it that on the night of Michizane's death in Dazaifu several thousand pines suddenly grew up overnight in the area northeast of the Kitano Shrine in Kyoto. The place name Senbon, or "Thousand Pines," still designates the district.

Standing joists of emerald.
All these, with corridor and worship hall,
Remain for view today,
Vividly recalling that time of long ago.
Known throughout the Capital
As Kitano—"North Moor";
In Naniwa, called Tenman—
"Heaven-Filling Shrine"—
The virtue and auspicious augury
Of its noble god
Gives divine assistance to our brush,
As briefly we recount the annals of this shrine,
Unrivaled in its glory.
Here in Japan, where passed to generations
Are Sugawara's secrets of the brush,
Before that lofty majesty,
Even now one stands in awe.

—end—

Third year of Enkyō (1746), eighth month, twenty-first day.
Playwrights: Namiki Senryū
           Miyoshi Shōraku
           Takeda Koizumo

A Note on the Puppets

Magicians never reveal their secrets, and Western theater often hides its mechanics in an effort to persuade an audience of the verity of what it sees on stage. This is especially true of the usual forms of puppet theaters found in the West, where manipulators and speakers and the sources of music and sound effects are rarely, if ever, seen by the audience. The Japanese puppet theater, or Bunraku as it is called today, tends in the other direction, coming close to producing a balance between the realistic thrust of the dramatic story unfolding and the inherent unreality of the appearance in full view of the spectators of both the handlers of the puppets and an enormously vigorous narrator providing a narrative recitativo as well as the voices of all the characters. Each puppet in a major role, and some in much less important ones, requires the close coordination of a team of three manipulators. Traditions surrounding various plays and scenes therein vary, but all manipulators usually wear black smocks and gloves and have black hoods over their heads, a convention that tells the audience they are meant to be invisible. Yet, in one of those difficult to explain phenomena, the puppets regularly seem to come alive on stage, even suggesting at times that they are struggling to free themselves from their keepers, as the audience falls under a theatrical magic that blends the handlers into the

The illustrations shown throughout are drawings by the late Miyao Shigeo and found in his book *Bunraku Ningyō Zufu* (Tokyo: Kanō Shokō, 1984). I would like to acknowledge with much appreciation the permission given by Messrs Miyao Yoshio and Miyao Jiryō to use these illustrations originally drawn by their father.

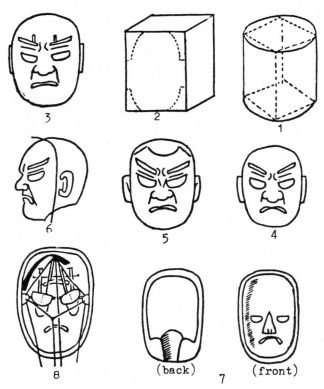

FIGURE 1. Stages in the construction of a puppet head. Heads are made of light weight, fine grained paulonia wood. A typical log section (1) is cut square (2) to approximate measurements of 12.5 cm. high, 10.5 cm. front to back, and 12.5 cm. across the front. On this is sketched the outline of the face and head shape, and carving progresses from rough to a more finished stage (3, 4, 5). The head is then split (along the line in 6) and hollowed (7), and cutouts are made for such movable parts as eyes, eyebrows, mouth, etc., as they may occur in a given head. Movable parts are then attached (8) with strings leading first to a spring (made of a thinly shaved section of whale tooth—the dark element at upper left in 8) and then downward. The front and back of the head are then glued together (9). The neck (10) is fitted into the hole at the base of the head (11) and attached with a bamboo dowel that permits the head to pivot in a nodding motion. Another thin section of whale tooth is affixed inside the head (12), providing a spring to return the head to an

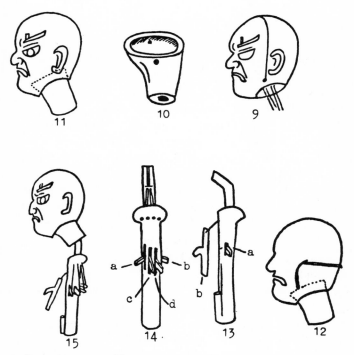

upright position in nodding motions. A neck handle, or *dōgushi* (13), for the principal manipulator to grasp is then made and fitted with triggerlike devices called *kozaru* (13a) to operate movable facial features and a sliding pull (13b) to nod the head up and down. For heads with several mobile facial elements, a number of *kozaru* may be provided, operating either a single action (such as rising eyebrows) or sometimes dual actions (as when a mouth opens and eyebrows rise simultaneously). In 14, the several *kozaru* are attached to strings that run through the holes at the top of the neck handle and thence to the interior mechanisms of the puppet head. When pulled by the manipulator's thumb they produce the following movements: rolling the eyes to the left (14a) or to the right (14b); raising the eyebrows or, alternatively, opening the mouth (14c); and simultaneously raising the eyebrows and crossing the eyes (14d), a combination often used to express strong emotion. When all of these elements are fitted together (15) and appropriate wigs and painted make-up are added, the head is ready for use on stage.

darkness and leaves the puppet figures in vital highlight. I can think of no other theater of inanimate creatures that realizes this illusion so completely and so convincingly.

The head is the most striking element of the puppet, for it is the primary source of expression, especially when fitted with such features as movable eyes, eyebrows, and mouth. There are at present only one or two artists who carve these works of art; figure 1 shows the stages in the construction of a puppet head. Movable facial features are more common in heads for male characters, but female heads may have mobile eyes and mouths, and in one spectacular case a winsome young girl is transformed by the movement of a single trigger into a fearsome demon with great eyes staring from red sockets, a gaping mouth filled with sharp golden fangs, and a pair of gold horns rising from the top of her head. Comic characters may have wiggling noses or ears, and one dull-witted shopboy displays an intermittently running nose. There are well over sixty different heads for men, women, and children in use in the Bunraku theater, and these are made the more varied by the use of some 117 or more wigs. Wigs are painstakingly made of human hair and the hair of the yak. By varying the particular wig and differing make-up, a single head may thus serve a wide range of roles.

Bunraku puppets are not small. They are approximately two-thirds life size, standing as much as some 120 centimeters tall (about 47 inches). Nor are they suspended by strings as are marionettes, but are carried about the stage by their team of three manipulators (figures 2 and 3), each operating a different part of the figure. The principal manipulator supports the puppet with his left hand, which holds the neck handle. He thus performs all the head and torso movements, while with his own right hand he operates the right hand of the puppet. He wears high wooden clogs on his feet to elevate both himself and the puppet, thus

FIGURE 2. Three-man manipulation of a Bunraku puppet. The principal handler, here in formal costume and unhooded, stands on high wooden clogs, which vary in height depending on the physical stature of a given manipulator.

making it easier for the other members of the team to function. Second in the hierarchy, and standing on the principal manipulator's left, is the operator of the puppet's left arm. The third member of the trio is positioned between the other two and handles the puppet's legs. Though he ranks lowest in the hierarchy (all puppeteers begin their apprenticeship working the legs), his task is both demanding and important, for inexpertly manipulated legs can ruin the overall impression of vitality.

Bunraku puppets in lavish costumes on stage offer little hint of the simplicity of their construction (figures 4 and 5). The body

FIGURE 3. Three-man operation of an uncostumed puppet, showing the more typical position of the three manipulators.

is given shape by a simple board for the shoulders (figure 6) and by a bamboo hoop at the waist. These are connected together front and back by sections of canvas cloth on which the name of a puppet manipulator may be written. Arms and legs are suspended by cords from the shoulder board. A sponge-like vegetable fiber (*hechima*, or snake gourd) is used to give roundness to the shoulders. Male puppets are larger and heavier than female characters, partly because with few exceptions only male puppets are equipped with legs. Since the long traditional Japanese kimono worn by women hides the legs and feet, actual legs and feet are unnecessary for most female puppets. The movement of

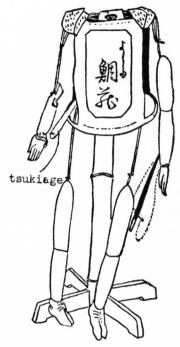

FIGURE 4. The basic construction of a male puppet, here supported on a bamboo stand when not in use on stage. The rod, known as a *tsukiage*, at the puppet's right is used to raise and lower the shoulders (as in shrugging, laughing, etc.) or may be thrust against the principal manipulator's right arm or chest to support the weight of the puppet during long periods of inactivity on stage.

feet beneath the kimono is suggested by the third member of the manipulative trio, who grasps the inner hem of the robe (figure 7) and moves it as though feet were moving beneath the garment. When the female puppet is seated on the floor, a small stuffed bag sometimes suspended from the waist hoop may be

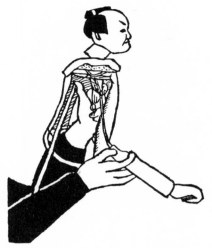

FIGURE 5. The *tsukiage* in use.

pushed forward to give an impression of the presence of legs beneath the costume (figure 8). More padding occurs at the shoulder than on male puppets, but arms are suspended from the shoulder board in the same manner. In the few instances where legs are used with a female puppet, they are usually suspended by light cord from the waist hoop.

The hands of a puppet can be highly expressive, and so there is a rather wide variety of types. Some ten types occur frequently in productions, with another two dozen hands for more specialized uses. All are made of Japanese cypress. As a rule, right hands are attached to a short forearm only, hand or finger movements being effected by a trigger in the forearm. Since the left-hand operator must stand somewhat to the side of the puppet to avoid interfering with the other two manipulators, a rod *(sashigane)* incorporating a similar trigger mechanism is attached to the left

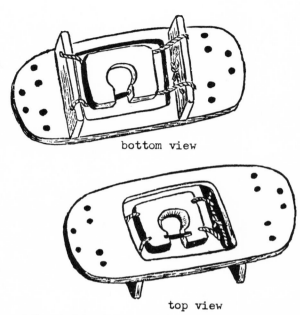

bottom view

top view

FIGURE 6. Detail of the shoulder board. The smaller wooden piece suspended within the larger cutout receives the neck handle of the puppet's
head. The holes are points at which cords holding legs and arms are
attached.

arm (figure 9). The principal operator's right hand is usually hidden inside the ample sleeve of a puppet's costume, but in cases
where the costume is close fitting (such as a soldier in armor) or
where a male puppet is fitted with a padded upper torso cover in
a role requiring him to be bare chested (a wrestler, for instance),
the projecting rod controlling hand and finger movements will
also be used on the right arm.

Arms having movable hands are essentially of two types. In
one, the fingers of the hand are stationary and the whole hand

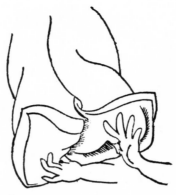

FIGURE 7. Manipulation of the inner hem of a female puppet's costume to suggest the movement of feet.

pivots at the wrist (figure 9). In the other type, finger and wrist movement occurs simultaneously. In some cases the fingers are fused (figure 10); in others there is an articulation of the fingers, producing a grasping gesture (figure 11). There are minor exceptions to this pattern: the wrist may be fixed and only the fingers move, either as a fused group (figure 12) or as articulated fingers (figure 13). Though the grasping action of some hands is quite realistic, the puppet cannot actually hold onto an object—a sword or staff, for instance. Accordingly, many hands are fitted with a leather loop known as a *yubikawa*, or finger strap. By slipping his fingers through the loop, the principal manipulator can grasp and wield objects so that the puppet appears actually to be performing the action (figure 14).

The variety of specialized hands includes those having a hole made to accommodate a particular item, such as a fan, a flowering branch, or drumsticks. One hand specifically for a demon has three claws. Some interesting ones are designed to simulate

COMPANIONS TO ASIAN STUDIES

INTRODUCTION TO ORIENTAL CIVILIZATIONS
WM. THEODORE DE BARY, EDITOR